110 Days

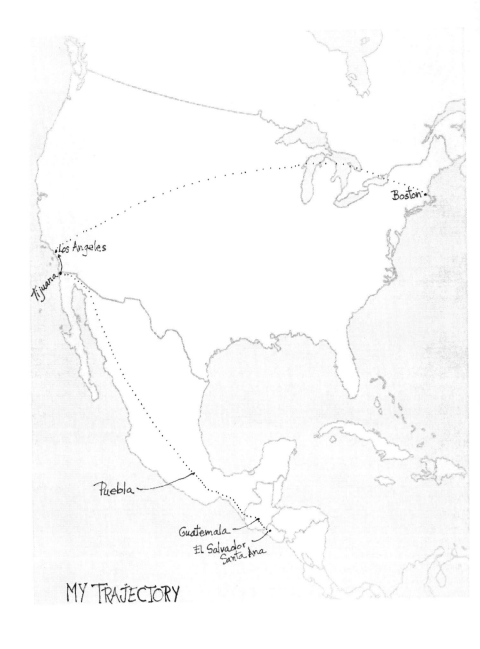

MY TRAJECTORY

110 DAYS

What Happens when an adolescent
Seminarian
lets blind optimism, naïve confidence, and
a disregard for uncertain consequences
determine his first year as an immigrant.

José Francisco Ruiz Castro

Editor: Elena Mercedes Ruiz
Second Printing Editor: Carolina Arango-Ruiz

2020

iv

First Printing: 2018
Second Printing: 2020
ISBN 978-1-71666-390-1
José Francisco Ruiz Castro
Boston, MA 02130
Ordering: Lulu.com

Dedication

To mi niña bella, Elena, who edited this memoir, correcting my English prepositions, questioning obscure meanings, suggesting better text organization, and deleting boring accounts, and to my patient wife, Carolina, who lovingly edited this second printing.

Thank you. Without your support and encouragement, I would have never crossed off this item on my bucket list.

Contents

viii

Acknowledgements

I have traveled several times to Puebla, Mexico to engage in extensive conversations with the cerebral and phlegmatic Gustavo Orellana, my seminarian classmate and best friend, and the members of the Rivadeneyra family. Their recollections of events helped give context to my memoir and helped minimize my exaggerations.

I would like to express my gratitude towards Eric, my first son, who insisted, contrary to all evidence, that I was a good writer and gave me the motivation I needed at the start of this project. I would also like to thank Alejandro, my second son, and his wife Kathy for providing the photo of the road on the front cover of this second printing.

Teto, my younger brother, gifted with an extraordinarily detailed memory, helped me bring memories back from obscurity and, his daughter, my niece Violeta, who suggested structural improvements to this second printing.

Last, but most definitely not least, I would like to acknowledge my daughter, Elena, for the countless hours she spent reading, meticulously line editing, and taking notes on my hyperactive spurts of creativity during our brainstorm conversations, and my wife, Carolina, whose revisions appeared on this second printing. I would especially like to thank them for talking me out of publishing too early and convincing me to wait another year to make this book the best version it could be.

Prologue

Today, January 02, 2010, is my first day of retirement and I am still not sure who I am or who I have been. By now it should be certain, given my age, that I would know the exact extent of my qualities, defects and limits, and that I would see when I am heading to failure, but it is not. I will accept this fact, for today I particularly feel insecure and unsettled. I feel compelled to look back on my life and tell my family my true unfinished story: the successes and glory accompanied by the embarrassing and shameful moments where the flesh governed the spirit, desire steamrolled ethics, and necessity suspended principles temporarily.

My family loves a version of me that is incomplete. I have always sought attention, love, camaraderie, respect, and admiration, but now through these words I wish to become a better-known person without hiding my insecurities, my sins, and my failures. Even now, I still ask, who am I? Where do I now belong? Where am I now going? Will the rest of my life continue being an adventure as it has been up to the present?

Not all members of my immediate and extended family, and friends, will agree on the manner the events recounted in this memoir unfolded, which may upset them. I must note that like all reconstructed memories, mine undoubtedly may have untrue elements and an imprecise timeline: events that might have happened sequentially may appear in my narration as concurrent and in different localities.

Some of the events in my mother's family history, the Castro Meza, were passed down to me by other family members and were not my first-hand experiences. I am also fully aware that memories change through time; this is unavoidable. People's perceptions of family misdeeds may become more demonized through time and their virtues, including mine, more sanctified. I ask my family members who may hold a firsthand knowledge of the narrated events that you keep this fact in mind as you read the following account of a piece of my life and my journey to the U.S. as I remember it, and as only I can interpret the events.

Needless to say, I am wholly indebted to those who appear in my memoirs. I love you. Again, please, take no offense at seeing your past as I have captured it.

❋❋❋

On my return to Boston from Miami with my family after Christmas vacation, my wife Carolina, 10 years younger than me, was already into her first week of work this New Year, and the lonely, unsettling silence in the house pushed me out the door to venture twice to the mall and supermarket during the day, with no purpose in mind, like a perfect French *"flaneur"*; out for an aimless stroll seeking stimulation.

This Tuesday morning started with bitterly dry, cold air that made me turn back to the house to fetch a thicker jacket and quickly understand the reason lucky retirees overpopulate Miami. But my duties as a father to a 12-year-old daughter had overridden my desire to escape to warmer climates until the winter made way for spring.

Dazed shoppers, their faces showing the same number of wrinkles, or maybe more and deeper than before the exhausting holidays, ambulated aimlessly at the mall. Their tired faces with black circles around their eyes, not unlike mine, were looking for some excitement to break the dullness of their lives after an ephemeral, overexposed holiday's excitement that left them with stale disappointment and inextricable tedium. Where else can one find meaning if not during the holidays? I couldn't figure out if the holidays' excesses were the culprit of these shoppers' permanent boredom, or if it was due to just old age. I strolled for a while along the almost empty mall corridors. Some young faces looked towards my direction. Maybe my ski coat gave me the appearance of a tan-faced, skier-want-to-be old guy, just back from a Vermont winter vacation. There were also college kids enjoying their winter break by shopping for some gear they probably didn't even need. "What do you think about this jacket, Mom? It's 50% off." The mother did not bother to respond, too tired from the holidays and from life.

The overall rhythm of the mall was somber and lethargic, as though people were walking with weights in their legs, or trying to wade through a desolate landscape flooded by a tsunami. The aftermath of the holidays on everyday Americans' faces surprises me every year. All that eating and drinking takes a heavy toll on their bodies and souls. I decided to sit down on a bench and observe my surroundings, to take it all in, to meditate. This was my first day of retirement and I did not know yet what to do today or for the rest of my life. I had failed my good friend Norman Edinberg's admonition, "Retire only after examining your life and knowing what you are going to be doing during retirement."

A deep sense of alienation took me over while sitting on that bench. The same feeling one would feel when going to a private party where nobody recognizes you, not even the host, because you ended up in the wrong house and instantly you notice that the dresses, hairdos, and physical postures do not conform to the images you are comfortable with, and you feel the strong urge to run away unnoticed, as the influential French writer, Marcel Proust, once put it. I had no doubt just landed in *"terra incognita"*.

My mind drifted towards English High School, from where I had just retired, and found comfort in that thought. I became certain that, out of habit, my colleagues and students would be expecting me at school after vacation. *"¿Dónde está Mr. Ruiz?"*, they would wonder, before remembering, *"Oh, sí, él se jubiló antes de las vacaciones de Navidad. El ya nunca va a regresar. Se me había olvidado. Dichoso."* Surely, the secretary would mark me absent just to realize later in the day that I wasn't going to come back, and even those who did not deal with me regularly maybe sensed that something was different around the school halls, a vacuum left by my absence, without being able to describe it. A warm feeling invaded my heart upon thinking that I may be missed, diminishing my loneliness.

From the mall's bench it was difficult to restrain from people watching. It was also equally difficult not to imagine and invent their personal stories. After all, I just retired and I was searching for some indications that the world would provide me with some emotional resonance to alleviate my alienation and otherness. These people wouldn't suspect in their wildest dreams the significance of this day. This was my first day that I did not need to report to work, a place I loved. I then eagerly looked for early signals, for compelling, concrete indications that could have predicted the path my life would hence forth take. No chance! Oblivion reigned in the atmosphere.

An overly made-up and perfumed woman in her fifties, well dressed, swinging a Gucci bag, walking slowly, passed in front of me. She sent a couple of tired and bored glances around her, as if recapturing her bearings. She left behind an aroma of mixed Neiman Marcus perfume testers. Maybe she was a housewife, a widow, or maybe on her day off, but definitely lonely. After just a fleeting moment, I decided that I knew this woman. I knew she was venturing to the mall to enliven her boring life. I also knew she was going to fix it by temporarily obtaining some fleeting happiness the only way she knew: by shopping and maybe spending tons of money at Saks Fifth Avenue during their 60% off sale.

Next, a group of young Japanese tourists with their melodic language conferred with each other in front of me and paused to take a group picture. What are they doing visiting Boston during this snowy, bitter, cold week? At a short distance, next to the fountain, several black babysitters, who looked to be nannies of white babies from the Back Bay area, sought refuge from the cold and sat to feed their charges while the children sat in their carriages.

Their clipped accents betrayed their origins, most likely from the Caribbean islands.

I guess, after the excesses of the New Year's celebrations, some people make the effort to go back to normal. I immediately made the first resolution for my entire retirement years: Never come to the Mall mid-morning during a mid-winter weekday. It is a depressing site with no consolation.

Next, I ventured into the Sony Style store, which at the present no longer exists. Not one clerk bothered to greet me, or annoy me with their sales pitches. God! They may have been in deep hangovers from New Year's celebrations, or just bored and exhausted, or just acting as they do every Tuesday mid-morning during the Winter. Uncharacteristically for Boston, nobody was in a rush. Nobody wanted to get anywhere. It seemed that the longer they took to go about their business, the more relaxing and the slower they went the better. Into what kind of social atmosphere was retirement pushing me? Were the retirees, the unemployed, the lonely housewives, the babysitters of other people's children, and the lost tourists reflections of my future state of being? This became scary. My body started to shake uncontrollably; I rushed out of the mall stunned by despair, wishing for the bustling halls and the noisy cafeteria of the high school with its fresh-faced, young inhabitants, the future of America, that gave me and the building life. I missed work profoundly. What the hell did I retire for? I then entered and walked through the supermarket absent mindedly, buying nothing.

Before I knew it, Friday had already arrived. Being the only person in my household who had just retired caused me to think deeper about my life situation. Today, my chest lacked some needed undetermined emotion. I was the perfect example of what some cognitive psychologists have known for some time: what seems to be unique thinking is rather a development or reaction to opposite or comparative experiences. In other words, my insights at that moment may have been produced in comparison or contrast with what others experience or what I just experienced previously. For example, take the case of the emotional and mental mindset of workers once Friday morning comes about. That feeling of great expectations for relaxation or excitement of things to come during the weekend, including the sense of freedom from the shackles of a 9 to 5 job, is felt only as a reaction, and in comparison, to the stress produced by the highly structured workplace in America. So deep is this anticipation that workers dress more casually on Fridays as if to pretend that the weekend starts Friday mornings, not Friday afternoons.

My first Friday as a retiree came and I wanted to feel again that sensation of anticipation. My body and my mind desired to feel that deserved rest was about to come after a week of arduous work, but did not. I was jealous of my wife feeling relief at the end of her week after I picked her up from work. "Aah! Today is Friday!" She sighed. "I can't wait to get home." Is this what retirement also means? Not feeling that excited about the coming of Friday?

I began to think that I would be missing something very essential to my happiness. The steady regularity of retirement life may erase the ups and downs of a life that once was entirely focused on survival, life's shortages and abundances. I may run the danger of making my retired life too even keeled. I don't think the caveman would be very happy with this. My evolutionary physical constitution is built for action, for fight and flight. I feared that if I didn't change this situation soon, I would die sooner than expected out of the shear boredom of it all. I decided that I would have to construct my daily routine in such a way that recreated that missing feeling of the advent of a great weekend. I thought that was fundamental for my wellbeing. I knew I would not feel the need to relax and rest if I did not work hard at something. I decided to create a life in retirement that was full of contrasts: rest after hard work, peace after high emotional excitement, dullness after long strenuous expectations, new successes and insights after unintentional failures and obscure experiences, and truth and reality after an imaginary ambiguous life. If there was one thing I knew for certain when faced with my new life as a retiree, it was to avoid monotony. As William Blake wrote: "*Without contraries is no progression. Attraction and repulsion, reason and energy, love and hate, are necessary to human existence.*"

Chapter 1: Maybe a job for retirees would help keep me sane

It was then only logical that three weeks into retirement I was already looking for a job, any job. The process of looking for any job transported me back to the beginning, to my past in Los Angeles. My life was markedly different then.

I had just crossed the border, more than 40 years ago, with a few dollars in my pocket, like thousands before me. I had no alternative but to get ready to fight for my daily survival. Like many new immigrants, due to my complete ignorance of the English language, I resorted to unconventional ways of communicating with English-only bosses in Los Angeles. My non-verbal communication, especially my body and hand movements, became extreme in those encounters. I soon became an expert on show-not-tell techniques. I didn't know how to say, "I am looking for a job." To the would-be employers, I looked desperate, naïve, starved, intense, and eager to get my hands dirty with any task.

My attitude then was not unlike the soccer player who trains arduously with his teammates just to spend most of the season on the bench until that moment comes when the coach sends him to the field, full of energy and optimism, but with no experience, and surprises the fans by scoring the winning goal. My disposition revealed an intensity possessed only by the hungry waiting for food and a readiness akin to that of a sailor who, after months at sea, finds himself back at port looking for action. Sometimes I joke with my family that the only way I could really achieve happiness during retirement is if they were to drop me in the middle of a random country with no money or understanding of the language and leave me incommunicado for a couple of years, just to recreate the need and impetus for daily survival.

In Los Angeles, three months later, Ernesto, a bright Mexican from Jalisco I met in my first ESL class in El Monte Adult Education Center, became my guide, cultural mentor, interpreter, and an informal English language teacher. Possibly, he had crossed the border many times during the past couple of years and had acquired some useful English phrases for survival. He made me practice, repeatedly, the phrase "I am looking for a job." This would become very handy ten months later in Boston.

In Los Angeles, prior to meeting Ernesto, my first job in the US was as a part time helper to the janitor of St. Luke's Catholic Church in Temple City, a small middle-class suburb east of Los Angeles. I found the job the day after I arrived on US soil. I got it not by enunciating very properly, "I am looking for a job," for I knew zero English at that point. Rather, that bright and early, fresh morning, after crossing the border, I felt very confident about myself and had an exuberant outlook. This optimism produced a force in me that made me believe that I could conquer anything, do anything and be anything; a feeling that spurred me to knock loudly at a church rectory, maybe just after the 6:00 a.m. Mass.

This was a perfect, Southern Californian day. The bright sun hit my forehead as I walked towards the church, not yet changed from my traveling clothes and looking gaunt, disheveled, and dirty. My eyes squinted as an automatic reaction to the silver reflections coming from everywhere. It appeared that Californians loved glitter. Cars were polished to a perfect shine, especially their wheel rims, front doors were surrounded by chrome framing, and the church steeple reflected like a mirror. Filth and grease were clearly not allowed in this city. As I walked to the church, I became aware of my front pocket and the $100.00 that were still there. My cousin Sandra was expecting her money back soon after I found my first job. *I should send it to her. I bet she has been waiting for it for a long time. I promised her.*

I was finally in America, the land of opportunity. I had just started what turned out to be the biggest adventure of my life. *"Al que madruga, Dios le ayuda."*

The parish priest, already in his late sixties, opened the door. He was thin, tall, and almost languid, with the whitest hair. I startled and froze. I was expecting a maid, the stereotypical Spanish-speaking maid. I did not know the American, culturally expected protocol when looking for a job or addressing a priest. After a couple of seconds of silence, however, the black cassock in front of me triggered an immediate reaction. It transported me back to my Seminary years in El Salvador and Mexico, and with a loud baritone voice, I blurted out in Latin *"Ego volo laborare!"* The priest immediately understood and it was his turn to be startled and taken aback upon hearing me speak in Latin, a dead language. With his eyes and mouth wide open in amazement at hearing those words come out of this disheveled and dirty looking young guy, he opened the door wide. I emanated a body odor that could only be produced after many weeks without a shower, and I looked not unlike those who are rendered unrecognizable to civilization after having trekked the Appalachian Trail. The priest suddenly grabbed me by my shoulders and quickly pulled me into the rectory as if to hide me and avoid the posh, middle class, white suburb of Temple City from noticing my arrival.

The priest paid me handsomely ($4.00 per hour) in comparison to the going hourly rate of the day ($1.00 or $2.00 per hour) for non-English speaking "dirty Mexicans". He saw it as a charity. He quickly assigned me to do the dirty job that the white janitor refused to do well: cleaning the parochial elementary school toilets, taking heavy objects out to the garbage dump, and cleaning the tables and floor of the messy cafeteria and sometimes the library. Yeah! This was my first job in America and my first job ever. I became one of many immigrants who did the job that many Americans, spoiled by their higher standard of living, refused to do well or do at all.

The janitor, Ron Cooney, quickly sensed that I did not have any experience doing any laborious work. He even doubted I could do a good job as a janitor's helper. He was right. I was already 20 and up to that time I had used my hands only for opening philosophy books often written in Latin. On the first day, the janitor noticed my hands and asked me to open them to show him their palms. He straight out said: "sissy." I only knew he was referring to my hands. It took me a while to understand what that meant. My hands were too soft to the touch. None of the expected calluses developed from hard labor were present. He decided to toughen me up by assigning me most of the janitorial tasks. I never saw him during the day after he walked around the building showing me the daily tasks to be completed. Maybe he went back home or to a hidden office somewhere in the back of the school to sleep.

During those first months, I was prepared to do literally any physical job possible for I was never sure I would have enough money to buy even a glass of milk the next morning. I lived with the idea that my efforts for survival could turn quickly into a monumental disaster. There are no doubt people in my surroundings sensed my desperation and some obviously took advantage of me. At this time, as a recent arrival, my mind and body were tuned in a state of high alert. Every inch of my body and every neuron synchronized in unison with charged intensity as I faced the outside world, similar to an alert Cheetah ready to charge towards its prey or an alert prey ready to receive the first blow and bite. I could have become either one at any moment. Once on the job, I worked the hardest to complete my assignments as diligently and perfectly as possible; an ingrained attitude forged at the Seminary.

In the minor Seminary Juan XXIII of Santa Ana, we had a saying about our daily activities and chores, "Do it as perfect as Jesus Christ would have done it. High quality and perfection are the only goals in your activities." Moreover, happiness was best achieved as Aristotle thought, defined by the pursuit of excellence (*arête)* or living up to one's fullest potential.

I therefore cleaned the school's bathrooms and toilets until they were sparkling white. The cafeteria's floor had never looked so clean and disinfected or the library's chairs and tables as tidy. My actions echoed Aristotle who once wrote, "quality is not an act, it is a habit." I came 30 minutes before starting time and left 30 minutes after my scheduled hour. I found myself often waiting by the main school doors for the priest and for the custodian to arrive. They looked at me inquisitively, suspiciously, trying hard to figure me out and read into my hidden agenda, which I had none. The language limitations did not let me explain my motives, my inside wishes and goals. I was always all too willing to please them by doing an exceptional job. I had been perfectly trained, tamed, and domesticated by the Seminary to be enslaved by this type of life: a life of following orders, respect for authority, and submission. This would become my modus operandi through the first years in this country.

One day before going home, a month after my arrival, I walked around the parochial school at the end of the day and discovered an upright piano against a classroom wall. I hadn't played the piano for over a year, felt very rusty, and decided to play a series of exercises Padre Chus had taught me in the Seminary, moving up and down two octaves alternating your fingers, especially the fingers 3, 4, and 5 of each hand. Padre Chus insisted that those exercises would help me totally separate those fingers controlled by the same tendon. I became completely absorbed in the playing and it served as a deeply relaxing moment for me. It brought me nostalgically back to the life I had left behind and reassured me that some things may stay the same no matter the distance or the inability to understand my new surroundings. I might have spent an hour playing that piano, with crescendos and decrescendos, with "ffff's" and "pppp's." When I finished, I closed it very gently and turned to exit the classroom only to notice that the janitor had been there listening to me in silence, sitting down in a small little first grade chair towards the back of the classroom.

Next day, as soon as I arrived, the priest John Birch walked me up the chorus balcony of the church, fired the electrical organ up, opened the *urtext* edition of the "*Inventionen Sinfonien,*" by J. S. Bach and asked me to play "*Inventio-1,*" one of the few Bach pieces that the Padre Chus had taught me well. After a couple of tries and a few minutes of warming up, I played it for him. I even managed to assert on the foot pedals.

He was pleased. He hired me to be the Sunday organist for the 11:00 a.m. Mass. I didn't have to say or sing anything. I would just play the list of songs, usually easy pieces by Bach, that Father Birch would mark on the book before the Mass with careful indications of when to play them during the ritual of Mass. Of course, I knew the ritual inside and out in Latin and in Spanish, but the English version sounded very strange to me and I had to constantly stretch my neck over the organ to examine the priest's position and movements at the altar. There were times when he had to send a quick nod towards my place at the chorus balcony to indicate the start and end times of my playing. He paid me $50.00 per Mass. All my payments were made in cash, under the table. I had been in America for over a month and I had already saved $550.00. This represented a fortune for somebody like me who had never worked a day in his life.

Ten months later in Boston, one hour after landing, drowsy from the red-eye American Airlines one-way #2507 flight, Ernesto and I started scouting for a job in the Back Bay area. The phrase "I am looking for a job" became my opening line as I entered every store, boutique and

restaurant on Newbury Street on the steamy, hazy morning of July 10, 1973. Ernesto walked up and down Beacon
Street hoping to find a job there. The Boston Gardens became our starting point.

In another time and place, I had felt the heaviness of
a steamy and hazy climate like the one we encountered in
Boston. Once I experienced such weather on my way to
the border, on a late afternoon, on the pacific coastal road
of Guatemala with my right thumb extended, trying to
hitch a ride. The other time was in Sonsonate, a town
down the skirts of the Izalco and Santa Ana volcanoes in
El Salvador, waiting for a chocolate-smooth-skinned girl
to dance a cumbia with me at the verbena celebrating the
beginning of lent. In both instances, the heat and humidity made me sweat profusely.

Under those weather conditions, it was not uncommon
in El Salvador for a young man to take his shirt off to cool
down and to keep his shirt dried and clean from sweat. If
one kept the shirt on, it was of great necessity to carry a
couple of handkerchiefs in one's back pockets to be pulled
out constantly to dry the sweat around the forehead and
neck, especially the neck, so that the shirt's collar would
not get stained with dirt. Mothers and wives would do the
laundry weekly by hand in order to make sure the men
never ran out of crisp white shirts to wear. Surprisingly,
Bostonians endured the same oppressive weather during
the Summer as I had in El Salvador, but I kept my long
sleeve white shirt on. Before I left Los Angeles, my friends
swore that Ernesto and I had to brace ourselves because
we were coming to a freezing Boston town, so I packed
shirts with sleeves. I had no idea what I was in for!

We soon found ourselves walking on Marlborough
Street. with our English-Spanish dictionary in Ernesto's
hand, constantly stopping to consult it, taking advantage
of each pause to dry our foreheads with our white handkerchiefs. One sign posted behind the first floor at 81
Marlborough Street caught our eye one block from the

Boston Public Garden, which was, unbeknownst to us, the most expensive and historic section of Boston. The building was constructed in 1865 in a French Academic style and had three floors with three bay windows on each.

"Ernesto, ¿Qué quiere decir 'let' en inglés? Mira en el diccionario. Ahí dice 'Room to Let'."

"Hijo de la chingada. Aquí en el diccionario hay dos páginas con la palabra 'let'. ¿Cómo voy a saber, cabrón?

"Bueno, ahí dice 'room', y eso ya sabemos que quiere decir cuarto. Entremos y preguntemos, porque se me hace que están alquilando el cuarto," I said.

A lanky, very pale, young man with slouching posture and long arms and hands opened the door at 81 Marlborough Street. Ernesto asked about the room. "Fifteen dollars the week," the man said. Two low, short twin beds without headboards and footboards, a small antique round table that had seen better days, and one nightstand without a lamp filled the room. A small kitchen that we didn't ever plan to use was built inside what could have been a large closet. One large window faced the Public Alley 420. "Yes," we both said, and the room was ours.

I clearly remember the steamy hot temperature inside the room. We never complained. We had entered a rooming house, what once could have been a single-family house inhabited by a Gilded Age fur baron but was now populated by disheveled out-of-state college students from different universities, there probably only for the Summer. There was one immense bathroom with an original bathtub and dull copper original classic fixtures, which looked much bigger than necessary, but were kept shiny and bright. In my recent trip to Buenos Aires, I saw similar white enamel cast-iron bathtubs in the historic apartments around the Recoleta district that made me think of 81 Marlborough Street in 1973. Here in Boston, the bathroom was located on the second floor and shared by all students. Uncharacteristically to college dorms, I never ran into any students while walking to the bathroom day or night. The floors were quiet, even though the lanky manager of the building, in his high-ceiling-spacious room on the first floor and what would have been the baron's family living room, played his grand piano and gave piano lessons. Later in the summer, I met some of the students who were studying music at Berklee School of Music. There might have been a strict rule imposed by the neighbors about instrument playing and practicing because nobody practiced their music in the house.

It took me less than two hours after landing in Boston to find a job as a dishwasher at the *Café Florian* on 85 Newbury Street., owned by a Hungarian émigré woman who had grown up in Paris. Café Florian was a small, bustling European café with and the only establishment on Newbury Street with city permits to keep tables and chairs on the sidewalk, mimicking a Parisian café. The tables were cooled by the shadow of an office building across the street on late summer afternoons. When I approached it that day, the small black marble table tops were filled up with such staples as a variety of French cheeses, pâté, fruit platters, and half-bottles of Cabernet Sauvignon. The mix of cheese scents and red wine aromas brought me instantly back to the Monsignor's banquets that I had often served as a seminarian waiter.

Café Florian took food seriously. There was a dinner course, including French omelets, and a sinful pastry cart exhibiting brandy-soaked brioches with peach custard stuffing. My taco-truck diet did not prepare me to understand such succulent and decadent displays of dishes. The Café was literally walled in by art galleries on the second block of Newbury Street. The customers had to walk down several steps to an almost subterranean niche. The restaurant space was long and narrow, with exposed brick and several antique mirrors hanging among watercolors and prints.

In the summer of 2016, I went on a trip to Italy with my wife Carolina and my daughter Elena, who had just graduated from high school. While in la Piazza de San Marco in Venice, we sat at the tables of the historic Café Florian for an afternoon coffee. At that moment, looking at the menu, it occurred to me that the Newbery Street. café's name was probably inspired by this one in Venice. The font used to write the Newbury Street. cafe's name on its menus was the same one used in the Café Florian of Venice. I imagined the owner of the one in Boston, at one time in her youth, maybe just after WW-II, sitting at the same spot where I was, dreaming about one day coming to America and maybe opening a Café just like this one in Venice. My memories of the beginning of my past are ever present, inspiring and redefining my present.

The French and Italian coffee and patisserie attracted a sophisticated Copley Square crowd. This café was the only place in Boston where patrons could savor Parisian pastries accompanied by a strong Italian cappuccino, with French chansons mixed with Mozart's five French horn concertos playing out of a large Akai reel-to-reel tape player, in an endless loop, in the background. Those concertos have since been engraved in my psyche and washing dishes by hand or machine at home never again have felt so enjoyable. *I must buy a cheap record player to listen to these concertos at home. I bet Ernesto could warm up to this music.* At Café Florian, I found an atmosphere akin to my Seminary: washing dishes and doing other chores while listening to classical music. This was way before Starbucks took over Boston with a coffee shop on every corner.

It was around 11:45 am when I entered Café Florian. Ron, the manager, took his white apron off and handed it immediately to me, interrupting me at mid-sentence of, "I am looking for a job..." "I need a dishwasher right now," Ron said with a big smile, spreading his thick brown mustache over his upper red lip uncovering his yellow teeth. "I can't wash dishes and at the same time manage lunch in this place." His face changed from a corrugated sheath of stress wrinkles to a smooth white paper. I was being sent by the gods to help him. As soon as he listened to my over-pronounced English, which I am sure was still mostly un-intelligible; he knew immediately the only reason for my appearance was to ask for a job. So much for my incessant practicing of that sentence!

That morning, just before lunch hour, the dishwasher had walked away from the job, but not before hurling dirty china against the kitchen walls in disgust, presumably fed up with the accumulated high piles of dirty dishes from breakfast. Ron walked me to the kitchen and looked in horror at the mess left by my predecessor. After a very short explanation, I attentively watched his non-verbal communication. He appeared to tell me to take over the dishwasher, a very small machine totally unknown to me, tucked under a counter in the corner. The main dining area was packed for lunch and a long line started to form waiting for sidewalk tables. I immediately had noticed that it would have been impossible to wash such a large amount of dirty breakfast dishes while waiting for the ma-chine to go through its cycles and be ready for lunch service. I opted for washing and drying the dishes quickly by hand and handed them one by one to Stanley, the cook, a very tall man with a crooked nose.

The waiters were soon pleased to see such rapid turn out of cooked meals. Their impatient, unforgiving, regular high-tipping customers, with only less than an hour-long lunch breaks, did not have to wait for their lunch orders any longer. "Two-ten the hour," Ron hollered, peeking into the kitchen door, his big face painted again with a wide smile that showed his rotten-smoke-stained front teeth, just back from the back alley for a cigarette break. I had seen rotten teeth only in the faces of poor, overworked *campesinos* in my family's *hacienda*. Possibly, before hir-ing him, the Hungarian owner might have thought that Ron's front teeth were a perfect match to those she had seen in the smoked-filled rooms of Parisian restaurants.

I left the café at 4 p.m. and met Ernesto at our new room. He had just found a job driving a van to distribute classical music sheets to multiple venues and individual musicians preparing for a concert. The historic, Boston Music Company, founded in 1885 by Gustave Schirmer, hired Ernesto. The van was white and new, with large blue letters on its sides and tastefully done music notation, with stylish Fa and Sol staffs. Years later, and just before it closed its doors at its main building, which was now property of Emerson College, I went there to buy my piano music sheets and thought about Ernesto's eager and happy face when I found him in the room, resting in his bed, deep in thought after landing his first job in Boston.

After our first paycheck, we each opened an account at the That's My Bank branch, at the corner of Boylston Street and Dartmouth Street. We made a pledge to save most of our money and looked for a way to continue learning English, but we didn't have any idea of where to go. Ernesto brought his Mexican guitar from L.A. and used it on his spare time to sit by the Copley Square fountain to play and sing Mexican folk songs. I left him there and walked to the Boston Public Library, one block from the fountain, got a provisional card, and walked down to the basement to listen to music tapes, any music. I did not find any tapes that would teach me English, which was my intention.

One day, I stumbled onto a musical about the American Declaration of Independence, titled "1776." I spent countless hours listening to the tapes with little understanding at first, but with time, I began to understand the main ideas of the songs' lyrics.

Later, I found another version of the musical that included the libretto to my ears delight. I repeated it many more times until I was able to follow the sounds of the music with its lyrics as I read them. To this day, I vividly remember the chorus singing in unison the following lines:

"Sit down, John! Sit down, John!
For God's sake, John, sit down!
Sit down, John! Sit down, John!
For God's sake, John, sit down!"
"Someone oughta open up a window"
"No, no, no. Too many flies! Too many flies!"

Several years would pass before I could grasp the real spelling and meaning of the word "*oughta.*" I put extraordinary efforts to learn the language because I had the suspicion, at that moment, that my stay in the U. S. would be long.

One job was not enough to keep me occupied. I felt restless after work. I wanted to feel exhausted and the only way was to work harder and longer. Soon I got an additional dishwasher's job, which was easy to find since there were plenty of jobs in Boston restaurants. Howard Johnson's on Boylston Street hired me. I punched 8 hours at Cafe Florian during the day, from 6:00 a.m. to 2:00 p.m. and 8 hours at Howard Johnson's during the night, from 4:00 pm. to 12:00 a.m. six days a week. Easy! I didn't have to pay for food, nor for transportation, only rent, and I slept like a newborn baby. Our room and the two restaurants were within a three-block radius in Back Bay. My savings account started to grow steadily.

Life became harsher for Ernesto, however. He spent the day driving around Boston, stopping for lunch at McDonald's, and buying food for dinner at the local supermarket on his way home, just to finish his day opening the door into an empty room. We started to see each other only on my day off to do things together. He started to resent his new lonely life and became quieter than usual. Once, I decided to bring food from the restaurants for Ernesto, to make him happy, risking losing both of my jobs. I did this a couple of times only. With my limited English, and by that time already undocumented, I felt less secure than Ernesto. He had a Green Card, which I suspect might have been fake, while my visa had long expired. A great fear of deportation took over me, which now I know was totally unfounded at that time in Boston, where all Latinos were assumed to be Puerto Ricans and never stopped by the authorities to show ID's.

Soon, almost subconsciously, Ernesto and I started to sense a distance between us. We had been brothers up to this time, forging our energies toward only one goal: to make it in America, but our lives were pointing towards different directions.

One night, Lester, the Howard Johnson's manager, sent me home earlier than usual. I stopped for a coffee at the Dunkin Donuts on Boylston Street before heading home. For a moment, I was tempted to enter the Paris cinema, a first-run art house on Boylston Street, showing a movie named "El Topo," by Alejandro Jodorowsky. I remember my big surprise at seeing a billboard of a movie in Spanish by a Argentinian/Mexican director I had heard about when I lived in Puebla. Are the Bostonian gringos so sophisticated to appreciate a movie in Spanish? I asked myself. I checked the showing times. The next showing was a midnight, impossible for me. I opted for coffee.

As I waited in line to order, the girl sitting on the first red stool at the counter fixed her blue eyes on me, looked away for an instance, then turned them again towards me. I ordered a cup of coffee with two old fashioned donuts and as I turned to leave, she asked me in a primitive Spanish where I was from and offered to teach me English. Remembering what I had learned at El Monte Adult Education center, I managed to ask her if she knew the name of the English verb tense in the sentence, "I would have done it". She failed. She asked me to give her a second chance to prove that she could be an excellent teacher to me. We set up a time for a lesson the next day, my day off, at 4:00 pm.

Ernesto came home next day after work and found me with this stranger, reading English aloud to me. At that time, I thought that I would expedite learning the language through transcribing entire books. I had started recopying by hand the entire text of Anna Karenina, from a paperback I found in a box next to the garbage in the back alley —among several nonfiction hardcover books — into a notebook. I didn't understand anything at first, but the process forced me to pay extreme attention to the words. I used the limited small dictionary we brought from L.A. to lookup words I didn't understand. The tutor was reading Anna Karenina aloud next to me as I followed the text carefully, when Ernesto entered the room. "My name is Claudia," she said.

   "*...had she contrived the most cunning devices to meet Vronsky, she could have thought of nothing better,*" Claudia continued reading. "I don't understand the structure of that sentence," I said frustrated. "Why is the word 'had' before the verb? What does 'could have thought' mean", I asked. The dictionary was of no use in this case. Claudia did not find a clear way of explaining it to me, but taught me how to pronounce "could have thought." You say, "coodov," she told me. "*Maldito inglés nunca lo voy a aprender,*" I said turning towards Ernesto who had been following the lesson from his bed. Claudia would later become my first wife and the mother of my first son, Eric.

   This was around the time when I wrote the first letter to my parents. It had taken me one year to do so for reasons that I don't quite understand. This insensitive, cruel delay could have been caused by my inability to convey any good news until now. I also had feared my stay would have been very temporary and not worth an optimistic letter home. Or maybe, I was too caught up in the immediate issues of day to day survival to have energy for international communication. Teto, my younger brother, tells me now that I was a jerk. My mother cried every night for a year, having thought me already dead, killed in the trek north. He tells me that the day my first letter arrived, my mother made a special chicken soup for the family and made the rounds through our entire extended relations to let them know that I was well and working in Boston, not Los Angeles.

Chapter 2: A New job during retirement?

When I reached my third week of retirement, I started looking for a temporary job. My friends and family did not cease to suggest activities to keep me occupied. Here are a few examples.

Friend #1
"Now you can audit all those courses at Harvard that you always wanted, especially the ones dealing with Scholastic Philosophy and Ethics. You also wanted to refresh your Latin and French. This is the time."

Friend #2.
"Now you have all the time in the world to practice the piano. You can take as many hours as you want while your wife is at work, no complaints from her. Learn those difficult classical pieces that you love so much. This time there are no excuses!

Family Member #1.
"Now it is the time to bicycle across America, the trip of your life. This you've wanted to do for a very long time. These two books are your retirement present: "Just the Two of Us: A cycling Journey Across America," by Melissa Norton and "How to Find Interesting, Rewarding, Fulfilling, and Fun Things to do in Retirement," by James Stafford. Please, read them."

Family Member #2.
"This is the time for you to work towards having your own private, small bilingual high school, baccalaureate granted, geared towards educating Boston's Latino youth. This is what you always wanted. You could make it into a

Charter School. This is the right moment. Strike while the iron is hot. The State and President Obama are in sync on educational reform with the new Race to the Top initiative. Start writing a proposal and get some people together to advise you."

Family Member #3.
"Don't do anything for six months. Use this time to reflect. Do some yoga! Relax!"

The intensity of the struggle I felt to survive during those first years in America could never compare to any other life venture in the subsequent years. Back then, I felt invincible and eternal, without letting anything pass by me, almost frantically devouring all experiences. The priest who gave me my first job showed great wisdom. He knew from the start that my job would be temporary. It lasted two months. Now I also know the reason why he paid me so much. As an act of charity, he decided to help me get my feet settled in America by aiding in my transition.

The priest, however, unintentionally created something greater in me. He created in me an unwavering faith in my future in America. My expectations about succeeding in America increased 100-fold after my first job. I became confident that anything was possible on this side of the border. Things were so easy here. Previous Salvadorian immigrants had been right when they would come back and talk about their successes in America. Easy! No obstacles! Success in America required only energy and motivation. *¡Ganas!* I know now that had I remained back home in Santa Ana, then a small town of El Salvador, I wouldn't have ever had a chance. Still, my thoughts at that time were to remain in Los Angeles as long as it took me to learn English so that I could go back home with some kind of marketable skill. I never intended to stay in America for more than a couple of years. I was convinced then that the Army would soon vacate the Salvadorian National University, indicating its reopening and a signal to resume my law studies that I had started soon after I left the Seminary.

The priest at Saint Luke's, Temple City, Father John Birch, may he rest in peace, wrote me a letter of recommendation on a postcard that I carried around in my pocket in L.A. and in Boston, and showed it to people as a form of reference whenever a job opportunity came up.

> *"This is to recommend Francisco Ruiz for any janitorial job. Francisco is a hard worker. He does not speak any English, but, when shown how, will do anything you ask him to do. He has been helping our church and school janitor to wash windows, sweep and mop floors, clean bathrooms and perform several other janitorial tasks. We cannot afford him anymore. Please consider him for a job."*
> Signed, *Father John Birch, 12/08/1972.*

When I read the card now, I burst into a melancholic smile. That person the priest described sounds like a distant, distorted echo of me: inexperienced, innocent, naïve, pure, still like a seminarian. The year I graduated from BU, I returned to Saint Luke's with my parents and asked to see Father Birch. I wanted him to be proud of me. I showed him my diploma. He did not remember who I was. I told him my story and said that I had come to see him to thank him for giving me my first job in America. The young priest who had led me to him later told me Father Birch had Alzheimer's and was not remembering much about anything those days. I had wanted him to see that I had made something of myself and that I had a future thanks to the start he gave me, but fate and time had other plans and it was clear that I had missed my chance. Despite the reunion not going as I imagined it over and over in my head, I still will forever be grateful to that priest who took a chance on a scruffy immigrant and set me on a good path.

Eventually, I may try to engage in the activities my family and friends have suggested for my retirement. For now, I decided on something less stressful and more structured, some kind of part-time job that could create a sense of purpose, provide a schedule of tasks to be adhered to, and formulate daily concrete objectives to be accomplished. I thought that the perfect fit for this would be to contribute in some capacity to the 2010 US Census. I had a stake in it. I wanted everybody to be counted, especially the ones who have been traditionally undercounted, such as Hispanics and Blacks of the inner city.

One early morning in Spring, I walked into the Regional Census Bureau Offices located at Copley Place, Boston. The offices happened to be in the same mall, above the same spot, where I had spent my first weekday of retirement, wandering around. It surprised me that I would be in the same place again. Was this a lucky omen, or just a coincidence? I had already vowed never to enter a mall again during a weekday, especially in the mornings, but I was determined to investigate this job possibility.

Hidden behind the decorative waterfall, I found the elevators. I took one to the third floor, where a serious, tall, and wide shouldered man in his thirties standing behind a counter asked me for my ID, as if to say: *What are you doing here? You don't belong here.*

"Your ID," he barked.

"I don't have one," I shyly responded, with some fear in my heart.

"You can't enter without an ID," he instructed me, as I became aware of his military gear: gun, bullets, earpiece, two-way radio, and boots.

"I don't work here, yet." I retorted, while other impatient men and women in their expensive business suits flashed their corporate ID's, a daily routine for them, almost spilling their macchiatos, making their way to their offices as if not to be late for their important meetings. The guard just gave them a perfunctory nod and let them pass. I felt utterly unwanted and unwelcome.

"Don't you have any ID?" the guard probingly and loudly inquired. I bet he made those perfumed women feel extremely safe.

"You mean any type of ID? I thought you were asking me for a special ID to be able to enter this floor," I explained.

By this time, I was already feeling really stupid. A group of annoyed executives and secretaries stared at me. I finally gave him my driver's license. He scanned it into a database and gave me a visitor's pass with the copy of my license on it. In retrospect, the encounter makes sense. After 9/11, all federal offices cranked up their security measures to ensure no one suspicious or threatening was let in.

This type of daily interaction with the police, guards and security officers may be very normal to most people, but not to me. Every time I encounter law enforcers, I flash back to my experiences in El Salvador, at the border between Guatemala and Mexico, and my trek to the USA, through Mexico. Guards, police, army, airport security, border securities, and anybody with a uniform, at any checkpoint, always trigger powerful and unwelcomed images within me that I try intensely to keep in check. I see violence and death in the faces of law enforcement officers despite the tremendous public campaign in the US to sanitize them, to make them community friendly. During such encounters, a turmoil of emotions unfailingly betrays me and, as a result, my reactions and responses, always tinted with anger, are automatic and never fail to surprise me. I become a Pavlov dog, instinctively reacting to a perceived threat or reward.

Law enforcement at any checkpoint makes me feel accused and guilty of crimes against humanity and this demeaning feeling turns into outrage that overtakes me. That was one of the reasons why I avoided discothèques

with bouncers while in college. This was one point of disagreement Saturday nights or weekends in NY City with
my college roommate Patrick, who often loved to put to a
test his desirable in-look and upper class European up-
bringing by measuring how long it would take Studio 54
bouncers to lift the red velvet cordon to let us in.

My deep seeded primal pride would not let any ignorant fool to get the upper hand. In Central America and
Mexico, I often fought forcefully with my logical verbosity
and stinging tongue. In America, however, my thick accent
sent some people away and intensified others' reactions
against me. At present, I have become a bit milder and
aware of my errant immigrant status and its perilous consequences. More often than not, I escape those situations.
However, in light of recent changes in the federal government under President Trump, these uncomfortable
interactions with law enforcement are coming back full
force once again.

On this account, I feel jealous of my younger brother,
Teto, now living with his wife and two sons in Cambridge. Teto, a veteran of the Salvadorian Special Forces,
never acquired negative feelings towards law enforcement.
Having been in the army, he feels part of their club. When
we travel together, I am the only one to be pulled aside for
further inspection and interrogation in the secret rooms at
airports. He walks past security laughing. This never fails.
This happened when we visited Jerusalem years ago for
my son Eric's wedding. It happened again on our way back
from a pleasure trip to El Salvador, and again when re-
entering the USA from Canada, and all over again coming
back to the US from my family's recent trip to Israel. I have
written multiple letters to the National Security Administration complaining. Because of my persistence, I have
received Redress Letters from those offices saying that I
am pre-approved by national security, which purportedly
would help me avoid those humiliating encounters. Nothing has worked. I showed my letter to the security officer

at the airport only to receive an indifferent smile while being escorted to the backroom for interrogations.

When visiting the Niagara Falls, my wife and I took a tour bus that crossed the border to the Canadian side of the falls in the summer of 1994. On our way back, one US immigration officer boarded the bus, looked around, and, of course I knew as soon as he stepped onto the bus, that I was going to be the only one to be picked for questioning. I loudly stated, "There are 55 white people on this bus, and because I look different you picked me. This is a blatant case of discrimination. Those white people behind me may be the ones without ID and are illegal, not me." My wife pleaded with me to be calm and to just give him my American passport.

On another occasion, in 1995, when I drove Teto to Needham to pick up my eldest son Eric from his mother's house one Sunday afternoon, the Needham police stopped me in the parking lot and asked me for my ID. This time I had had enough and was ready to fight back and even go to jail. I argued with the police officer forcibly and at length. I told him that he did not have the right to stop me to ask for any identification, and that I was going to sue him for violating my civil rights of free movement. I came close to his nose and loudly asked him how he could be so blatantly racist and show no shame and if whether or not the entire Needham police culture was contaminated with the same nasty, racist pollution.

This time it wasn't my wife who pleaded with me to be reasonable in front of the officer who already had handcuffs out. Teto, in an act of brotherly betrayal, defended the cop's behavior in front of me by saying, "the officer is just doing his job. Please, show him your driver's license." *"That is not his job,"* I said. "He needs to explain himself. Why is he stopping me to ask me for an ID?" By this time, a group of people had already gathered around us to witness the exchange, most likely assuming that the officer was trying to protect their pristine neighborhood from a criminal. That's exactly what people in the suburbs feel, especially when dealing with outsiders. The officer mis-read the crowd's intentions and, fearing that he was making a big mistake, put the handcuffs back into his belt. Noticing his concession, I did regrettably show him my driver's license. Teto and I continued our walk to pick up Eric.

It never fails. For certain, I fall under numerous ter-rorists' profiles unknown to me. That is the only explanation possible. My face shows features that fall un-der a category universally understood as non-white. This feature greatly amused me while in college, where I could pass as Japanese, Chinese, Indian, Cambodian, Turkish, Palestinian, Filipino, but never as a Latin American from El Salvador. That also explains why I had a college girl-friend from each of those countries. Or, maybe my nervousness is so visible that it causes officers at check-points to become suspicious of my behavior and inevitably trigger their profiling protocols.

✳✳✳

The 2010 Census Bureau was hiring census takers, but that central office was not distributing the applica-tions. I was kindly directed to go to my neighborhood public library for a basic skills test and, if I passed, a sub-sequent application process. I was hired, but decided not to do it. I had lost the impetus.

Nowadays, I have fallen into a typical daily routine in my retirement, waiting for Carolina to retire. Sometimes I joke with her and say if I had known of the consequences derived from marrying a woman 10 years younger than me when it came time for me to retire first, I would have had second thoughts about her. To keep active and delay men-tal decay, I keep my daily calendar full of activities: teaching Spanish at Brookline Adult Ed. at night, taking

French literature classes during the day, taking Tango lessons, volunteering at Centro Presente where I teach Citizenship, keeping up with my bicycling, reading and re-reading Spanish literature, and trying to finish this book. However, these social engagements have not been enough. My new venture at present is a teaching position at Boston Latin School as a permanent substitute for the French teacher on sick leave. I have learned more French in the past three months from trying to keep up with French 3, 4 and AP classes, with extremely bright students, than I have during my years studying French at Brookline Adult Ed. Want to learn something? Teach it. Today is Friday, and I just regained the feeling of anticipation of rest and fun that I had lost. It is blissful.

Chapter 3: La Caminata. At the Border between Guatemala and Mexico. Talismán. Part I

My experiences with authorities in the US, however, pale in comparison with a series of encounters with law enforcement during my unexpected three-month walk to the United States from El Salvador. It all started one hot day in the middle of August, 1972, when the rainy season was at its fullest. I awakened way before sunrise to the pleasant smell of wet soil and a citric aroma sent by the lush vegetation of our traspatio. Those delicious scents attenuated the jittery effects of last night's fearful, restless sleep. Years ago, might have been around my birth, my mother had planted a mango, a lemon, a banana, an avocado, a cinnamon and an orange tree in the traspatio, where my mother found solace and distraction from the pains of her daily life. She planted and replanted and waited for *la luna tierna,* to do her grafts. She did them at night and brought me to the traspatio with her, as if my presence would conjure Mother Earth to be kind to my mother's vegetation.

The night before, three members of the infamously brutal Salvadorian National Guard, led by Lieutenant Monje, had come to the house to get me. The guard left word with my father that Lieutenant Monje wanted to interview me about the events prior to the military occupation of the national university. I was lucky. I was nowhere to be found because of late I had acquired the habit of walking to the hideout of one of the groups of the revolutionary movement, for a late-night meeting with *el Roperón,* one of my university classmates. After the closing of the University, with much more time on their hands, the revolutionary student and professor movements had adopted an intense planning period to devise a new strategy for facing military repression. I had become restless day and night, and looked for something to replace the routine of the university, to take my mind away from the deadly events of the military occupation, while also trying to make sense of my relationship with my then-girlfriend, Norma. Thinking about the university made me look towards the future, while obsessing about Norma's relationship brought my attention to the present, complicating a life already in turmoil. Attending the revolutionary meetings provided me with a purpose unconnected to both, university and Norma.

Lieutenant Monje's visit to my house clarified further my future. Monje had come to my house that night to arrest me. Escaping from Santa Ana was the only option. On that aromatic morning before sunrise, I frantically threw a few of my possessions into Teto's green army duffle bag, stepped out of the house, and never looked back. Destination: North. After my escape, the Salvadorian National Guard, financed by the US government and under the flag of anti-communism, went on a murderous rampage for almost 20 years, provoking a civil war that killed thousands and disappeared hundreds of young people. I had just escaped what was soon to become the bloodiest period of Salvadorian history.

Flashing forward to almost a week into my trek, I wondered about my mother's reaction when learning that I had left again. I don't remember hugging her goodbye. She had never gotten used to my previous long absences. At this moment of uncertainty and possible danger, I felt the need to have Teto, my younger brother, with me. His street smarts, weaponry, army recognizant, knife throwing, and black belt karate skills were legendary in Santa Ana, as well as his dope dealing of mostly marihuana that he hoisted from *La Hacienda Los Apoyos* vía la IRCA, the train that made a stop at the Laguneta station. *La mara,* soon started to call him *"Teto Mariguana"*. Teto never lost a bar or street fight, with or without knives, sometimes against three opponents. He had escaped death several times.

Once, he was left for dead bleeding profusely out the side of his abdomen, his body against the street curb in the notorious *Barrio Santa Barbara,* after having fought four opponents with knives. One of his mistresses ran to our house to let my mother know of Teto's condition. The doctor later said that the knife miraculously had not puncture any vital organs. Once in a while nowadays, he complains of a sharp pinch on his left side after doing exercises. *"Nunca regrese a la casa siguiendo las mismas calles",* Teto's admonition now echoed in my mind.

I arrived at a border and stood in the middle of no man's land, in the crossroads populated by smugglers, drug traffickers, and professional *contrabandistas.* The border between Guatemala and Mexico trapped me with a group of destitute people, many escaping from their undesirable home countries' economics and politics, others looking to lay low for a while, hoping to cross over unnoticed by the Mexicans. Once in Mexico, their hopes were to use it as a springboard, or transitory bridge, to the US. It was evident that with the right amount of money, one could bribe Mexican immigration officials, all men, from the one working at the counter stamping the passports to the general in charge of customs, especially the general. Mexican corruption was legendary and well known by foreigners. *"El que no tranza, no avanza."* "Just give them a *'mordida',"* people told me. "They will let you cross the border. No questions asked." If only I had the money!

The rainy season had arrived and continued vigorously. After I left home, I chose the hottest, the muggiest, and least populated seashore route leading to the Mexican border because it was the shortest, at around 300 miles. The other way would have been attempting to cross the border between Guatemala and Mexico through the mountainous, treacherous, overgrown, *selva* of the ancient Mayan trails that led to the Usumacinta River, through the Lacandón jungle; a much longer trip. This less traveled route was known to be absent of border posts and checkpoints. The Mayan-Quiché communities straddled both Mexican and Guatemalan areas. One could walk from one country to the other unnoticed if one spoke the language and wore the right tribal apparel. My father's maternal grandmother was a pure Mayan. *If only I knew how to speak their dialect. Once at the riverbanks, I would hide in the crowd and cross into Mexico.* Several high, rickety suspension footbridges, not unlike those bridges seen in the Indiana Jones movies, were used to cross this river.

The inevitably vertigo-inducing walk on those suspension footbridges would have represented a problem for me. I spent my childhood school vacations around the Lempa River in the Santa Ana Salvadorian province, where I crossed a similar, badly maintained, sagging bridge with roped sides and a wooden-slat floor with huge gaps due to missing planks. I never got used to it. The trick then was never to look down to the white-water torrents that could make the bravest of us want to turn back. One or two very small campesino children, while playing away from their parents, would fall through the cracks every year and disappear in the tumultuous rapids bellow.

The locals, however, were very adept at crossing this bridge running with heavy bundles of farm products on their backs and heads, jumping over the gaps, as if crossing a well-paved road, while the bridge would swing side to side. This bridge which was located next to the Laguneta train station terrified me. My cousins and I played around the bridge and dared each other to run across it, knowing that the Hacienda property ended at the start of the bridge and there was no need to go to the other side. There were times when I froze in the middle of the bridge, unable to jump over its wide gaps. As a child, I could not reach the rope sides to clutch them with my hands. I used only one side and would walk sideways to cross the bridge. My older cousins, especially Neto, would have to come back to my rescue, making fun of me all the while. Later on in my adult life, my susceptibility to vertigo became more apparent, which explains a lot about why I suffered so much on that small bridge, but I ended up somehow crossing it anyway.

There was a good reason why I chose not to take the path with the bridge, but the mostly flat and hot-steamy CA2 route through Guatemala, which proved to be much longer than anticipated. A direct trip, at that time, would have taken no more than 10 hours by car from Santa Ana, El Salvador to Talisman, Mexico. It had already taken me five days. Hitchhiking definitely was not the fastest way to go north. With an empty wallet, however, hitchhiking was the only present solution.

I did not know back then the existence of the freight train, now nicknamed *"La Bestia,"* that was very popular with migrants from Central America. I would have expected to take it once in Mexico. Who cared if the wagons carried pigs and cows, petroleum or deadly chemicals! I am sure that in 1972 the trip on this train would have been very uneventful. It takes just a quick jump to board this train, while it makes its way through the mountains from Southern Mexico to the US. Today, desperate children and young immigrants jump on this train, and climb to its roof to go North, hoping to find their mothers and a job. Nowadays, taking *La Bestia* is a death sentence. Migrants call it the "Death Train," or "Hell's Train." Smugglers and criminal gangs roam its roof, in silence. Some cry inconsolably, others pray continuously, unprotected, knowing that *La Bestia's* subtitle could very well be "Here Hell begins." After many days without sleep, some succumb to exhaustion and fall off the train to their deaths, while others die from decapitation by tunnels.

On my trip through Guatemala, long waits for vehicles to pass by gradually brought me into a state of unbearable tediousness. The forest and the tall grass alongside the road produced an incessant, numbing hum broken at times with a soft wind whistle that accentuated the uncharacteristic silence of the road. Now and then one car would rumble past, but I was alone on the *carretera* for the most part. Sometimes I had to stand and walk for two to three hours under the burning sun, only to be interrupted by a humid, violent thunderstorm that left me drenched to the bone with water and salty sweat, before any vehicle would pass. Adding to this misery, the *chicharras* never rested from their constant, high pitched drone. At other times, a *campesino's* dog would bark at a distance, rejecting my presence and warning me that I was about to breach his territory.

I was afraid of farm dogs. The bites I had suffered by Tío Paco's dogs as a child traumatized me. The multiple times my mother took me to see her favorite brother, his dogs found a way to escape his control and run towards me to grab my scrawny calf behind my mother's skirt where I would quickly hide, seeking protection. Since then, I have been terrified of unfriendly farm dogs. The stories of rabid dogs that at one time were common in Chalchuapa had increased my fear. These dogs created an uproar of panic in Chalchuapa's barrios. I would hear how the dogs would be promptly killed by an attentive resident's gunfire. I knew rabies was a serious danger to the community because after those incidents the *alcaldía* launched a vaccination campaign.

One would think that I shouldn't be afraid of dogs after being raised with many. One in particular, Buck, was a German Shepard mixed with other native breeds named after Buck Rogers, my father's favorite childhood comic strip that appeared daily in the early 1930s in *La Prensa* newspaper in combination with Buck, from Jack London's book The Call of the Wild, one of my father's favorites. Buck was born one year before I was. Since the moment of my home birth, we were inseparable. Buck was my full-time protector and left my side only to take his meals in the traspatio. Right after I was born, my mother would complain that Buck was frightening away all her relatives who wanted to visit and meet baby Chepito. Later, when relatives came unexpectedly, as was always the custom, they had to wait outside the house while Buck was taken away to the traspatio. Our guests wouldn't enter the house until being assured that Buck was securely leashed to the mango tree.

I spent hours playing with Buck and sometimes was nasty to him, but he never protested. Buck became my horse, my pillow, and my running buddy. I pulled often on his ears and tail. I have an early memory from when I was three of me peeing on Buck while he stood immobile, no protest. He could have bitten my penis off, if he wanted to. Buck never complained. Another recurring routine with Buck took place when we drove from the city to our farm. Sometimes my father refused to bring him with us because Buck fought the farm dogs and regularly came back home bloody. Buck often sensed this decision and would wait hidden around the house just to bolt through the front door seconds after we drove away, slipping through the maid's' legs before they had time to stop him. Two or three blocks down, thinking about Buck, I would look through the small rear window and suddenly see him running after us at full speed, trying to catch up with our Chevrolet pick-up truck. I would yell at my father, "Buck is coming! Buck is coming!" My father would slow down to let him jump up into the truck's bed. Wagging his tail, full of happiness, he would plop himself down just below the small rear window to be next to me.

One spring day, Buck disappeared. My father tells me that when he looked for him all over Santa Ana, a friend told him that they had seen Buck joining a pack of wild street dogs. Another friend said that a Guatemalan thief had kidnapped him. I cried for Buck with desperation, but gradually I forgot about him.

One day during dinner, around six months later, my father heard a knock at the front door. It was Buck, whacking his tail against the wooden door, begging to be let in! The story, as told by my father, is that Buck walked hundreds of miles from Guatemala City to return home. When Buck stumbled his way back, he was unrecognizable. Looking like a skeleton, long gone were his muscular chest and hind legs, his fur infected with scabies, and his parched tongue stuck out of his mouth. Buck entered the house, paced very slowly through the patio, without greeting anybody, crossed the kitchen, and stopped under the mango tree in the traspatio. He remained prostrated down by the tree for weeks, moribund, without acknowledging the presence of my father or me. It was my mother who gradually nursed him back to health and, once again, I happily rode him like a horse without him protesting. Up until now, we don't know how Buck found our house, supposedly from a 200 miles distance. It's quite a miracle.

Back on the highway, no rabid dog jumped into the road to bite me like I feared. At times, I was sure a driver would pick me up as he slowed down on his approach only to ignore me or swear at me, *"¡¡¡Cabrón mariguanero, hijueputa!!!"* Young men with long hair would be considered hippies under the influence of LSD or marijuana in those years, especially while hitchhiking.

After a couple of days of walking with no ride, a truck picked me up after the sun set, just outside Mazatenango. I had been walking all day. Soon after, the truck veered off the main road to deposit me in the center of Retauhuleu. Exhausted, I laid on the first green wooden bench in *El Parque Central,* under a leafy tree full of hundreds of green parrots that had decided to perch there for the night. Despite the birds chattering, I slept soundly. Early morning, I walked back to route CA2 thirsty and hungry. This time I did not wait long. A small green Ford pickup truck, driven by a young Mayan with a big smile and carrying another stranger on the truck's bed, gave me the last ride I needed to reach the Talisman checkpoint on the border between Guatemala and Mexico.

Ironically, 16 years before, while living in Guatemala City, where my alcoholic father had forced the family to move, I had slept in the Retauhuleu *Parque. Central.* My father had stationed the family mini cooper by the side of the park late at night and ordered the family to get some sleep in the car before continuing our summer vacation trip to the beaches of Champerico. Overexcited by this trip, I stayed awake all night. My mother and my three other brothers checked into the local *pensión* across the cobble street, but my father and I slept in the car. He feared the mini cooper was a unique, exotic car and an easy prey for thieves. I lay down on the back seat and watched the moisture of my breath fog the windows and divert the rays of the dimmed yellowish streetlight as they formed squiggles like slow moving worms of transparent shadows on the car upholstery. I don't remember hearing the parrots chattering that night, I suspect they were already sound asleep.

Once in the Mayan's green pickup truck, I became elated. This other young guy from Nicaragua was also on his trip North without money. He mentioned California. I mentioned Puebla. I felt stronger. I had company. Surely, once in Mexican territory, I knew the rides would come by more frequently because many roads, from different directions, converged at the same border crossing: *Talismán.*

Upon seeing my Salvadorian passport all in order, and noticing multiple previous Mexican student visas I had used during my Seminarian years, I was positive the Mexican immigration officer would let me pass, no questions asked. After all, I had crossed the same border many times with Gustavo on our way back from summer vacations to the Seminary of Puebla without a hitch. At that time, however, we both were wearing prep school jackets and ties. Despite my unkempt look this time, I expected the same treatment. I couldn't have been more naïve and wrong.

I joined the long line and when I finally reached the counter at midday, I presented my Salvadorian passport to the border official and smiled, already thinking about my next ride north.

"Can I see the $100.00 that you will spend in Mexico?"
He said with scorn.

My stomach clenched into knots as it dawned on me
that I needed to prove that I had at least $100.00 in order
to cross the border.

"I don't have that amount. I am a poor student going
back to Puebla."

"Then, for sure, you must have tons of money. Show
me at least $100.00."

"I have all my money saved in the bank of Puebla. I'll
be there tomorrow."

"Show me your bus ticket, then."

"I don't have one."

"Guard! Guard!"

Immediately, a guard with a Belgium-made G-3 rifle,
the preferred weapon at that time for all Central American
National Guards, came up and escorted me out of the
building to push me back to the Guatemalan side.

I was not deterred. I had to cross that border. Where
would I get $100.00? I had only one solution: to humiliate
myself and beg like a hungry stray dog to every rich trav-
eler passing by for the $100.00, a very unlikely event. Who
in their right mind would give me such a high amount? To
a wealthy vacationer who was very protective of their
money, I could appear to be a thief, a con artist, or somebody just scouting for rich travelers to later rob them as
they stopped to sleep on the other side of the border. My
problem was figuring out how to convince people that I
wasn't a thief. No one was going to believe me.

I dreaded the possibility of rejection when asking
somebody for money, especially when I needed it so desperately. This was one of the responsibilities I couldn't
stomach while I was in the Seminary. Priests lived out of
charity and Sunday's mass donations, but occasionally,
there was the need to meet with a rich donor to haggle for
a bigger donation. I accompanied my mentor, Padre Chus,
to perform this job a couple of times during my Seminary

years and would ask rich heiresses of coffee plantations for money. I invariably considered those negotiations demoralizing and demeaning. When the parish priest assigned me the task of selling lottery tickets for such and such excursion, usually to Guatemala's town of Esquipulas, where there is a historic miraculous black crucifix deeply venerated by Central Americans, I would ask my brother Rafael to go house by house in our barrio to sell them because I couldn't stand to do it myself. Under the current circumstances, however, as I stood on the opposite side of the border, I needed to be brave. It was strikingly clear I could not afford to be proud.

All vehicles, cars, busses, trucks, and 18- wheelers had to stop to unload their passengers just before crossing the Mexican border. Travelers lined up to show their papers to be stamped for admittance into Mexican territory, the vehicles had to be searched by customs. All merchandise passed through. One needed only to be versed in the art of the perfect *mordida*: payoff and anything could be accepted through without any fuss.

I decided to stand in a strategic spot where I could canvas people without being noticed by the Mexican and Guatemalan National Guard or any other border official. If the guards were to see me, they would become suspicious of my activities and take me as a fugitive on the run or an armed robber waiting for the right moment to pounce on unsuspecting travelers. From my vantage point, I took a deep breath, and began to beg.

Chapter 4: At the Border between Guatemala and Mexico. Talismán. Part II

"**E**xcuse me! Can you help me?" I began to plead, "I know you have a lot of money. Could you lend me $100.00 just to show it to the immigration officer? I have all my papers in order. I have a visa. I really need to cross this border. As soon as we are on the other side, I'll give the money back to you. Please, trust me."

I tried to talk to anyone who would listen, but no one would register my words or even glance in my direction, until finally someone approached me and peaked my hope.

A tall and thin white American man in his thirties, with the bluest eyes and yellow hair, Richard Widmark Hollywood star look alike, and with an almost unintelligible Gringo accent, stopped to talk to me in Spanish. He pulled me aside, hid behind a tree, inserted his right hand in his front pants pocket, and took out a wad of unclipped, half-folded, lose $100.00 bills. He spread them using his thumb as a poker player does when carefully examining his dealt hand. He kept the money low and close to his pants, avoiding a straight view from the distant guards for fear of raising suspicion. *This is how hundred-dollar bills look like.* I had never been so close to so much money in my life. I was ecstatic! My long wait would be finally over! Surely, with so much cash, the man could afford to see one bill go.

"You are looking for one of these, right?" He smirked, holding up a hundred-dollar bill.

"Yes. I'll give it back to you as soon as we reach the other side. I just need to show it to the official." I explained.

"Too bad for you, I am not giving you one cent, you stupid bastard!" He cruelly stated, as he mockingly swaggered away with pleasure and satisfaction after seeing my stunned and deeply disappointed expression. He quickly joined the immigration line and gave me a final look of disdain. I often wonder what makes people feel pleasure while humiliating others. It must be a survival instinct. Maybe there are some groups more prone to sadism. A sense of dread came over me upon thinking that this cruel Gringo could be an accurate representation of the true nature of all Gringos. I cried with desperation. That was my last attempt. It was better now for me to turn back home, to a life without a future and if I stayed out of trouble, the Salvadorian National Guard would ignore me.

Alongside the road that ended at the border gate, a row of *posadas* and *comedores,* some inside shelters made of adobe with low straw roofs, others within cement walls with rusted tin roofs, populated the area. Food was served out of these places at all times of the day and night. The air wavered in a constant stream of smoked wood, fresh hot corn tortillas, cooked black beans, and cilantro. It appeared that in El Carmen, a shantytown at the Talisman crossing, everybody was traveling north. How far north? That was to be decided by persistence, endurance, and a little bit of luck.

That night, after eating some toasted thick tortillas topped with cheese and black beans, offered by a *pupusera*, who I had befriended, I slept under an *Amate* (wild fig) tree situated half a mile away from the border. I used Teto's green army duffle bag as a pillow. It did not rain, as it had every other night, which was a small blessing after a day of misery. Before falling asleep, I examined my unfulfilling immediate past and nurtured agonizing doubts about my future. I was known to my friends and family as a person who often entered lapses of extreme introspection, and, at times, melancholy. At 21, I felt I was a total failure and I think there were good reasons for it.

In moments of great insecurity, one tends to play the unavoidable and well-known "what if" game and imagine the road not taken. What would have happened if I had not deserted the Seminary after nine years of intense studies and profound commitment to my path of becoming an ordained priest? It is something like rewriting history, a recent popular idea as of late. How would the world look now had Hitler won the war? What might have happened if JFK had not been assassinated? Where would we be in our course of scientific discovery and progress if Copernicus never placed the Sun rather than the Earth at the center of the galaxy?

I spent three years in Puebla, Mexico, under a scholarship, obtaining a bachelor's degree in philosophy. By all accounts, I had a bright future within the ranks of the clergy. However, I walked away from the Seminary, as soon as I got back to Santa Ana from Puebla, Mexico, with my diploma in hand. The first day in town, I learned that the bishop, Monsignor Barrera, had changed his mind. He refused to send me, as it was promised and expected, to the Université Catholique de Louvain, Belgium, where I would have studied four years of theology for a doctorate degree. His decision filled me with a bone-deep disappointment that I never resolved.

I had returned to Santa Ana with my head full of simple but transcendental philosophical questions. I had struggled to reconcile in my mind the philosophical definition of a person as taught by my professors at the *Seminario Palafoxiano* in Puebla during my last year of philosophy, and its implications to the celibacy requirements of the priesthood. Their philosophical definition of a totally fulfilled person included free will, independence, and the intimate relationship with another person. How could I have been a complete human without falling in love and living in the sanctity of matrimony? I asked. Will I be condemned to be an incomplete person for the rest of my life? The solution presented at the Seminary dealt with a supposed process of sublimation, that when successful, the priest would consider himself married to his parish flock--to his congregation, to the people of God-- and the nuns, emulating Saint Teresa of Avila, would consider themselves to be married to Jesus Christ and blessed with the love of the father, God. The church is the bride of Christ. Just as a married man must give the whole of himself to his wife, a celibate priest must give the whole of himself to the church. I doubted my spiritual skills could bring me to a successful sublimation and ecstatic divine love on purely philosophical grounds, but I had put those questions to rest as I entered Santa Ana. I was determined to follow my vocation and finish the career.

Bishop Barrera of Santa Ana provided me with a catalyst. His decision to not send me to Louvain was a big blow to my self- esteem. It made me doubt my capacity to be the best and to succeed. God sent me a message and I had to listen. Bishop Barrera, I learned later, feared I would become radicalized while in Louvain, a traditional and conservative institution with a progressive philosophical department. He did not need revolutionary priests in his midst. Priests too aligned with the terrestrial conditions of the poor were not welcomed. The last couple of seminarians on scholarships, who had come back recently as priests from Louvain, had exhibited strong revolutionary tendencies according to the bishop. These priests, among them, Padre Walter Guerra (*el chele Walter*), Padre Camilo Girón, and Jesus Delgado (el padre Chus), were the most talented and educated in Central America.

I shared my reasons for leaving the Seminary with Padre Camilo and Gustavo recently when our vacations coincided in Santa Ana. Both told me that Bishop Barrera was very conservative and stubborn, and not known to change his mind once a decision was made. I never had a chance.

"The Louvain admissions office has sent two scholarships for two seminarians of high academic record. I think Chico (my seminarian nickname) should be considered," Padre Chus announced to Bishop Barrera one afternoon in my presence.

The bishop did not budge. My community of local priests and seminarians at the Juan XXIII Seminary of Santa Ana had thought my quick departure for Louvain to be a *fait accompli*. I walked out of the *palacio episcopal*, hurt, embarrassed, and disappointed. On this 1970 late July afternoon, I slowly walked with heavy legs, confused, lost, fearful, and depressed on a bright humid afternoon towards home. My family lived on a third-floor three-room apartment of the *multis*, a compound of new apartment buildings on the city limits of Santa Ana, and that was where I headed, one foot at a time, leaving as much space behind me as possible. I never looked back.

I just recently achieved some psychological closure when my wife and I visited Leuven (one hour by train from Brussels), entered the university classrooms, libraries and dormitories, and imagined taking copious notes as the professor imparted a lecture on scholastic philosophy. I imagined sitting there in 1970 and speculated about what could have been. Teto tells me that I would have come back to El Salvador, joined the revolution, and most likely been assassinated by the government. I phoned Padre Camilo on our return to talk about my Leuven visit. Camilo laughed and, at times his voice cracked, as we spent, one hour, reminiscing about his years in Leuven in the 1960's.

I never went back to the Episcopal Palace to talk to Bishop Barrera. He never made an attempt to come and fetch me either, as a good father would have done with love and understanding, as my heart deeply desired. I needed him to orient me, to advise me, to have a conversation with me, his spiritual son, about my future and options in life. He was never that personal as many Catholic clerics are not. This is due to their lofty, outside of real life, religious training. He gave up on me so easily. He discarded me, as if I had been all along just an appendix of Gustavo's future. Gustavo had already deserted; he had written him a letter of resignation before I came back to Santa Ana. If

Gustavo had already failed to live up to his commitments, there was no need to try to save me. I was rendered of questionable value. I was part of a package and the bishop assumed I had also resigned.

Totally abandoned by the bishop who I saw as a strong father-figure in my life, out of a regimented seminarian life, and with nothing to do, I spent several months closed in my room, shell-shocked, staring up at the white ceiling, in great darkness. The real world outside of the Seminary was incomprehensible to me; a foreign land with an undecipherable social language and alien cultural conventions. Its inhabitants seemed extremely preoccupied with daily living. All this sounded to me like gibberish and trivial monotony.

I straddled the cusp between sanity and a total psychological breakdown. I became a deep-sea diver who returned to the surface too quickly, almost unconscious, not having been provided with enough time for decompression. This life-shift almost killed me. I did not find a place to escape the oppressive and disappointed look of the entire community. Teto was the only one who dared enter my small room, my refuge, to entice me to join him in worldly affairs. When he came into my room, he would find me in the same position in my bed, with my nose pointed to the nearest wall, and my unblinking wide-open eyes fixated on a distant point in the horizon. Before it had been the ceiling, but this had already lost its curse or magic spell. I was an easy prey to anybody, anything, at this moment.

"Come on. Why don't you try the fresh marihuana that I cultivated in a hidden plot in the hacienda? I smuggle it in the train every weekend." "Why don't you go to the rock concert given by our cousins' band in the center of the city?" "*Vamos donde las putas, cabrón. ¿Por qué putas no se sale de este cuarto, cabrón?*"

Rafael, my other brother, the poet, in trying to understand my condition, resorted to writing sad poems and long disappointing short stories about my depression, which much later he read aloud to me. One of his stories was titled "The Fallen Hero." I was his hero, he wrote, his Odysseus. It pained him to see incomprehensibly how a hero can become totally defeated by life circumstances. He was deeply disappointed in me, in my weaknesses, in my inability to stand strong. My aged religious aunts and my mother, with their white handkerchiefs at the ready, irrigated their tanned and withered cheeks with a teardrop every time my name was mentioned in their afternoon coffee reunions. Pirri, my youngest brother, remained oblivious to my suffering, too distant to comprehend.

What followed was a long period of deep depression, social maladjustment, and ineptitude. My entire extensive family's hopes for a sure seat in heaven, a common belief among catholic families when one of its members becomes a priest, disappeared overnight. My obsessive, devout aunts, who woke up every morning to attend the 6:00 a.m. mass at the *Apostol Santiago* church in Chalchuapa to receive communion, and who often saw me helping the priest in mass, cried with despair and decided to increase their penance. I was already 20 and had absolutely no knowledge about the outside world after having been cloistered in a Seminary for almost nine years. I was a virgin physically, mentally, socially, and most importantly a virgin of the heart.

"Chepito, get out of the house and do things like the other boys do. Stop helping me in the kitchen. I don't need help," my mother would often exhort me during those days, when I dared to come out of my room to get something to eat and to seek comfort in her presence.

Chapter 5: Norma I.

As it typically happens, it took a girl to shake me up from my somnolence. Girls were treated like beings of another planet in the Seminary, aliens whose unexpected volatile movements could carry you to destruction, emotional spells, carnal knowledge, despair, and hell. One way to avoid a girl's curse of the original sin, was to idolize and sublimate her as the virgin daughter of God. Girls were entities that needed to be kept at arm's length, with respect, but always far away, with an effort to depersonalize them for fear of disastrous personal involvements. The absence of sisters deprived me of intimate glimpses into the feminine world and its mysterious personal psychology. This readied me to accept the idealistic and unrealistic framework put forth upon women by the Seminary: an idealization of women bordering on the views held by the knights of the Middle Ages, whose courtesan code aimed at serving and pleasing them by proving themselves worth of their love in the battlefield. My romantic attitude at that moment could have been compared to Balzac's General Montriveau at the time when he meets La Duchesse Langeais, in *La Comédie Humaine*.

> *"Il était, à son âge, aussi neuf en amour que l'est un jeune homme qui vient de lire Faublas en cachette ... mais de l'amour, il ne savait rien ; et sa virginité de sentiment lui faisait ainsi des désirs tout nouveaux."* ("At his age he was as much a novice in love as the guy that has just been furtively reading Faublas, but of love he knew nothing; and thus, his sinless romanticism created on him new desires")

I had never carried a potent, sexually charged, long conversation with any girl, until Norma. She and her close friend Yolanda crossed my path one day when I had just descended from the *multis* third floor, building A, Apt. 34. Out of the dark cave of my room for the first time in months, I was on my way to the Cathedral with the intentions of talking again to God. I wanted to know the reasons for my abandonment. The rainy season had just ended taking away its oppressive humidity. Today rushes of crisp air hit my face, sharpening my senses and attuning me to my surroundings, clarifying my purpose for the day. Norma's eyes sparked as they looked up to examine my face, showing their dark pupils through a strand of blonde hair, to quickly lower them timidly. She allowed Yolanda, with her open white face and sparkling green eyes, leveled with mine, to do most of the talking. Their blond waist-long hair flapped on their cheeks. Norma seemed to prefer her face partially covered by it, while Yolanda kept clearing it off her face. The girls were on their daily beauty promenade around the block, which they performed religiously to flirt with the neighborhood boys after their morning classes at school.

At noon, at that time, Salvadorian children walked back home for lunch and, if needed, a half-hour siesta. At 2:00 p.m., they returned for two classes to complete their school day. Some students played hooky in some afternoons, especially the upperclassmen in high school, and used this time to see their lovers. Norma and Yolanda did just that.

My irreverent brother Teto, knife thrower commando, war survivor and street fighter, told me recently here in Boston that Norma and Yolanda were known in the multis as *"amontonadoras,"* girls whom most of the multis boys had already hugged and kissed and maybe touched intimately, but never gone all the way. Rafael, my other brother, had already experienced Norma's hugs and kisses. When the girls noticed the arrival of a new boy, they couldn't wait to compete to get a piece of him. In their walks, the extremely endowed Yolanda and Norma changed their school uniforms for their shortest skirts and lowest necklines to display as much skin and cleavage as possible. At their sight, the bored boys and some unscrupulous married men, practically drooling, directed loud whistles from their balconies.

The echoing narrow horseshoe shape, that gave form to the four story *"multis"* and its courtyard, did not let any-body escape from public scrutiny. There was always a housewife or an old lady watching down from a balcony. The entire *"multis"* neighborhood and others later said that the whole town of Santa Ana knew Yolanda and Norma. The married women at the corner bodega com-mented in horror about the new decadence of morals. The modest and timid girls, religious or not, kept on a leash by their parents, wished with a jealous countenance to enjoy the same freedoms exerted by Norma and Yolanda. The barrio boys took bets on who would score first or next.

The rumors commented that Norma and Yolanda usu-ally preferred well-nourished rich young men from outside the barrio who circled the area with their new cars, full wallets, expensive jewelry, and exotic smells, looking for a one night of excitement, or so it was rumored in the *multis*. My mother, who never accepted Norma, complained aloud that the girls were whores and that everybody knew that they jumped into those cars because they liked older, well-built, hairy, and corpulent fellows, from the rich areas of town.

In this afternoon, with coquettish smiles accentuating their adventurous eyes, the girls approached me to offer me an invitation for an impromptu afternoon walk up the wooded hills of the city called *el cerro Santa Lucía*, to the west of the *multis*.

"We know you are going to become a priest. We have not seen you up close in a long while. We have been watch-ing you at a distance with a strong desire to meet you. You looked so serious with your black 'sotana,' that blue band around your waist, how do you call it?... and those spar-kling black leather shoes. You seemed always to be pressed for time, as if the world would end if you didn't get to your destination. We have taken only quick glances at you when crossing your path. We didn't want to get in your way. We were fearful of you. We thought for sure you could guess all our sins just by looking into our eyes. And, of course, we didn't want a man of God to sin on our account," Yolanda, the talkative, loudly pronounced ending with a mischievous smile. "Where is your *"sotana?* Don't tell me that you have decided to keep your black habit hung in your closet permanently!"

The thought of some of my neighbors hearing the echo of Yolanda's loud voice made me flinch. I still had a reputation to uphold.

"But, look, today we are literally running into you, almost bumping into you. *¡Qué casualidad!* We couldn't resist. We had to start some place; don't you think *padrecito*?" she continued.

I accepted their invitation out of courtesy. My desire to escape the peering eyes coming from the balconies of the *multis* that pierced through my skin like thousands of minute metallic shots provided a strong incentive. In small communities such as the *multis,* nobody was immune from the peeing eyes of his neighbors. *"El qué dirán,"* caused people to be in their best behavior in public, but *"a escondidas"* one could get away with murder.

Girls were not what I had in mind when I got up that day. The tall and svelte Yolanda talked loud and continuously as we made our way up the hill, measuring her words as to avoid her usual profanities, but her marked *mercado central* accent attested to her humble origins. The short and plump Norma walked at her side, away from me, looked down most of the time and let her long hair cover her left cheek. I felt stripped, light footed, unprotected, and immodest, but fresh, without the extra pounds of my black *sotana.*

The *cerro Santa Lucía* was the wooded hill that gave shelter to secret lovers escaping nosey neighbors and to catholic high school students who often used it after school to explore each other's pubescent love before running home for dinner. The students knew that their parents and The Daughters of Charity nuns of the girls-only *"Colegio La Medalla Milagrosa"* and, right across it, the Salesian priests of the boys-only *"Colegio San José,"* would never allow them to venture into the *cerro Santa Lucía's* wooded hills. It was not uncommon, despite parents' vigilance, to see a couple of early-pregnant young-girls disappear in the middle of the school year to only re-appear in the middle of the next one. Their babies were left in the care of the young girls' mothers to be treated publicly like their new siblings as not to jeopardize the young girl's future marital prospects, and life would go back to normal.

At the summit of the hill rested an old Spanish colonial house whose terrace provided a romantic view of the city below, especially at night. This house used to be a bourdelle, *"el Mirador,"* now turned into a restaurant. This bordello, the only lit house on top of the cerro, was very popular with the rich married men of the city during the 1940's and 1950's. When I was child, *El Mirador* was one of my father's favorite places for a night of heavy drinking, mambo and chachacha dancing, and lengthy sexual escapades accompanied by his poor lower-class friends, whom he wanted to impress by vulgarly pilfering my mother's inheritance. Today, as I walked up the hill with Norma and Yolanda, I couldn't help but look up to the summit and focus on the house's terrace imagining my father telling his jokes and singing his songs, and impressing the crowd with his exceptional dancing, a true bon vivant. For a moment, I felt my resentment deepening further and my anger exploding. How can life be so unjust? I could only think of how comfortable our lives could have been if my father had chosen a sober life.

We trek the uphill dirt path that bordered some *"cafetales,"* with their trees already heavy with the red grape coffee fruit, which bent down their branches by their weight, brushing the ground, weeping bloody tears, just waiting for the harvest soon to come. We stopped on a green grassy open area sprinkled by rocks of different sizes mid-way up the *cerro*, but high enough to get a good view of the city. We found a rock with soft indentations evidently made by many others before us. Yolanda sat on my left pulling her tight short blue skirt down as if wanting to cover her knees, looked carefully at her *chancletas* inspecting her toe nails, polished with a loud red, afraid that they had not survived the dusty trek. Norma, who had yet to utter a word, sat on my right and did the same with her purple skirt. Both sat very close to me. My body trembled. I retreated slightly and clasped my hands together as if ready to pray the *pater noster*.

I quickly understood the purpose of the climb. As near as I could tell, both girls were competing for my surrender. *El padrecito* for sure has desires. I felt more comfortable with the quiet, short and slightly plump physique, protected by a shy demeanor, that Norma possessed, only to break it to smile at Yolanda's jokes to quickly resume a hiding position slightly behind her as if looking for protection. Whereas, the exuberant, with high cheeks and a striking tall body that could have passed as a model under any international standards, but loud without restraint, full of vulgar speech of Yolanda's character, scared me.

"I am not sure I want to become a priest anymore. I have been studying in Puebla, Mexico for the last three years. I am not going back," I said. "I am searching for another future. The accidental properties of my life are clouding its substance. I have lost grasp of the essence of things. I am not sure anymore whether their essence is immutable. I am starting to think that dogmas are a pure invention of man and as such relative in their foundations. I am about to reach the conclusion that there is no permanent substance of things like Parmenides thought. All life is made of flux and constant change, just like Heraclitus believed. I feel God abandoned me and I see only darkness ahead of me. For sure it is a punishment for my mortal sins, for my violating the Ten Commandments. This may be the time to listen to Nietzsche, through Zarathustra, to become an overman, free from all the prejudices and moralities of human society by creating my own values. Maybe I will enroll at the local university and become a defense lawyer, which is closer to what I studied in the Seminary."

The girls attentively listened to my life story, even though almost nothing made sense to them. Their poor or lack of schooling had not prepared them to understand what I was saying and referring to. Teto would later tell me that if I wanted to make some conquests, I needed to dump down my vocabulary, complicated language patterns, useless intellectualism, and keep at bay topics of conversation that only other seminarians would have understood.

Definitely, barrio boys and girls, even young high school and university students of those times would have thought I was out of my wits. When speaking, oblivious to the presence of my audience and its background, I tended to sermonize, to assume a professorial posture, and to behave not unlike a schizophrenic mumbling about obscure worlds and scenarios. I might have seemed too far removed from the girls, so distant, so unattainable, completely *ido de la cabeza*. I belonged to another world, an unknown world, and they were right. They didn't yet know my inner turmoil and my desire to wake up from a nightmare. I needed a remedy to sooth my pain. Deep down my soul was invaded with an impatient eagerness to catch up with lost time. The girls listened immobile, respectfully; trying hard to understand the turmoil in my heart expressed by my nonsense, and doubted the effectiveness of their conquest and saw no prospects with me. The barrio boys were easier.

After my monologue, I noticed in Yolanda's eyes hesitation and uncertainty of how to proceed. Regardless, a decision had been made beforehand that Norma had to have the first pick. Yolanda's luminous unusually big green eyes blinked at me almost imperceptibly as if to encourage me to make the first move soon, because Norma was anxiously waiting. She had been the front, the hook, the mesmerizer, the pitcher of the sale, the pimp. Norma sensed that her turn had come up. Her short breathing lifted and lowered her supple chest at a rapid rhythm with deep intakes of air ending in an inaudible sigh as her eyes brimming with desire pierced my soul. Yolanda's intentions not to compete with Norma made sense later. I learned that Yolanda was the adopted one, "*una hija de crianza*," a sort of live-in maid, but treated like a sister. She had to defer to Norma in their competition to attract lovers. Like a Seminarian with celibacy integrity, I swallowed hard, froze in place, let dead time elapse, kept silent and did nothing, which only increased Norma's desire.

The cerro Santa Lucía covered the yellowish rays of the approaching sunset, dimming the city below. Up the cerro, the lights of the terrace of the bordello, now a restaurant, turned on earlier than I would have expected. Dogs were barking in the distance waiting for their masters to return home. Soon, workers would start coming home from work. Their wives' peaceful moments would start to change into a hectic kitchen dance as they anxiously started to prepare dinner, which was usually a small plate of black beans, white rice, and sweet fried plantains accompanied by queso fresco, *crema salvadoreña*, and a pile of handmade hot thick tortillas. The smell of just cooked soft corn dough "nixtamalized," treated with an alkali, like ash or slaked limestone (called *cal)*, stirred my stomach. "We have to go back. My father comes home early today and he may expect a well-cooked dinner," Norma whispered.

As it darkened, we started our descent, again with one girl at each side of me. I decided to go with the quiet one, the one with a lisp, the one who spoke in a permanent whisper. I, still resisting, very hesitantly grabbed Norma's trembling hand to continue the march towards town. Is this what it means to succumb to temptation? I thought about some of the advice given by Thomas Kempis in his "Imitation of Christ," that little book that looked like an agenda book that some of us seminarians carried in our white shirt front pocket, consulting it several times during the day.

> *"En resistir, pues, a las pasiones se halla la verdadera paz del corazón, y no en seguirlas. No hay, pues, paz en el corazón del hombre carnal, ni del que se entrega a lo exterior, sino en el que es fervoroso y espiritual."* (True peace of heart, then, is found in resisting passions, not in satisfying them. There is no peace in the carnal man, in the man given to vain attractions, but there is peace in the fervent and spiritual man).

I had the clear sentiment that an entire period of my life, the seminarian period, was reaching its end. Grabbing Norma's left hand was the demarcation. I had crossed to the other side, the secular one, whose code of conduct was unknown to me.

Grabbing hands was considered a monumental action and expressed a desire to make the relationship official. I suddenly let go of Norma's plump left hand when the first houses had started to appear at the end of the *cafetales*. It was too soon to make public our accidental decision to become a couple. Norma gave me a confused and almost fearful look. She had not conquered me yet. I had resisted it. I had sworn chastity. I had stayed away from women, away from terrestrial sinful love since taking my seminarian vows. Today, however, like Hippolytus meeting Aricie, I had succumbed to the desires of love. Today, I was re-entering, more precisely, forced to enter, the mundane world. I felt like a prepubescent boy, like from one of those Hollywood movies, raised inside a well-stocked bomb shelter sent out to get some needed supplies, only to discover that the A-bomb was never used above ground, and that the war was over. He did not know it at first, but people in the outside world were greatly surprised by the incredible naiveté he showed regarding worldly matters and social relationships, and by his out-of-date, classical, and overly polite language.

Socially, among teenagers, my holding hands with Norma meant a love declaration that needed to run its course. This affair with Norma would turn out to have a drastic change in my life. That day, I never made it to the Cathedral. It took me 20 years more to step inside it again. Norma and Yolanda innocently lived up to their roles as the biblical women who spoil men's intentions for chastity and propel them towards sinful carnal knowledge.

Had I decided to kiss them and make love to both, one after the other, as Teto tells me he would have, I would have encountered no resistance, for inviting someone to the" *loma*" meant just that in the "multis," , but those sinful thoughts never entered my little head of mine that day.

Chapter 6: At the Border between Guatemala and Mexico, Talismán. Part III.

Tonight, however, a close distance from the border, I fell asleep not in my room staring up at the ceiling, but lulled to sleep by a black night illuminated by a bright canopy of stars, their rays filtering through the leaves of the *Amate* tree, in no man's land, unsure about when my ordeal at the border would end. My head whirled with all the worst possible outcomes. I wondered how Gustavo would take my unexpected visit if I ever got to Puebla, and how Norma, who had months before immigrated to Los Angeles, would take my arrival if I ever got there, which was an even longer shot than Puebla.

The early morning was pleasant and fresh. Somewhere, in a distant tree, a flock of parakeets had started their racket, signaling the start of a new tropical day. I breathed in the scent of the flower of *Izote* and was surprised by how attentive I had become of my surroundings. I walked down to the *pupusera's* stand. Pale sunlight reflected from the chassis of the parked trucks that waited to be inspected by the Mexicans before crossing the border, some with Panamanian and Costa Rican license plates. The *pupusera* offered me breakfast. She felt sorry for me. A crowd had already formed in a long line waiting to cross the border. Others decided to rest before crossing, hoping for the lines to diminish. Many were hungry and eager to buy breakfast from the pupusera: fried eggs with refried black beans with the distinct flavor of Guatemalan or Salvadorian sour cream on top, and a cup of hot and strong Guatemalan coffee.

Business had increased dramatically as of late, she told me, and she attributed it to my arrival. "*Yo sola no doy abasto,*" she said, hinting at me that if I wanted to stay there and work for a while, I was welcomed. I was a very different and unusual young boy, who looked and spoke differently, not like the others. I had brought her luck. To her, I had become a little good-luck charm she never wanted to give up. The belief in talismans, witches, apparitions, spirits and their influence on daily life are strongly held by many campesinos in Latin America.

"*Bachiller, tal vez hoy usted cruza la frontera,*" she wishfully stated with a wide and innocent smile that only the earthy *campesinas* are able to form.

"No. I have to start making my way back to Santa Ana," I sounded already defeated, as if I had ridden to battle, only to be turned back again.

"No diga eso, vaya rumbo al norte," She said full of cheerful, inextinguishable hope. "Mucha gente menos preparada que usted se va hacia el norte y estoy segura de que ellos llegan hasta California," she consoled me. Fed daily by the pupusera, my long stay at the border became less stressful. Now and then I would help her turn her pupusas over at the comal.

Strangers have often helped me in the most crucial moments of my life. I have been trying to understand for a very long time the reason why I inspired sympathy from strangers, especially in those unknown moments of an uncertain destiny. Now into my retirement, I search for people who knew me at that time to ask their interpretation of this phenomenon. Some have commented that my baffled, vulnerable, and outwardly defenseless innocence and incomprehensible lack of life experience beamed so bright out of my eyes that they were compelled, almost as a necessity, to help me.

When just recently we reunited after 40 years, thanks to Facebook, Ernesto told me that he and other people helped me during the time he met me in Los Angeles in 1972 because of my clean, unstained, untouched essence that shone about me like a gleaming aura. According to him, I was a sort of antidote. I looked innocent, defenseless, and anxious to devour life. I was transparent, a virgin, void of life experiences, and above all, pure. There were no mean spirits in my bones. I inspired tenderness and love. I was one of those people who evoked a need to protect, to shelter. I acted not unlike Voltaire's Candide,

> *"c'était un jeun métaphysicien, fort ignorant des choses de ce monde, et il* (the King of Bulgares) *lui accorda sa grâce avec une clémence qui sera louée dans tous les journaux et dans tous les siècles. »*(He was a young metaphysician, entirely ignorant of the world and therefore, out of [the King's] great clemency, he condescended to pardon him, for which his name will be celebrated in every journal, and in every age.)

In other words, I was a complete ingénue, almost a total loser.

Ernesto didn't think twice before bringing me to the welding factory where he worked immediately after he had met me during our first English as a Second language class in el Monte, California. He also made sure the foreman hired me even though I had never touched a welding gun before in my life. Ernesto ended up doing my job behind the foreman's back for a week so I wouldn't fall behind, until I learned how to weld ornamental designs for house gates and fences.

After my job as a janitor's helper ended at the Saint Luke's Catholic Church in Temple City, I visited all public and private schools in the area looking for a similar occupation. I already had assumed great competence in the janitor's helper profession. After hearing my petition for a job, Sharon, a volunteer secretary at a catholic elementary school in San Gabriel, was eager to help me with everything on the spot. A month later, for other added reasons, she would bring me to her single-level beige home and convinced her husband Jorge to let me live with them until I found a good job. I ended up staying with them for two months.

Later in Boston, there was also the time when on my day off from washing dishes at Café Florian and at Howard Johnson's, I would venture to Kent's, a restaurant facing Copley Sq., for a nice dinner. This middle-aged Irish waitress did not let me pay for my meal since my first visit there, "Come over every day if you want to. I'll pay for your dinner, love." Sure, I did just that on my days off. She never told me why, and I never asked. I wouldn't have understood anyway. Her tender smile, full of happiness, without saying a word, received me every time I entered the restaurant and she made me feel loved, safe, and happy. There was even a special table assigned for me: the same small round table next to the window facing Boylston Street, looking at the Romanesque Trinity church and the beaux arts Boston Public Library. She just brought me the most expensive meal offered at Kent's and finished it with a float, a dessert consisting of scoops of vanilla ice-cream floating in a cold glass of root beer. I might have reminded her of a son who lived far away or had died, or maybe she did it as an act of religious charity. I never knew.

Even the circumstances of meeting my first wife, Eric's mother, Claudia, a daughter of survivors of the Jewish holocaust, attest to these weird experiences. She told me just before our definite divorce that when she met me she felt an irresistible urge to do something for me and couldn't help but to teach me how to excel in the English language and adjust to my unfamiliar cultural surroundings.

Another time, during a scorching day in July, I attended an outdoor Flamenco show in a Cambridge parking lot on Harvard Street next to Central Square. This time one of the young flamenco dancers, at the end of the performance, jumped off the stage, cut through the crowd, rushed up to me and directly, almost authoritatively, pleaded with me to fly to Spain with her that same night to study flamenco in Seville, all expenses paid, and live with her as long as I wanted, no commitments. She wanted me in her house. By then, I was a senior at B.U. and I had to resist the temptation. My extreme-period of adventure had already phased out. If not, I would have left with her.

What the *pupusera* did for me long ago at the border became a pattern in my life as I made the transition from El Salvador into the American society. Those surreal experiences are still fully unexplained to me.

✳✳✳

From the *pupusera*'s stand, I spotted the arrival of a charter silver *La Galgo* bus, with air conditioning and padded upholstery. We called these types of busses in El Salvador "Pullmans". The bus pulled in front of the immigration offices. Its top banner read "*Ciudad de Mexico*". I hastily gobbled down my last tortilla.

"*Espero que nos veamos pronto, pupusera,*" I said in farewell, before I quickly ran towards the bus to observe the faces of its passengers.

They were all female elementary school teachers in their early forties, well dressed, loud and happy. A haughty man in a blue suit briskly stepped out of the bus, eager to engage the officials. His confident air told me that this was just a routine stop for him. *He must be the guide.* He then turned back on to the bus and told the women to wait until he came back. First, he had to announce the bus arrival to the official in charge to summon his entire crew and get ready to receive and promptly process a large group of excursionists. I knew, no matter what, no matter how much of a *mordida* they gave to the guards, the women's wait would be long.

I didn't hesitate. I intercepted this confident man as he made his way to the building. I dropped my bombshell request. I spoke very seriously, almost somber, using the most   proper   Spanish   grammatical   structures, pronunciation and cadence, found only among members of the clergy and university intellectuals. It worked. He agreed, but at a cost. I had to pay him interest for the $100.00. He was after all an executive and never ready to be easily taken advantage of. It did not matter that I would have possession of the money just for a few moments. It was a loan that needed to be repaid quickly and with high interest. I was to reap high benefits after all. Actually, he wanted the interest before he gave me the money. Like the many others I had approached before him, his fear of my running away with the money was immediate.

"Give me $5.00 right now, put your duffle bag inside the bus and use my seat," he ordered.

"I just have 5.00 colones left in my pocket," I nervously pleaded.

He grabbed the money and continued on his way, as if nothing had happened. Or was it the other way around? Maybe he had just bilked me. I didn't care. I decided to board the bus and sat in his seat, the first seat behind the chauffeur, under the inquisitive eyes of all those women passengers. If he came back to kick me out, I was going to shame him in front of them. I had just become part of the excursion. Most likely I had been wrong about this man. *I bet, instead, he will pity me and find me a permanent seat all the way to Mexico City. I know the women will not protest. They will mother me and feed me, and maybe caress me, even more, maybe pay me to stay with them once in Mexico City and ask me to be their young chaperone. I can't believe my luck.*

The guide came back. The plan was very simple. I was to be his helper, expected to keep my mouth shut, walk a step behind him and just in front of the group of women. If he gave me an order, I had to execute it. "Don't look towards the guard," he hissed in my ear as we approach the entrance to the border building. *I don't think the guards will remember me. Even if they take a second look, the context is different. I am part of an excursion. I couldn't possibly be the same boy they kicked out a week ago.* Moments before I stepped out of the Pullman bus, the guide had slipped a $100.00 bill into my hand and asked to check my passport. Everything was in order. We walked in a straight single-file-line formation towards the official. My mind froze with fear. I could see in the distant the guards with their G-3's, leaning against a *Ceiba* tree waiting for excitement.

"*El siguiente, por favor,*" the immigration official bellowed.

Chapter 7: At the Border between Guatemala and Mexico. Part IV.

As expected, the Mexican official took a couple of seconds to examine my passport. My Mexican visa was in order. I showed him the $100.00 bill and he barely looked at it, ignored me, stamped my passport, and hurried me through. The ruse had worked. I obviously was part of the tour of women, their guide's helper. After he had waved me along to the side with apparent jealousy of my company, the official perked up, assumed a higher air of importance -- the stereotypical Latin macho posture -- buttoned his tired-looking uniform, and eagerly started to summon the women. They looked their very best after having managed to freshen and doll themselves up before stepping off the bus. The women wore various perfumes that made many other travelers' heads turn and my lungs suffocate. The official couldn't resist flirting with them, *"de dónde salieron tantas bellezas?"* as the effeminate guide looked at him with impatience.

As soon as Customs was done perfunctorily inspecting the insides of the tour's valises and suitcases, including my duffle bag, a whistle sounded indicating that the bus was ready to cross the border. I joined the group on its walk towards the bus. Just before reaching it, the guide, who had kept a close eye on me all this time, blocked my way and stood in front of me with Teto's army green duffle bag in hand. He asked me for the money back while taking a deep breath of relief as if his life had just been spared. *"Good luck on your way up north,"* he mumbled, almost feeling sorry. I was already on the other side and that lessened my disappointment of not getting a chance to ride with the tour group all the way to Mexico City. Maybe if I had flirted with the guide...?

It was just before noon and I could faintly sense the burnt aroma of toasted tortillas, black bean soup and cilantro emanating from the pupusera's shack at the other side of the border. *She must be thinking about me.* I fought a strong urge to walk back, to throw it all away, and re-think this ridiculous adventure. I thought about Gustavo in Puebla, and Norma in Los Angeles, and regained my resolve. After crossing, the possibilities of getting a prompt ride abounded in this spot. Immediately after the border, there was already a very congested area with pickup trucks, buses, and 18-wheelers. I extended my arm and lifted my thump. The first small Toyota pickup truck invited me up. I swung the duffle bag over the truck's bed and jumped in it with a single swift movement as if propelled by the bag's momentum. *"Take me as far as you go, as long as you go North!"*

I stood on the bed of the pickup truck, leaning forward against the rear and top of its cabin. The warm salty tropical wind flapping against my face filled my lungs with hope and made my long, hippie hair whirl over my face, accentuating the sense of speed. A sudden, unusual, adrenaline-induced vigor seized me. Now, I felt free and unstoppable again. The flapping sound of the wind on one's face gives the exhilarating sensation that one is in the midst of a great adventure, exploring the unknown world. It didn't make a difference if I never arrived to my destination. I imagined myself in full flight high in the sky as I did those times I galloped on my horse *Gallina* down the prairie towards the river Lempa in the hacienda, or when I was 4 years old bicycling down the paved hill next to our house in the city, while my father looked on from the sidewalk.

This happy sensation caused by the wind on one's face may be due to the fact that humans share a common ancestor with the birds that take flight towards the deep blue horizon. *I bet this truck will catch up with the tour bus, pass it, and the women will smile at me with surprise,* I thought to myself. *If I get quick rides like this one, I could be having dinner in Puebla by tomorrow evening with my compatriot*

Gustavo Orellana. I can't wait to see his face. It has been two years since last I saw him. I can't believe I almost turned back.

✳✳✳

Gustavo and I were the only two seminarians sent to study philosophy at the *"Seminario Palafoxiano"* during the bitter cold winter of 1967-1968 in Puebla. We were not sent, but rather we were escorted by Monsignor Barrera from Santa Ana, El Salvador to Puebla, Mexico. It took us three days to get to Mexico City after an exhausting, more than 1,000- mile trip on the ill-maintained Pan American Highway built in 1950. The brand new and improved, German made, top of the line, lotus white, 1967 1300-cc VW beetle carried Gustavo, a priest we had picked up just coming along for the ride, and me in the back seat. At front, there was the chauffeur and the Monsignor. This small little car was equipped with a top rack towering with belongings and valises of five. Up to this day, I am in awe with what that small, low-powered vehicle accomplished the trip with no incidents even though we over exceeded its cargo capacity by many pounds.

For reasons that I never understood, the preparations for this first trip to Puebla had been done in haste. The Monsignor met with Gustavo and I to tell us our future soon after having excelled in our private academic examinations. Before that meeting, I had successfully formed, from the poorest barrios of Santa Ana, a boys' choir that sung *"villancicos"* Christmas Eve at the Cathedral, and had spent two weeks in the mountains preaching, living in a mud-and-wattle hut, eating raw chicken eggs and mangoes, and drinking water out of *tecomates* brought to me by the *campesinos*. Seemingly, the Monsignor was impressed by my creativity, community development strategies, and dedication. I did not see it that way.

One of the mottos of the Seminary, drilled into our heads every morning, was R.I.O. It stood for Responsibility, Initiative, and Observation. To improve our community, we needed to observe what needed improving, take the initiative to find a solution, and be accountable

Segmento de Cadáveres Ambulantes

for those solutions. Every year the Seminary held a contest putting R.I.O in practice. Is there anything in our community that could be improved? How could it be improved? Who would take responsibility to improve it? The seminarian with the best observation and plan of action, judged by the rector and the bishop, would be declared the winner. Some thought of a way of keeping the toilets sparkling clean. Others dwelled on making the daily schedule more efficient. Some came out with a weekly publication, *El Semanario,* to highlight seminarians' position papers, poetry, short stories, and humor. Others planned to stage theatrical *veladas,* including *zarzuelas,* more often.

Cadáveres Ambulantes (excerpt below) became one of the most celebrated *zarzuelas*, written by a Salesian priest in the 1950s, that we staged for the Santa Ana community and sometimes in small towns, as was the case during our December break in Tacuba.

This motto gave me handles, boundaries, and a structure for my outlook on life. It didn't occur to me at that time that a strict adherence to R.I.O would have translated into the qualities the Monsignor had noticed in me. After my good deeds, he could not ignore me, but his favorite was Gustavo. He might feel too homesick and fail. Gustavo needed a partner, and I fulfilled that purpose nicely in the Monsignor's mind. The passport pictures were taken and the visas were procured overnight, a perk of being members of the Clergy. My father was ecstatic to hear the news and my mother proud but broken hearted because I had to depart within two days. Her first son was leaving for who knew how many years.

Upon hearing this news, my mother's eyes filled with tears of nostalgia for wealthier times, and with good reason. Her honeymoon present had been a trip to Mexico City via Pan Am. My parents spent two months enjoying the music and nightclub scene of the late 1940's Mexico City, whisking through cabarets, theaters, and dance halls. Their favorite nightclub was the *Teatro Blanquita*, where my parents could see on any number of nights Pedro Infante, Maria Victoria, Toña La Negra, Cantinflas, and other artists of the Mexican Golden Age.

My mother had corresponded with one of the greatest actors and singers of that time, Jorge Negrete, during her teen years. Jorge Negrete was one of her idols. Jorge ended up sending her a paid plane ticket inviting her to come to meet him. Her father Rosendo, Papá Chendo, refused to send a *señorita*, with or without chaperones, to the decadent scene of Mexico City. She had hoped, now just married and on her honeymoon, to finally run into Jorge Negrete, but it never happened. When recently visiting my

94-year-old father, he showed me his black and white wedding pictures. I took a long look at my mother's face. There was no doubt her 1940's black and dense hairdo, her thick lips painted with an intense, loud red, and her jewelry combined with her proud posture would have made her a great Mexican star. My brother Teto corroborated that sentiment when the other day he unintentionally let some tears roll down his cheeks while watching a 1940's black and white Mexican film with the famous comedian Cantinflas. Cantinflas' love interest looked exactly like our mother would have looked at that time, he said.

My mother had a grand ole time in Mexico City with my father, just a bit disappointed for not having met Jorge Negrete in person. The couple had a grand finale of their honeymoon frolicking in Acapulco, spending two weeks here, the Mecca of fun at that time for all *latinoamericanos*. This honeymoon was made possible thanks to some of my mother's inheritance. My father's only contribution to the trip was his white *lino* suits, tortoiseshell sunglasses, two tone leather shoes, and his insatiable thirst for partying and alcohol. Teto, a former alcoholic, but now thanks to AA sober since April 25th, 1995, had deep conversations with my father while getting obscenely drunk together. Teto tells me that my unscrupulous bastard of a father cheated on my mother even while on their honeymoon, with women that the hotel bellboy would sneak into adjacent rooms while my mother slept. My father had married my mother solely for her money, and maybe some love. After my mother died, I gradually kind of forgave my father, as I concluded that it was unfair to be angry towards an old man.

Jumping several years ahead of those weeks in Mexico, Teto and I came back from my father's funeral in El Salvador. My brother Rafael tells me that my father's last words before he closed his eyes were, "*Ahí está Rosita.*" He died thinking about my mother. Those days in the warm sun of Mexico had been the greatest of times. Barely a decade later, after I was born, they were not sure they had enough money to buy next morning's milk for their children. It had taken my father only ten years of daily drinking, stupid engendering of children with other women, frequent traveling, nightly gambling, and a pathological sex life, to lose my mother's fortune.

When it was announced that I would be going to study in Mexico, my parents' honeymoon memories came alive once more, and I understood the added force when seeing my mother crying with joy and my father coming out of his alcoholic stupor. My scholarship to go study in Puebla had come as a big surprise. The Monsignor had not given any hints. Surely, Gustavo and I were made of what it took to become great priests and monsignors and the Church was willing to invest a lot of money in our philosophical, theological, and spiritual training. Padre Camilo, our Rector after Padre Chus in Santa Ana, told Gustavo and I over coffee at Santa Ana's Mr. Donut recently, that we were sent to be educated and become the next bishops and archbishops of the church.

Three years later, however, Gustavo deserted the Seminary and remained in Puebla. He never came back to live in El Salvador. He fell in love with the most beautiful Mexican girl in town, Elsita, during an Evangelization Campaign launched by the Seminary. It was towards the end of our BA of philosophy. He couldn't bear to leave his love behind; neither could he face the Monsignor were he to go back to Santa Ana. Instead, Gustavo cowardly wrote him a letter explaining his decision to explore the world before a definite, ecclesiastical commitment. Although the letter might have caused deep pain and disappointment in the Monsignor, he understood. Taking a year off was often recommended before seriously commencing the required four-year theology studies, a requisite for ordination. One week before I left to return to El Salvador, Gustavo walked to the curia in Puebla to withdraw money from our line of credit and moved to a Puebla guesthouse. He later told me that I gave him my share to pay for his food. The night before I left, I spent it talking to him about our lives and futures. Conflicted, he cried in his bed as I rested on the sofa all night trying to console him.

His decision was monumental. It would define the rest of his life. He would have to live with its good and bad consequences. We competed fiercely academically, but had become close friends, and treated each other now like brothers. It is generally harder for the one who stays put than the one who leaves. At this moment, Gustavo's future had become very uncertain, while mine was clear. I saw myself in Louvain, Belgium, by September. That same night, he pleaded with me to desert and stay with him in Puebla. He had already procured a teaching job at the private *Liceo, Colegio Benavente,* and he assured me that I could also teach in the same institution. We fell asleep around 4:00 am. I was determined, however, to go back, with the hopes of soon leaving for Louvain.

The cerebral and phlegmatic Gustavo walked me to the bus depot the next day at 8:00 am. Mercedes, a classmate at the Colegio Benavente, also appeared. There, he cried again. After nine years of sharing an exact military-like routine, our brotherly ties, for the first time, were about to be severed, maybe forever. He was terrified to be left alone. The Monsignor had been right. Teamwork had been our mantra. For so long, I had been his only connection to Santa Ana. I felt he was being irrational and impulsive, so unlike him, the phlegmatic one. He was exhibiting traits that belonged only to me, according to my ancient Greek category of a sanguine temperament.

Our temperaments show their differences even in music. Gustavo and I listened to Bert Kaemfert while studying for the government high school private exams at the Bishop's Palace in 1966. I liked That Happy Feeling, a happy and lively song and Gustavo loved "The Wonderland by Night", slow and melancholic, that went with his. The records had been brought by visiting Monsignor (Graziano) from Italy and we used his record player.

During those nine years together, our competitiveness came out often, in class or in the soccer field. We showed no mercy and forgot all about being humble in the manner of Jesus Christ. Sometimes Gustavo would strike my cheek, and other times I would strike his, but neither presented the other cheek to receive the second blow. We thought to humiliate the other, and make it known to others that we were better. All of that was subtle and metaphorical. Except one day when they put me as a goalkeeper on an impromptu soccer game outside the city. Gustavo and I had ended up on the same team. The opponents, much better than us, scored 6 goals, one after the other, in a short period of time. Feeling defeated, I, as a goal keeper, wanting no longer to go through more pain, decided unfairly to change sides as a striker. I wanted to be a winning player at the end of it all.

That cowardly act of mine proved unbearable for Gustavo. He endured his anger for a few hours. It waited until we were back at the Seminary. Upon arrival, he saw me walking next to the sidewall of the chapel, decided to attack me by pushing me against it, with an unexpected rage. I accepted his anger and rage as something I deserved. It made me think of my actions and how easy it was for me to abandon my commitments. I had shown little integrity of character. You never betray your team.

Another time, much older, during our propaedeutic year in Santa Ana, I annoyed Gustavo to the utmost degree by practicing in the second-floor piano-room where he had decided to hide, seeking complete silence to concentrate on his Latin and Greek final exams.

"Chico, *por favor, ¿tú puedes dejar de tocar el piano? ¿No ves que estoy estudiando?* he asked widening his blue eyes, more visible now through his thick glasses as if he were looking through the bottom of a wine bottle.

"Este es el único momento que tengo para practicar. Estoy tratando de aprenderme el Danubio Azul. Estudia con mi música." I said pedantically.

"*O tu paras de tocar el piano, o yo te paro,*" Gustavo blurted out as he pushed his desk with force and started to walk towards me from his corner.

I heard the sharp sound of his steps as he rapidly moved across the shiny ceramic tiles. I turned around, stood up with my closed fists, and forcibly kicked the bench back against the piano, which responded with all its chords, producing the most unsettlingly dissonant of sounds. The seminarians studying on the first floor might have thought we were being sloppy in our moving the piano to the rehearsal choral room. I remember rushing towards each other, encountering each other in the middle of the room kicking and punching, and continuing to the opposite corner as two jousters on their horses would do with their lances. We repeated this encounter several times, kicking and punching in the middle of the room and then retreating to the opposite corner. Our kicks and punches were muffled by the black, long skirts of our cossacks. I don't remember how this ended, but one of us left the room. Neither Gustavo nor I remember if we ever actually hit each other. I think we never did. This was the highest moment of our animosity.

The year of propaedeutic led us to moments that opened our eyes, waking up from our holiness, even if only momentarily. One of those experiences occurred when Imelda, Padre Camilo's younger sister, decided to visit him every Sunday. the day the nuns gave her permission to leave the Santa Cecilia boarding school. This feminine presence soon triggered instinctual responses from Gustavo and I.

We started to compete for her attention since the first moment we laid eyes on her from our perch in the main corridor, where we did our homework on Sundays. Seeming to float through the air like an apparition, she graciously made her way across the sunny patio, turning her head slightly towards us to give us a surreptitious, timid look that sent luminous reflections our way. The loud rhythm of her high heels as they hit the patio tiles accompanied a slight but distinctive hip swing that made her blond hair bounce. We followed her every movement from the entrance to the seminary to her disappearance at the end of the patio as she turned towards her brother Camilo's quarters. Perez, the Seminary's doorman, had just opened the front door for her after an insistent ring.

The same scene repeated itself every Sunday that year. It didn't take much time at all for both of us to develop a strong crush on her. As soon as we would settle into our usual spots in the main corridor to do our school work, we, like Pavlov's dogs, would experience a hot rush in our lower bellies even before we saw her.

One Sunday, Padre Camilo was out of town. I, as the student prefect that year, was keeper of the keys to all the rooms in the Seminary. *"Perdone joven que lo moleste. Me dicen que Usted podría abrir el cuarto de mi hermano,"* Imelda asked me, looking adorably into my eyes. This was the first time I became acutely aware that there was another gender. One thing led to another and we ended up sitting on Padre Camilo's bed next to each other, talking endlessly about her courses innocently holding hands while feeling unfairly kept restrained by a cage like two *tortolitas*, only hoping for the door to open to instinctively fly away.

The cerebral and phlegmatic Gustavo had been watching all my moves that day and as soon as he noticed that I was nowhere to be found, became suspicious and decided to burst into Padre Camilo's room. Gustavo found us sitting on the bed. I got startled and immediately stood up. *"Algunos seminaristas te andan buscando para pedirte permiso para tomar un recreo y tú te has perdido todo el día,"* Gustavo said disapprovingly, as his dark mind was probably imagining us embracing, kissing and lying in

Padre Camilo's bed. That day Imelda's hands made my heart skip a beat and, from that moment on, I awaited her Sunday visits with breathless anticipation.

On another Sunday, Padre Camilo invited Gustavo and I to jump into his VW buggy for a ride around the Santa Ana volcano. Imelda sat in the front. We parked next to an open volcanic hill to go for a hike. We made our way up and down century old lava boulders along an imperceptible trail. Inevitably, all dressed up in a long yellow dress, Imelda felt ill equipped for the trek. Gustavo and I took turns offering our hands for support as we climbed up. Imelda had already implicitly made up her mind and preferred my hand. Gustavo became incensed with jealousy. On our way back to the Seminary, the VW radio blasted with the newest popular songs. Rafael's *"Yo soy aquel"* and *"Yo estoy aquí"* were repeatedly played and instantly became Imelda's songs.

Our infatuation with each other did not go unnoticed. It was not long after the short trek around the volcano that Padre Camilo summoned me into his office. He asked me with a stern face if I loved Imelda and if I wanted to marry her, because if I wanted, he would be very proud to have me as his brother-in-law. Camilo's question surprised me. Were devout Christians supposed to get married after merely having held hands? This struck me as too precipitous and scary. I did not know what romantic love was, but I was sure what I felt was not what I expected love to be: a crazy uncontrollable and unstoppable passion. *"No. Yo tengo vocación para ser sacerdote. No me quiero casar,"* I said.

Imelda stopped coming to the Seminary on Sundays from that day forward, until the time during school break for *las fiestas julias* when I became sick with the mumps and was quarantined in a secluded room at the far end of the patio. She begged Padre Camilo to let her come to visit me every day to bring me reading material. She brought me several books, but the one that made a lasting impression on my feverish mind was a copy of the poetic Christian Andersen fables and short stories. Tears rolled down my cheeks at the end of the "Under the Willow Tree" story.

As children, Knud and Johanne play under the old willow tree whose branches cover the little stream that flows into the sea in the town of Kjöge. Sometimes they both just sit under the tree while Johanne sings to Knud. The town admires her angelic voice. Once they become teenagers, Knud declares his love for Johanne who tells him that she loves him like a brother and nothing more. Knud, with his heart deeply broken, leaves Denmark for a long journey around Europe to forget her. Several years later, he finds himself inside Milan's opera house and who does he see? Johanne as the prima donna of the opera. The audience goes wild. The people sitting next to him tell him that she is the most famous singer in Europe. He decides to wait outside the opera house after the show with many other people to see her walk towards her carriage. She shakes hands with many of them and comes to Knud. He looks into her eyes and says "Johanne". She looks into his eyes, shakes his hand, but does not recognize him. A very elegant man, her fiancé, gives her his arm and walks her to the carriage. Knud, all defeated, decides to walk back to Kjöge to see his parents even though it is the dead of winter. All exhausted, halfway to his destination, he finds a willow tree next to a little stream and decides to rest. He has a happy dream with Johanne and feels the branches of the tree holding him with fatherly love. He wakes up for a moment, but asks the tree to lull him back to sleep to continue dreaming his happy dream with the one he loves. The villagers find him frozen to death under the willow tree the next morning.

The first time I sat under a willow tree in the Boston Garden, my thoughts went back to that sad story, and to Imelda, and how ready I had been to leave it all behind to follow what I thought was my calling. I was renouncing incipient love to accept a religious life, but I doubt it was a deep inner conviction, but rather I might have been adopting a position that reflected what was expected from me. Imelda read this story and several others aloud to me as she sat on the edge of my sick bed. She ordered fresh fruits and purees from the kitchen and left suggestions of what diet was best for me to follow. I never saw her again after I got well. Gustavo now tells me that Camilo really wanted me to marry his sister and did all he could to leave me alone with her. A few years ago, 50 years later, fate brought us together again. Gustavo and I met in Santa Ana, El Salvador, with Padre Camilo at the Mr. Donut coffee shop. Imelda arrived late, glamorous as always, with a sincere wide smile and romantic eyes. We both, Gustavo and I, ran at the same time to kiss her and hug her. I paused, looked closely with an inquiring expression, and said: "*Finalmente llegó el momento de elegir entre Gustavo y yo.*" We three burst into a happy smile remembering the long gone days full of youthful palpitations of our tender hearts.

❋❋❋

The Toyota pick-up truck stopped suddenly and woke me up from my reverie. *Why are we stopping? We have been traveling for no more than half an hour.* We had come out to a deviation, a fork in the road, just after the town of Tapachula. The green uniforms and the hard helmets were unmistakable. The clunk of their boots, the ruffling of their rifles, the curved bullet cartridges, and the sparkling handcuffs, sparked intense fear in me. A small, pitched-roof wooden hut not unlike the ones used in American country fairs to sell ice cream, stood in the center of the fork. It turned out to be an improvised Mexican National Guard post. *If I run as fast as I can and get lost in the woods...No, most likely they will shoot me dead. How funny! I escaped the Salvadorian National Guard just to be killed by the Mexican.* The guard ordered me down from the pick-up truck.

"*¿Pasaporte! Quiero ver los cien dólares que llevas para gastar en México,*" the eldest soldier with the machine gun asked me. He knew the answer. The officer at the border had just radioed him to look out for the truck. They both were expecting a *mordida,* from me, thinking that I had kept the $100.00. Their scheme failed. My pockets were empty.

Strong dread knotted my stomach and sent my heart pounding in my eardrums. The handcuffs felt colder and heavier than expected. Teto's army duffel bag was thrown from the truck and landed next to a ditch. The younger guard slammed the rear of the truck with his left palm to indicate to the driver that he should continue with his trip.

Chapter 8: Kicked Out of Mexico

The Mexican guards put me into the backseat of their green military double-cabin pickup truck. I was riding in yet another Toyota, but this time I did not feel free and unstoppable. My t-shirt soon became soaked with sweat, my lungs labored to breathe the stale air; paradoxically my body became fully alert while my mind was quickly pacing towards despair. My immediate future had just become again dangerously uncertain. The scenery looked very familiar. The guards had decided to drive me back to the border following the same route I had just covered.

Their Captain had not arrived to work yet. It was already late afternoon. The guards threw me into a small room behind the Mexican Guard Station of the border town of Santa Clara. I did not sleep that night. The floor was too humid. The rain leaked through the seam between the adobe wall and the dirt floor. I kept the duffle bag on my upper back all night, leaning against the driest wall I found. I was not fed. Nobody talked to me. *Is* this *how it feels the first time you are arrested?*

"Why are you coming to Mexico with a tourist visa but no money?" The captain with a black, thick mustache and cheeks like an inflated, angry toad ready to secrete his white slobber---like the ones my brothers and I used to see around the *"Laguneta"* de Chalchuapa--- asked me early next morning once in his office.

"I am trying to get to Puebla to see a friend. I have money in Puebla," I responded loud and clear.

"You speak like a very educated person, like a university student. I don't know why you are insisting in breaking the law by coming to Mexico without money. You must show me at least $100.00 to be able to continue. You, Salvadorian people think that Mexico is just a corridor on your way up to *Norteamerica*."

Now, he was hoping for the $100.00 that I did not have.

Next, the captain asked his guard to search my duffle bag. Inside he found three, thick, scholarly philosophy volumes written in Latin: *"Philosophiae Scholasticae Summa."*

"¡Hijo de la chingada! ¿qué es esto?"

"As I mentioned before, I lived in Puebla for three years studying philosophy in the Seminary. I was studying to become a priest. I borrowed those books two years ago and failed to return them to their owners. I don't want my friends to think that I am a thief. The books are very expensive."

"I don't believe *un cura arrepentido* would want to break the law," the Captain insisted. "Guard! I will not press charges against this *muchacho*. Walk him back to the bridge at the border and make sure that he walks safely onto the Guatemalan side."

Chapter 9: Guatemala City Part I

Defeated, hungry, and thirsty, I started my way back to Santa Ana, but not before visiting Guatemala City. Ashamed, I walked as fast and as far as I could to avoid the pupusera's face. *She will cry as soon as she sees me, of sadness or happiness. I don't want to find out.* The black pavement shimmered on the horizon. I extended my arm and lifted my right-hand thumb up, praying for someone to give me a ride. Three days later, I walked around Guatemala City, Fifth Zone, looking for my uncle, Tío Chepe's, house.

My father had seven siblings in El Salvador and seven siblings in Guatemala. He was born in Escuintla, Guatemala, a product of a union between an adventurous Salvadorian shoemaker, Rafael, and a pious, evangelist, Guatemalan woman, Esther. My paternal grandparents' union lasted six years before they decided to part ways. My father was brought to El Salvador by his single father when he was five years old.

Family history has a way of repeating itself, and it so happened that I was left alone in Boston with my first son Eric, when he was 4 years old after his mother and I parted ways. My paternal grandfather, Rafael, remarried in El Salvador while his ex-wife, Esther, did the same in Guatemala. They both, as if living parallel lives, had seven children each: three boys and four girls on both sides. My father became the link between both the Guatemalan and the Salvadorian families. Coincidently or not, children were born on both sides of the border at the same time and were assigned corresponding first names. Beyond their ages, corresponding children also shared the same skin tones. There was one blue-eyed and blond-haired uncle in El Salvador named Miguel, (Tío Michel) and a Miguel in Guatemala the same age, one dark-skinned Tío Chepe in El Salvador and his homologous Tío Chepe in

Guatemala. There was a wide-face, stocky aunt in Guatemala, Tía Lupe, and another one in El Salvador named
Nena. The youngest in both sides was called Jorge. In my
family conversations, one had to specify the country to
avoid confusion when talking about uncles and aunts: *"Tío
Chepe de Guatemala. Tío Chepe de El Salvador."*

Tío Chepe de Guatemala, his wife Tía Estelita, and his
daughters Sonia, Sandra, and Alicita were devastated to
hear of my adventure at the Guatemala-Mexico border
when I finally made it to their house. In their minds, they
still placed me at the Seminary in Puebla. It had been already two years since I had deserted and 6 years since last
I had seen Tío Chepe and his family. There was plenty to
catch up on. After dinner, I explained my present life well
into the night.

At the Salvadorian National University, as a freshman
pre-law student, I became sorely aware of the horrible living conditions of the *campesinos* in the big haciendas,
including *Los Apoyos,* my childhood hacienda. Growing
up, I did not make anything out of how the campesinos
addressed us: *"Buenos días, niño Chepito."* They would
take their hats off, bow to my cousin Neto and me, and
make sure to stay away from the main house because they
were always fearful to cross that deep invisible moat that
existed between the social classes, especially between the
landowner and those who worked his land. In practice, we
lived in a *de facto* feudalistic society in which the campesinos had to pay a tax to the master.

At the university, I also became aware of the plight of
the urban poor, most of them campesinos looking for a
better life in the city. During my years in the Seminary,
the conservatism of the Catholic Church did not allow me
to become aware of social inequalities. The Church was
aligned with the aristocracy of the local country, and the
poor were positioned as the people who had not yet been
blessed by God. I read incipient articles, on what would
later be called Liberation Theology, in the Seminary, but

only as an intellectual exercise to help me form an opposition to the prevailing conservative current espoused by my seminarian professors in Puebla, who were all trained in Europe, many at the Gregorian University in Rome. Ironically, the isolation of the Seminary with its abundant food, cozy shelter, and classical education formed a social bubble that insulated me from an experiential understanding of how, outside its 12-feet wall, a large group of people struggled daily for survival and lived in subhuman conditions. One could have thought we lived in the Middle Ages.

The seminarian professors never pointed out to us that the only reason we could live so comfortably was the large Sunday service collections, which were gathered mainly from the poor. The university, on the other hand, made that reason clear to me.

The closest I came to rebel in the Seminary was when I adopted Camilo Torres, the Colombian priest turned revolutionary, as one of my heroes, which alarmed one of my seminarian professors, Padre Landa. He ended up slapping me hard on my left cheek one day before entering the cafeteria for lunch upon telling him loudly that love was more important than his rules as a dean of discipline, and that Camilo Torres was the future of the priesthood. This was after he had admonished me for being a couple of minutes late for lunch. I went in the dining hall perturbed and humiliated, crying profusely, while the other seminarians looked at me with deep consternation.

"*¡Ay! ¡Qué malo ese cura!*", Sonia, my cousin, commented, placing the palm of her right hand on her mouth at the end of the word.

At the National University of El Salvador, on the other hand, most of my pre-law professors had obtained philosophy and economic degrees from the University of Moscow and La Universidad de la Habana. All were Marxist indoctrinated. It took pains to adjust to my new environment. I endured a gradual redefinition of my intellectual and moral positions, touching the core of my own identity as a seminarian. Listening to the professors' supercharged Marxism created in me an unsettled cognitive dissonance that I could only resolved by debating them.

When I enrolled in the National University after finally coming out of my depressed stupor, my seminarian scholastic philosophy was still fresh in my mind, and I couldn't help but to debate the professors' sociological positions in public, during class, in front of the other 100 freshmen using the debate syllogisms, rules for reasoning and argumentation, taught in formal logic. These professors quickly learned that I wasn't going to be an easy convert to Marxism, as many other impressionable freshmen were. Teto, at that time a senior in high school, later told me that his university friends commented on my valiant and unconventional behavior undermining the professor's intellectual authority, a no-no in Latin American academia.

My intense arguments with the tenured professors, especially with Luis Guevara, the Philosophy 101 professor, became legendary during that semester. "God does not exist," Guevara announced in one of his lectures and continued to prove the nonexistence of God using fundamental Marxist tenets: "matter is the supreme and unique cause of everything; the economic structure is the carrying structure of all the other structures that compose society." Prof. Guevara then drew a table on the blackboard putting the word "economy" as its base; and "man is the supreme being." I couldn't resist the urge to present the scholastic point of view in front of the class, among which there were many devout Catholics. I stood up and loudly proceeded to present several of the cosmological and teleological proofs advanced by Santo Tomas de Aquinas, influenced by Aristotle, and the ontological arguments put forth by San Anselmo, all very fresh in my mind: *"there is efficient causation in the world and the first efficient cause we named God; the end-directed activity of natural objects which shows an intelligent design a purpose understood only by the existence of God."*

The students, after a moment of shock, applauded and the Professor Guevara, with a doctorate from the University of Moscow, assumed a mute, stiff position, stunted by my audacity, and did not advance any counter arguments, as it would have been expected in the seminary. It gave me the impression that he had never heard the scholastic philosophy arguments to prove the existence of God and thus couldn't formulate any counter arguments on the spot, or maybe, so taken aback was he, that his mind blocked. The students were flabbergasted to witness a daring affront to magisterial authority and the inability of the professor to utter any response.

"Sonia, traéle a Chepito un vaso de agua", Tío Chepe commanded my cousin who all this time had been looking at me with her big blue eyes, trying to understand the importance of my story.

After this day, students sought me out during recess breaks between classes in the halls and the cafeteria to discuss philosophical and sociological issues. I knew little about Sociology, the Seminary taught only one semester course on the matter. My philosophy courses, however, had debunked Marxism as an illogical, deterministic, and reductionist theory. It argued historical materialism was fallacious and the laws of dialectics were fundamentally flawed. Communism with its atheism was obviously abominable. Marxism, as a theory, purport to explain all of society and its economics as much as Psychoanalysis portents to explain all psyche phenomena. Each theory fits very neatly into their logical systems, but they can't ever be proven right or wrong. They attempt to explain everything without proving anything scientifically. They have zero predictive value.

During our daily heated oral debates in classes, however, I was inevitably forced to reexamine the unacceptable social conditions of the poor by using the professor's' argument that the causes were the economic forces fueled by the hegemony of the landowners, the Church, and their military protectors. Seeing the Church as a cause of poverty was anathema to me and I could not accept it. After many years of peacefully demanding social change, only a true-armed revolution would create a new man and new social order, the university professors argued. Here lay my problem: Was violence an acceptable means to obtain social justice? Despite this, I soon started to view the very poor not as souls to be saved from sin, but as physical bodies that needed to be fed now. At the conservative Seminary in Puebla, my philosophy professors avoided the subject of something akin to Liberation Theology, which had not yet been clearly defined as such. Who would have thought that I would read its tenets at the atheist National University?

***

"Chepito, what were you doing getting into a dangerous, revolutionary movement? Didn't your father ever talk to you about what prompted the *matanza* of 1932 by General Martinez, the last Salvadoran dictator? -Tío Chepe interrupted me in the middle of my story with a serious intonation.

Meanwhile here I was despairing without seeing a clear way out of my wandering situation. What do I do? Do I go back to Santa Ana? What if the dammed lieutenant Monge is watching my house? What if they put me in jail? What do I do? Where do I go? – I asked to myself.

"I have been reading the daily newspapers. El Salvador is in deep turmoil and chaos right now and martial law has been instituted. The military kills first and asks questions later." -my Tío Chepe declared.

Looking back and forth between their father and me, my three wide-eyed cousins waited for me to continue my story.

Chapter 10: In Guatemala City. Part II

I t became easy, almost natural and logical, to transfer the undiminished fervor and passion I felt
during 'evangelization campaigns'---first in the
mountains of El Salvador and later in the native Indian
towns around Puebla---to the leftist political rhetoric
needed to organize university students to vote for Napoleon Duarte, running for the first time as the Salvadorian
presidential candidate, supported by a coalition of moder-
ate and left leaning parties. At the university, I was elected
treasurer of the student union, *La Sociedad de Estudian-
tes del Centro Universitario de Occidente,* or SECUO.
Students trusted *'el padrecito'* with their money. This
turned out to be a non-political, behind-the-scenes job, in
charge of collecting students' union dues before class reg-
istration. One added responsibility was, however, to
attend nightly meetings with the rest of the student lead-
ers and some professors who met at different houses on
the outskirts of Santa Ana to brainstorm strategies for getting the word out to elect Napoleon Duarte.

El Roperón Moreno, a short man with wide shoulders,
a solid, muscular chest, and working as an elementary
school teacher, was assigned the task of being my tutor on
socialism and Marxism, and to collect me every night from
my house on his way to the meeting.

After hearing the often long and almost incomprehensible Marxist analysis of the Salvadorian economy and
society, and the urgent need for land reform at the political
party meetings, *El Roperón* and I would take the long walk
back home to continue our conversation. Lingering for a
long time just outside my front door, we questioned, analyzed, and planned. The yellowish, dim light coming from
the light post reflected on Roperón's square face, accentuating his sharp, indigenous features.

Our voices were deep, loud, and easily reverberated throughout the narrow streets and over the colonial roofs of Spanish tiles, keeping several of our neighbors awake. I imagine now that there were some neighbors who carefully listened to our conversation, possibly some government spies among them tuned in with consternation, and some others annoyed, wondering why we took so long just to say our goodbyes. '*El Roperón*' would finally leave well past midnight, sometimes frustrated by my arguments against his Marxists analysis of the Salvadorian society. As a recent member of the student union leadership, I still had kept my conservative seminarian outlook. The group, especially the leader *Chepe Cacho,* was suspicious of my motivations and wanted to make sure I wouldn't act as a rogue member, uncoordinated and unvetted by, what I later learned was, the '*Movimiento Nacional Revolucionario*' political party."

"Communism is not the answer," Tío Chepe de Guatemala interrupted, "I have the answer for the problems of this earth in a religion I just joined. Let me read what the Bible says about *la política* on this earth. I know you know the Bible. I bet; however, they didn't teach you how to read and interpret it the right way in the Seminary. Jehovah Witnesses have taught me the right way."

That night, my story was cut short by Tío Chepe's response to it. I ended up listening to his long readings and interpretations of the Old Testament that I had yet to read carefully, let alone understand. Nothing he read aloud or said hit an available space in my mind. I just politely listened to his long sermon full of a tirade of biblical quotes. "*On Hebrews 4:3 the Bible says.... On Samuel 8:10 the Bible says...,*" while actually thinking about how to slip through the Guatemalan border into Mexico without money.

Tío Chepe's eyes, this time, did not reveal his happy-go-lucky attitude that made me gravitate towards him when I was a child. I got to know him better during one of my Minor Seminary summer vacations, when I became his helper on his daily medicine-delivery route around Guatemala City. He worked for Sterling Products International driving a white company van with a red, black, and white logo reading "*Mejor Mejora Mejoral.*" On the weekends, he drove further away from the city, into the mountains, escorting the bicycle races sponsored by the company. I met several of his friends during these trips and listened to conversations during the after-race parties with a bounty of beautiful women and liquor that caused me to increase my visits to the confessionary. Tío Chepe was a joker, an imitator, and a teaser. Women loved him.

During that summer vacation, I became the *de facto* babysitter, or protector, of my cousins, Sonia and Sandra, 14 and 13, who loved having me around. It gave them an excuse to liberate themselves from beneath Tío Chepe's thumb. A male cousin, almost a brother, in their house brought them excitement. One afternoon when we were left alone, Sandra taught me the basic Tango steps, the figure eight. After that, in the afternoons, just before Tía Estelita came back from the food market ready to make dinner, Sandra would power the smallest of record players to the highest volume, Sonia would join, and the two would dance Tango with me until we couldn't stand the sweat in our clothes any longer. During our pauses, I insisted to teach them the "*do, re, mi, do, mi, do, mi, re, mi, fa, fa, re, mi, fa...,*" a song adapted by el Padre Chus from the musical "The Sound of Music," that we loved singing in the Seminary.

Tonight, however, I sensed that an unknown force had possessed Tío Chepe, a more conservative, authoritarian, dogmatic, dictatorial, erudite, and self-righteous force. This time, he did not tease me or joke about my Salvadorian accent like he used to. Instead, he locked his fiery eyes on mine and challenged me to contest and argue his minute doctrinal biblical points, with a thirst that could only be satiated by making ever so clear, in front of my cousins, the obvious, limited, and corrupt hold the Catholic Seminary still had on me. He relentlessly put down my type of religious background as if to reassure his own newly discovered faith, taking me by surprise. I came face to face with a possessed human being and understood then the effects of religious fanatism: a total blindness towards reality, and an unabated desire to impose on others one's narrow view of the world.

Tío Chepe de Guatemala, many years later, would build his own Jehovah Witness "Kingdom Hall" in California, and become a wise elder in the church whose members would pay generously for his spiritual advice. "So, why are you so set on going north, anyway?" Tío Chepe finally asked, sensing my mental and physical exhaustion and disinterest for engaging him in a religious battle that I did not have a chance of winning. "You could stay here, if you want, until all the racket subsides in El Salvador."

Chapter 11: Guatemala City. Part III

"**N**ow that the military again controls the country and has invaded the University, I don't think there is a future for me in Santa Ana," I said in response to my uncle's invitation to live with him.

I continue my story, trying to prevent Tío Chepe from starting again with his biblical quotes. "The military invaded the university while I was in my office finishing the collection of the money that I had saved in the bottom draw of my desk. There were 2,000.00 colones of students' dues there. I should have brought that money home that night because the next day nobody could enter the campus since it was being protected by a regiment of soldiers brandishing machine guns," I continued with despair, as the feeling of loss and pain returned to me from that day. "I bet the army captain stole the money that I could have used to escape," I said with disgust. "I know if I continue my trip North, I could stop in Puebla and find a job teaching Latin or philosophy. Gustavo, my *compañero* from the Seminary, co-owns a Colegio in Puebla, but my final, true destination is Los Angeles," I explained. I did not say that persecution by the military was forcing me out of El Salvador. Neither did I mention that there was this girl named Norma that was pulling me towards California almost as strongly as the army was pushing me away from home. I was feeling a double force that pointed me towards the North.

Norma was by now living in Riverside, California, and would have never suspected that she was still on my mind, and that she was one of the reasons I was about to walk across Mexico. When her mother came to El Salvador to fetch her against her will, our relationship was declared over. Resigned to this decision, I was then determined to continue my university studies to become a defense lawyer specialized in criminal law. My university life had replaced her, but the military invasion of the University changed my future.

"You could study here at the Universidad de San Carlos! According to some people, it's the best national university of Central America," Tío Chepe suggested with an illuminated expression, as if a light bulb had turned on in his head and he had just come up with the solution to all my problems.

"But the same thing is happening here! La Universidad de San Carlos is frequently invaded and closed by the Guatemalan army. I think it was just reopened, after being closed for six months, but that doesn't mean it will stay that way," I argued.

"Maybe, we can help you another way," Tío Chepe paused to think.

My three cousins had been listening to our conversation without missing a word. Sandra, the middle child, already 21, and the most talkative, looked at me with her green, tender, big eyes, and gave me a full smile. Then, turning to her father, her heart skipping a beat, as she said all in a breathless rush,

"I want to help."

"*You? How?*" Tío Chepe de Guatemala exclaimed, eyes widened incredulously.

"I have worked at the pharmacy on Quinta Avenida, demonstrating and selling Revlon cosmetics for two years now. I have saved all my paychecks. I want to give Chepito the 100.00 Quetzals that he needs to cross the border," Sandra responded, again flashing me a luminescent smile.

"Sandra, you are amazing! I promise I'll send you the money as soon as I get to Los Angeles. I'll use my first paycheck to repay you," I said, my heart overflowing with gratitude.

After a long pause, Tío Chepe agreed. For me, this was practically a miracle. The next morning, I accompanied Sandra on the bus to downtown Guatemala City to wait for the bank to open.

"Chepito, I am very glad to help you, but do not forget to repay me. One hundred Quetzals is a lot of money to me," she said.

"I will never forget what you are sacrificing for me. I was considering going back to El Salvador, defeated with no real future. You have given me my future back. '¡Gracias mil!' When I come back, you and I have to dance the tango again. Remember?"

"Oh, Chepiiiiiiito," she said with a watery laugh.

I kissed her cheek goodbye, turned around, and started my walk towards the outskirts of the city. Once on the double-lane Pan American road, I again extended my arm and lifted my thumb. *This time I will not be stuck on the border between Guatemala and Mexico, and I'll make sure of that.* Four weeks later, I was knocking at Gustavo's door in Puebla. I had finally made it.

Chapter 12: Mexico. Puebla I

G ustavo's ancestors, the Orellanas, arrived in El Salvador from western Spain, probably from the Extremadura province, in the late 1700s, most likely as part of the Spanish migration to the new world, pulled by the promise of gold, land and riches. He tells me that his last name Orellana has its origins in the town of *Orellana La Vieja*. Unlike most the indigenous peoples who lived away from the Metapán Mountains towards the plains, beyond the volcanoes of the pacific coast, The Orellanas settled around the northwestern mountainous region of El Salvador, close to the border with Guatemala and Honduras, attracted by the silver and iron mines of the region.

They found the northern, narrow fields on the skirts of the small mountains of Metapán to be the ideal site for the farming of corn, beans, and squash, and the breeding of small herds of cows and goats. Agricultural advantage was valued, but what attracted Gustavo's ancestors the most were the metals hiding deep in the mountains, waiting to be dug out. These Orellana farmers and miners were self-sufficient with almost no contact with major economic centers of the region. Later their products included, to a lesser extent, indigo (añil- a natural dye) for exportation to Europe. Some of these Spaniards and *Criollos* (a word for people born in Central America of Spanish parents), including Gustavo's ancestors, did not usually mix with the indigenous, Nahuatl speaking, Salvadorian people (the Pipiles, who were conquered later by the Mayans) in the Metapán enclaves. Some Spaniard groups remained in the jungle, lost and ignored by the larger population, and did not mix as much as others.

Nowadays, there are some remnant descendants of those isolated groups that still exhibit identifiable body features inherited from their Spaniard ancestors. Gustavo is one of them. At 6'2", with light brown hair, and blue-green eyes, he breaks the typical image of the short, darker, Salvadorian mestizo. With a lanky body frame and a smooth, steady, bouncing gait, he looks as if he is descending to the city from the mountains with an oversized and overweight bundle of harvested crops, topped with some gold and silver ore, on his shoulders like his ancestors before him. Some say that the rocky nature of the mountainous paths creates the bouncing characteristic of this campesino walk. Others attribute the campesino walk to horseback riding since early age.

By virtue of his small rounded cheeks and large central incisors, we called him "el conejo" (the rabbit) in the Seminary. Other nicknames were "la jirafa", slim and tall as he was, he moved slowly like a giraffe, and "guara" (macaw) for his colorful yellow hair and red cheeks. Gustavo's walk still gives the impression that he never left the mountains. Contradictory as it may seem, when el padre Camilo and Gustavo met me in Santa Ana in February of 2016, Camilo, upon seeing Gustavo for the first time after 50 years, remarked that he looked like one of those blond ceremonious professors he had had in Leuven, Belgium. That image was created by Gustavo's protruding abdomen and slightly hunched, intellectual posture, which concealed his campesino past. Another Salvadoran could have easily mistaken Gustavo for a European, as the citizens of Puebla still currently often do.

At the time of this arduous trip to Puebla in the early autumn of 1972, it had been five years since our epic trip with the monsignor in the small VW buggy, and two years since I had left Puebla to return to El Salvador with the hopes of being sent by the Bishop to study in Leuven.

Once in Puebla, I found Gustavo already well assimilated among the intellectuals of the city and married to Elsita, who was then 7 months pregnant with Gustavito. He talked and dressed like a well-to-do poblano and most of his friends were members of the few criollo, devoutly Catholic families that still controlled the economy in the city. He had met them, and other foreign students, at the Colegio Benavente, a La Salle-run private high school, where Gustavo had landed a job teaching psychology and philosophy.

Gustavo was often mistaken as a poblano Spanish Criollo, a gachupín. The truth is that these so-called gachupines were the white descendants of a large immigrant wave from Italy, Germany, and Spain that arrived in Mexico in the middle of the 1800's, and settled around Puebla. Gustavo preferred not to correct their mistaken impression on him. Only the closest of Gustavo's friends knew his humble Salvadorian and campesino mountain roots. "He doesn't like to talk about where he was born. He can relate to me, another rural guy. He even brought me to El Salvador during one of our university vacations, to meet his family," one of his friends, Felipe, told me in confidence when I recently paid Gustavo a visit.

The petite and vivacious Elsita gave birth to two boys and one girl during the happy years of their marriage, but Gustavo's professorship at el Colegio Benavente, and later at *La Benemérita Universidad Autónoma de Puebla*, presented a serious strain on their relationship that ultimately led to a divorce. Elsita and her sister Gloria told me that Gustavo couldn't resist the temptation of the gachupín female students' love advances, which were many, and finally succumbed to a series of love affairs.

They tell me that Gustavo's life was spent meeting female students in the coffee shops that surrounded Puebla's historic central park, neglecting his three children and Elsita. Evidently, Gustavo was a rarity and a very coveted international guy by women in Puebla. Often after his lectures, women would leave behind their underwear on his desk.

Gustavo absolutely denies he had any affairs and that Elsita's uncontrollable jealousy fueled by her sister Gloria's gossiping drove them to a divorce. He met his students in Los Portales because he loved a strong cup of coffee accompanied by unrestricted cigarette smoking, and found it relaxing to tutor students outside the confines of the Colegio and the university. Elsita loved to spend exorbitant amounts of money, squandered the family weekly budget, and all together stopped loving him. He told me that he never forgets the time when he gave money to Elsita to buy new shoes for his three children telling them that they couldn't choose the most expensive pair of shoes because the budget was tight, but Elsita once at the shoe store, exhorted her children to buy the most expensive shoes "*antes que tu padre se gaste el dinero con sus amantes.*". Gustavo said that had Elsita still loved him and respected him, she would have insisted his children follow his directives.

✳✳✳

Strictly speaking, Elsita's father, Don Natal Rivadeneyra, was a *gachupín*, but not a Spaniard. His mother immigrated to Puebla from the German Alsace region before War World I. Elsita is very proud of her French and German ancestry. "I am trying to become a German citizen," she told me last year when I visited Puebla. "Nowadays, I spend around 4 months per year in Hamburg where my little sister, Lourdes, lives with her loving German husband. He is crazy about her. I babysit for her children and cook delicious mole Poblano. I think I can get some German admirers to propose."

Don Natal managed roads construction for a Mexican international company in Puebla that did business with Central American countries. Fortuitously, Don Natal's employer sent him to El Salvador to coordinate the construction of the *litoral* road that crosses the country alongside the Pacific Ocean. He brought his much younger wife, Reina, to this hot, humid, lush, and mosquito-infested seashore of southern El Salvador. Two of Elsita's siblings, as fate would have it, were born in the pacific port of La Libertad. The Rivadeneyra family would spend eight years in El Salvador, the time it took to build *la litoral*.

Elsita inherited the dark complexion and plumpness from her Mexican mother, and the eloquent and quick tongue from her Mexican/French/German father. Short, round, vivacious, and always ready to speak her mind, Elsita awakened the phlegmatic Gustavo and kept him on his toes.

"Do you know what, Chico? Today, in our evangelization rounds out in the community, I knocked at one of those small houses next to the Seminary. The most beautiful and kind girl opened the door. I spent hours talking to her because she couldn't stop talking. Her brother and sister were born in El Salvador and she made me wait until her father came from work. He never did, so she made me promise to visit this Saturday in the afternoon to meet the whole family. You've got to come with me," Gustavo eagerly commented one day before our evening prayers in the Seminary.

"We can't go out just like that! What reason would we give to our Rector, father Huesca, when asking permission to leave the premises?" I asked.

"To continue our evangelization, Rector Huesca would give us permission. We have an excellent pious and academic reputation," Gustavo, the always clever troublemaker, explained.

After that Saturday, Gustavo and I spent every Saturday afternoon at the Rivadeneyra's house during the 1969-1970 School year, purportedly evangelizing their entire barrio. Elsita had a younger sister named Gloria. The four of us managed to spend many undisturbed hours eating mole poblano, listening to a variety of popular Mexican, French, and American music, and most of all, talking about ourselves. The parents assumed that their daughters would be safe with two seminarian evangelists. The mother believed that it might do them some good.

Our friendships soon turned into a platonic infatuation. It was our last year of philosophy studies: the year of doubting and experimenting. One needed to be absolutely sure about becoming a priest before embarking into the next phase, the four years of theology, so we innocently experimented.

Gustavo and Elsita, and Gloria and I, invented all sorts of mental and innocent physical games throughout those hours. The fruit was prohibited either way. How far could our actions go without turning it into a sin? We played with fire. That year, we must have taxed the psychological strength of our seminarian spiritual mentors. Elsita and Gloria couldn't always resist the impulse of testing the strength of our vows. We couldn't and didn't know how to resist. We had never been tested. Would holding hands be considered a sin? What about a snug goodbye hug that lasted just a second too long, with the urgent need to never let go, and which left a rosy perfume scent lingering within our sinuses forever? Or, would a kiss placed on the cheek that, momentarily, purposely, slowly, and softly moves closer to the lips be considered a sin? Nowadays, I often wonder how Gloria's kisses would have tasted to me at that time. Yes, of course, I resisted. I would sleep on the cold marble floor of the Seminary's dormitory praying to Jesus to help me dominate my carnal desires. I was solidly committed to becoming one of his servants and soldiers.

Despite all our efforts to resist, that year Gustavo and I lived intensely. We started to buy secular literature, veering away from our book *Philosophiae Scholasticae Summa*. That was the time when we fought over the only copy of *Don Quijote de la Mancha*. We wanted to know if Don Quijote would finally get a hold of his imaginary "*La Dulcinea del Toboso*," and laughed surprisingly at Sancho Panza's daring farts to stop Don Quijote from another crazy adventure.

We also took turns with *Pepita Jimenez*, by Juan Valera. Luis, the protagonist, kept us in a permanent suspense. Would he choose to abandon his vocation by leaving the Seminary to marry Pepita? It was around this time that we also became enamored with Shakespeare's sonnets (in Spanish), especially, for unknown reasons, Sonnet #18, *Shall I compare thee to a summer's day?* We felt the power of these sonnets without having a physical representation of a woman. We were just in love with romanticism itself. We romanticized Dante's Beatriz and Shakespeare's Lucrecia.

We were especially absorbed with the poems of Gustavo Adolfo Bécquer, his short *"Rimas."* We would memorize them and recite them late at night in our rooms after having finished our homework on the existentialism of Nietzsche, Schopenhauer, and Kierkegaard. Is the idea of God really dead? Is the "will" more powerful than reasoning? Could a religious commitment be the only salvation from the absurdities of this world? Would all these mean that our vocation to become priests is obsolete?

The rhymes of Bécquer's poetry made us vibrate with their rhythms and we found that poetry was not difficult to understand when it dealt with romance. In a sense, these literature œuvres helped us understand the other side of what it meant to be human. We discovered in the company of Elsita and Gloria that we were full to the brim with theoretical and mystical experiences, but utterly limited in the practical knowledge of the world.

Rima XCI
> *"Podrá nublarse el sol eternamente;*
> *Podrá secarse en un instante el mar;*
> *Podrá romperse el eje de la tierra*
> *Como un débil cristal.*
> *¡Todo sucederá! Podrá la muerte*
> *Cubrirme con su fúnebre crespón;*
> *Pero jamás en mí podrá apagarse*
> *La llama de tu amor."*
(The face of the sun may darken forever,

The oceans run dry in an instant of fire.
The axis spinning our planet may shatter
Like so much brittle crystal.
Yes, all of that may happen! At the end, Death
May cover my flesh with her funeral shroud;
But none of it will reach within my soul and snuff
The bright flame of your love.)

The one poem we recited the most was this,

Rima XXIII
"Por una mirada, un mundo;
por una sonrisa, un cielo;
por un beso... yo no sé
qué te diera por un beso."
(For a glance, the Earth,
for a smile, the Heavens,
for a kiss... I don't know
what I would give you for a kiss!)

Another went like this,

Rima XXI
"¿Qué es poesía?, dices mientras clavas
en mi pupila tu pupila azul.
¿Qué es poesía? ¿Y tú me lo preguntas?
Poesía... eres tú."
(What is poetry? you ask, while nailing
your blue gaze into mine.
What is poetry? You ask it?
Poetry... that's you.)

And another,

"¡Los suspiros son aire y van al aire!
¡Las lágrimas son agua y van al mar!
Dime, mujer, cuando el amor se olvida
¿sabes tú adónde va?"

And finally,

Rima LIII
> *"Volverán las oscuras golondrinas*
> *En tu balcón sus nidos a colgar*
> *Y otra vez con el ala a sus cristales,*
> *Jugando llamarán.*
> *Pero aquellas que el vuelo refrenaban*
> *Tu hermosura y mi dicha a contemplar.*
> *Aquellas que aprendieron nuestros nombres,*
> *¡Esas... no volverán!"*
> (The black swallows will return
> to nest on your balcony,
> and with their wings they will knock
> playfully at its windows.
> But those who slowed down in their flight
> to contemplate your beauty and my happiness,
> those who learnt our names...
> those.... will not return!)

During those Saturday afternoons, with Elsita and Gloria, under the fog of a Pall-Mall-smoky living room, we discovered the Beatles, the Platters, and Frankie Vallie and the Four Seasons ("Can't take my eyes off you"). They made us listen to the top 10 songs in English of 1969, the top French songs of the year, such as *"Et Maintenant," "Je t'aime...moi non-plus," "Blue, Blue l'amour est Bleu," "Toute les Garçon et les Filles», «Un jour, un enfant,"* and those of Mireille Mathieu, our favorite song being *"La Dernière Valse"*. Somehow Gustavo smuggled a small transistor Hitachi radio into the Seminary that we kept during our studies tuned to *Radio El Mundo,* the Mexican station specializing in European pop music, dominated mostly by French chansons and Italian pop. Gustavo learned by heart the song Il Cuore è uno Zingaro by Nicolo Di Bari. I recently asked Elena, my daughter, to create a Mireille Mathieu radio channel on Spotify, the music-streaming program. Surprisingly, she started to dance to the beat of the 1969 French chançons. "This is the kind of music that is easy for me to dance to," she declared.

On some Sundays instead of continuing with our evangelization efforts, we sneaked into a movie theater. Puebla's movie offerings were populated by European films, mostly French and Italian. We sinned by watching the almost topless scenes in the 1969 French film "*La Piscine,*" starring Romy Schneider and Alain Delon. We laughed at Ugo Tognazzi in his "*Straziami ma di baci saziami*" comedy.

During those afternoons with the Rivadeneyra family, we also discovered the opera. Don Natal played Tosca, his favorite opera, for us repeatedly on his record player and gave us mini-lectures on the music. It was 1969, but Don Natal played the 1953 Maria Callas recording as Tosca, repeating many times the sections when Tosca calls desperately for her lover Mario. He was so pleased to find an inquisitive, educated, and captive audience. That year, we couldn't get enough of the Rivadeneyra's. During that time, we discovered that there was a powerful, enticing world beyond the walls of the Seminary and that it would require the utmost personal strengths to resist it. We, in many occasions, were not successful at resisting it.

❋❋❋

Once in Puebla, I entered Gustavo's apartment, and took a good look at him and Elsita, next to him, pregnant.

"It was love at first sight." She says. "My father and my mother knew I had fallen in love with this seminarian the first instant I opened the door. He wanted me to go to church and enroll in Bible courses taught by the seminarians. Look at my *panza*! This is what my Bible study gave me," she laughed. "I am hoping for a boy. I will name him Gustavo."

Gustavo and I, almost at the same year of our lives, descended from a religious, chaste, lofty, mystical, platonic, and spiritual sphere to a physical relationship with a woman, grounded in real experiences.

Chapter 13: Romantic Escape

One restless Spring night, Gustavo and I did not sleep thinking about the duplicity of what we were about to do the next day. The exhilaration of tomorrow's adventure captured our sensual imagination while, at the same time, presented us with a high-stakes risk of expulsion; in effect ending our academic seminarian life. We were not sure we wanted to end it yet. We loved the Major Seminary. However, after the well-planned premeditated deed, what kind of excuse could we come up with to tell the monsignor? We feared and we trembled, as I would imagine a first-time parachuter would feel at the edge of the doorway, the wind whipping his hair and gear around, just before jumping out of the plane.

We were on the move just before the roosters started singing and way before the first bus started clacking at the *"Central de Autobuses del Oriente."*

"Let's just bring our backpacks with the minimum amount of supplies necessary. Really, all we need is a towel and our bathing suit, no pajamas, no change of clothing, our toothbrush, definitely our toothbrush, and money," I said sounding very austere, "it'll be very hot, and it is only for one night. I can spend one night sleeping on a tree branch or on a bench in the central park, who cares."

"Elsita is bringing sun tan oil," Gustavo said.

"Why would anyone need oil?" I asked

"Elsita wants to come back to Puebla looking like a real Aztec Indian. She and Gloria are spreading this oil all over their bodies to bronze their skin. It is something that girls like to do, I guess." Gustavo said.

"Is their skin going to turn darker and softer?" I asked.

"I think it gradually becomes shinier and slippery, too. When we get there, there is only one way to find out," Gustavo, the quiet troublemaker, responded.

The roosters had not awakened yet at 3:30 in the morning. We crept stealthily up to the door leading to the main stairwell that would take us down from the second floor to the intersection of the cross, the Christian shape formed by the buildings adopted by the architects that designed the modern structure of the Seminary. There was the danger that at any time one of the 300 seminarians might have decided to get up very early to study or to walk towards the chapel to pray. Any of the 20 priests, our professors, could have also been up preparing their philosophy and theology lectures, which was not very unusual. The doorman, however, Juanito "*Malacara*", almost 85, a cantankerous old devil, would certainly be asleep, and if not, being deaf and almost blind, he wouldn't present a problem for us.

As we descended and reached the ground floor, we found the wide and long corridors deserted and darker than I would have imagined. At first, I thought it was the moonlight, but instead, a stark yellowish light emanated from the inner garden lights, faintly sifting through the floor-to-ceiling glass panes that formed the walls of the widest corridor. The rows of rectangular pillars at each side of this corridor -- that represented the vertical line of the cross and led to the main entrance of the building – could not clearly be seen. We decided not to walk down this corridor. Any seminarian or priest already up in the upper floors of the building that formed the horizontal line of the cross could coincidently look down through his window and suddenly have his attention drawn by our moving silhouettes framed by the inner garden lights.

We decided, instead, to take the riskier path: the narrower, longer corridor that passed in front of the classrooms on the first floor. Any awkward movement made by either our bare feet or our backpacks could produce an echoing noise from the cold marble tiles and alert the light sleepers in the rooms above of our rebellious presence. The tiled floors were always maintained sparkling clean and resonant thanks to the desire of Seminarians to complete weekly chores with exceptional pulchritude. We proceeded soundlessly and slowly, shoulders hunched, head bowed, like two black cats slinking in the shadows of an alley, Gustavo leading, and I just behind him. It took us more than ten minutes to reach the end of the corridor and find the unlocked back door facing the soccer fields. The building doors were always unlocked, for the 25 acres of land that surrounded it were enclosed by a thick 12-feet perimeter wall.

Once out of the main building, we still had to cross three soccer fields to reach this wall. The only light, the yellowish one, almost imperceptible, came from one street light post that was intended to light up the beginning of the narrow dirt country road that ran alongside the north wall of the fields. The Seminary was situated where the city ended and the countryside started.

❇︎❇︎❇︎

At this time, recent memories disturbed my mind. I thought about how we had walked that very same dirt road in the opposite direction at 4:00 am, three years earlier in 1967-1968 school year, the day after Gustavo and I arrived at the Seminario Palafoxiano of Puebla. That day, the seminarians were set to go on a 30-mile hike North to climb the 14,640 foot *La Malinche* mountain as a community-building exercise. Hernán Cortez had once passed on his horse through this same road. "*La Malinche*" was named after the Aztec Indian who was a slave, interpreter, secretary, and mistress of Cortez, and who became the mother of Martin, the first mestizo, and in other words, the first "Mexican."

That day, Gustavo, victorious, reached the snow-covered summit of this extinct volcano first, with a small group of other seminarians. I was not so lucky. A sudden dizziness, nausea, and excruciating headache overcame me mid-way up the volcano as I fell victim to altitude sickness. No wonder, since we had just arrived the day before from Santa Ana, El Salvador, which is situated at a mere 650 meters (around 2,000 ft.) above sea level. The group left me behind at 10,000 ft. after a lengthy respite and discussion about my condition.

"Have an extra shot of tequila, it will do you some good," some Mexican seminarians urged me. "We have been drinking tequila since we were babies," they informed me. They had also been drinking it since we left the compound with no apparent ill effect. "It'll keep you warm. You won't feel a thing. You'll feel stronger."

I didn't know any better and drank three shots of tequila and lay down under a solitary *ocote* tree, at the start of a vast area of basaltic formations, next to a ravine. Defeated, I urged them to continue to the summit, the cold thin air crushing my chest. An icy cold wind whistled down the rock formations, watering my eyes, and numbing my ears and fingers.

Gustavo became concerned, not wanting to leave me alone, but he pressed on, not being able to resist the impulse of discovering snow for the first time. I would have to wait six more years to have my own first snow in Boston. I stayed under the tree next to the trail most of the day, hallucinating and thinking that the group might have left me behind for good. I swore I saw a herd of wild boars stamped towards me, heard the "*Llorona*" with her wailing cries for her babies at the bottom of the ravine, and witnessed a vulture circled above me ready to dive and tear my eyes out. I clearly remember the constant clattering of rocks making echoing sounds down the ravine that added to my wild hallucinations. I remained in this tequila/altitude induced drowsiness all day.

Gustavo was happy to see me still alive on his way down and helped me get up from the roots of the tree. With his aide, I started the long descent with him, feeling better with each step. The Mexican seminarians descended the mountain at a brisk pace and once back at the compound they gathered in small groups, happily chatting about their adventure, while I, disheartened, moved aside, feeling inadequate and weak, like an unpopular boy who shies away from others in the school cafeteria. We entered the compound way after dinnertime. The nuns made sure to leave some dinner for us, which I devoured frantically despite the jalapeño-spicy-hot flavor that perforated my stomach.

❊❊❊

During those first weeks of the first year of philosophy in the Seminary in Puebla, I sensed that my presence in the group rubbed some native indigenous seminarians the wrong way and were set to treat me with some contempt, "We want you to know that we are better than any other Latin American country, especially the Central Americans whose countries at one time were part of Mexico. You may feel special with your scholarship, but you are not better than us." Later, the same group would smile as they watched me suffer at the dinner table when I made a grueling effort to eat my meals. The nuns would regularly concoct Mexican specialties, overdoing it with the jalapeños and a mix of chilies found only in the Puebla countryside to please their indigenous clientele. Everything tasted like jalapeño peppers, even the milk, with scents of *chile poblano* and freshly boiled and ground maize.

There were some white Mexican seminarians, from major Mexican cities, with last names like Arenas, Bello, Crivelli, Cosío, Medel, and Guizar, that made it a point to

aid us in our social adjustment, but the indigenous seminarians made our lives difficult. They were right about us.
Gustavo and I felt highly capable and better than the rest.
Sensing this, the indigenous Mexicans took every opportunity to squash our air of superiority.

"Do you want to try boxing with me, Puchiquita?" Itztli
said one morning while we were making our beds before
going to mass. My *Puchiquita* nick named was tagged on
me by the Mexicans due to my salvadorean slang word *púchica*, which I repeated often. Gustavo was called la
Puchicona.

He pulled a set of 4 brown-leather gloves out of his
bureau and helped me tie a pair around my wrist. I approached the challenge lightly, but with naive enthusiasm.
Whereas, for Itztli, boxing meant something totally different: a serious physical activity through which personal
scores were settled with honor. He ceremoniously helped
me tie my gloves around my wrists and soon after inserted
his dark, heavy hands into his, asking the seminarian
watching attentively from his bed to help him tie them and
serve as a referee. Itztli showed me how to assume a
fighting position, moved a couple of feet in front of me and
without notice or warning, while I was waiting for the referee's instructions, he punched me with an expertly
launched right hook on my left cheek and nose, knocking
me down. Blood started to run profusely on the floor.

The seminarian-referee ran to the infirmary to get
some gauze and alcohol to revive me and clean the blood
on my face. Itztli, unable to control his pent-up desire to
humiliate me, to graphically show me that I wasn't better
than him, had knocked me down without giving me a
chance to defend myself, breaking the rules of sportsman-
ship without remorse. He stood immobile with a mean
smirk of satisfaction on his face, defiantly staring at the
seminarian-referee who didn't hide his absolute disapproval. Itztli might not have been academically successful,
but that day, in a premeditated action, he showed me that

he and his indigenous classmates were stronger and street-wiser than me, and by association, Gustavo.

Later, Xipilli and Itztli would often choose to be in the opposite soccer team during our indoor tournaments to have the opportunity to show us that they were physically stronger, opting for playing very dirty in the field, kicking, pushing, elbowing, and kneeing us at every opportunity we found finding for the ball. They were disciplined often, exacerbating their frustration, for they felt that the seminarian-precepts were very lenient with us, treating us with white gloves as not to offend us. Gustavo and I, truth be told, often took advantage of our "otherness," getting away with infractions for which the Mexicans would have been punished severely or expelled. Gustavo was even given a private room as a freshman, which were reserved only for upperclassmen. He claimed that the common dormitories were too cold at night, making him sick.

Towards the middle of our first year in the Seminario of Puebla, we became well known, special, different, and proud of it. We were international students on a scholarship and exuded an academic aura of craftsmanship, effective study-habits, motivation, and intelligence. We didn't disappoint, and once again as in Santa Ana, competed for the first three highest class ranking positions, which in turn, gave us more social capital, which in turn, created more discontent among the Mexican indigenous seminarians, who were mostly recruited from the indigenous communities around Puebla, and among other nationalists, who felt that foreigners like us shouldn't receive any academic honors.

※※※

"Come on! Hurry up!", Gustavo whispered almost too loudly, bringing me back to reality, just after I landed on the soft dirt road from my jump over the peripheral wall of the Seminary. The chill in the air and the silence of the atmosphere, combined with the high adrenaline levels in our brains caused by doing the forbidden, invigorated our long walk to the bus terminal. We got there in time to board the 6:00 am ADO bus to Veracruz. Unusually jittery, Gustavo became very talkative and impatient during the six-hour trip, delving over the prospects of becoming a priest. The excesses of the clergy in Puebla, especially the ostentatious opulence of the Archbishop, rubbed him the wrong way. His campesino past could not reconcile with what he considered to be conduct going against what the humble carpenter Jesus Christ stood for.

"Did you notice the limousine, the garb, the protocol, and the submission of the Seminarian priests towards the Octaviano Marquez, Archbishop of Puebla, when he came to give mass during our spiritual retreat?" Gustavo said with disgust.

"Yes. That's normal for an Archbishop," I responded.

"He even waited inside the car until his private secretary priest placed a thick red carpet next to the door. That behavior tantamount to royalty revolted my stomach," Gustavo said, making a vomiting gesture.

Gustavo saw all the pomp and circumstance as a symbol of hypocrisy, not unlike the historic complaints of corruption and sinful behavior laid down against the church hierarchy by the likes of Martin Luther and Voltaire. At that moment, the thought of Elsita's sweet kisses waiting under the salty sun of the Veracruz beaches was also adding another element to Gustavo's disenchantment against the priesthood, forcing him to over rationalize his emotional state.

In a way, for him it was morally more desirable to leave the Seminary than to risk becoming a corrupt priest. Money and pleasures could be obtained in secular life while maintaining one's own moral commitments and without jeopardizing one's integrity. What was better, to be perceived as a just person, or truly be one? Even our

Rector, Padre Huesca, who later would become Puebla's Archbishop, did not look as pious as we expected. While officiating mass in the Seminary chapel in the mornings, he seemed to be going non-devoutly through the rituals, as if he never meant it, as if he did not believe it, and without bothering to conceal his indifference.

I came out of his services uninspired and miserable. It was clear that Gustavo was onto something that I was not ready to accept. Could Unamuno's priest-hero in his short story, *"San Manuel Bueno, Mártir,"* who did not believe in God, be not uncommon among Catholic priests?

One day, Rector Huesca showed the true face of the catholic church when he veered from the mass ritual to discuss with us the day after a political manifesto with six demands was published by university students in Mexico City on August 27, 1968. Huesca might have been afraid that the manifesto would have found resonance with the seminarians because he painted the student movement as driven by a bunch of degenerate hippies who wanted free sex and drugs, mortal sins, and gave little attention to their courageous humanistic demands. This also showed what Gustavo had already concluded, that the Church was always on the side of the government and the rich.

The Mexico City university students' manifesto encompassed basic liberties and rights: free speech, a halt to state violence, accountability for police and military abuses, the release of political prisoners and the beginning of a dialogue with the government. Absolutely, these demands were tame but powerful. This was the first time that anyone had cared to question the recurrent and historic undemocratic actions of the government. The entire population was in favor of the students except the government and the Mexican catholic church.

On the second day of October, The Mexican government ended up squashing the student movement by military force, killing hundreds of students in one night while they gathered and rallied in Tlatelolco, an area of tall apartment buildings. These killings went down in Mexican history as *"La Matanza de Tlatelolco."* The Mexican people are commemorating its 50th anniversary as I write these pages.

The extravagance shown by the clerics in Puebla did not affect me as much as it did Gustavo. I was convinced that I could follow a more austere life, a revolutionary path, as a priest who would fight for religious authenticity, poverty, and economic austerity within the catholic hierarchy as an attempt to reform it. After all, these were the years when thoughts akin to a Liberation Theology had started to permeate the lower ranks, like us the seminarians, of the Catholic Church. Some young clerics, such as the Colombian Camilo Torres, became well known for joining armed guerrillas in the jungle and paying the ultimate sacrifice: getting killed by the military and striking a chord in the hearts of many young seminarians. Rector Huesca was right in perceiving this threat to the status quo.

✳✳✳

We may have smoked Raleigh's and Paul Malls more than usual on our bus trip to Veracruz. Puebla had made us sinners and smokers. Stepping off the bus at the terminal, I felt nauseated; cigarettes never agreed with me, it was just something to kill boredom. I quickly wanted to detoxify from the bitter, acidic, rancid nicotine taste in my mouth.

Pedro, one of our classmates at the Colegio Benavente and a native of Veracruz, was waiting for us. A week before, he had offered us his house, eager to show his historic city. There was no time to waste. I was desperately seeking for something to sooth the bitter taste in my mouth. Gustavo suggested stopping at a cantina on our way to Pedro's house to have a couple of martinis. This was around the time when Gustavo and I had become addicted not only to cigarettes but also to martinis thanks to our *tertulias* at the Rivadeneyra's house. Their father, Don Natal, liked them dry, using World War II Diplôme Dry Gin. We used José Cuervo's tequilas. Pedro took us to his corner cantina and after a couple of them, I felt reinvigorated and ready to face hot Veracruz.

At his house, we deposited our backpacks and set out to walk around the beach. Gustavo told me, the last time I interviewed him for my memoir, that during that walk on Boulevard Avila Camacho, I didn't stop talking loudly as if I wanted the world to know that I was free, and that the martinis made me euphoric, losing all inhibitions, causing me to approach whichever girl crossed my path to drop them a pick up line. Unbeknownst to us, Pedro was well known around the beach as the most flamboyant homosexual of Veracruz. We suspected it, but didn't care. Gustavo tells me that the girls laughed, amused to hear *piropos*, mixed with Bécquer's rimas, so lovingly uttered by what they suspected were three gay men out for a stroll.

We spent Sunday with the Rivadeneyras at the Villa del Mar beach with a view of both the *Isla de Sacrificios* and *Isla de Pájaros*. Don Natal pitched an oversized tarp to accommodate his large family and us. Elsita's mother had brought food to feed an entire regiment. Nobody noticed the time when Gustavo and Elsita got lost within the crowd only to come back for lunch. I stayed with the family talking nonsense and waiting to see what would happen with Gloria. Nothing happened, other than the pictures Don Natal took of us. Gustavo and I stood together with Elsita and Gloria, each with our right arm around their naked shoulders. That was our great romantic adventure.

Last year, 45 years later, I visited Puebla and when I spoke to Elsita and Gloria, they remembered our time on the beach with nostalgia and regret that nothing more had happened.

We took the bus back to Puebla the next day, climbing the wall just before midnight, again unnoticed, and went straight to bed. I don't remember what we told our

classmates and prefect about our absence. Gustavo thinks
that we told Rector Huesca a lie: we had spent the weekend with Padre Camilo, our rector in El Salvador, visiting
Puebla for a religious conference.

I just came back from Puebla again recently. On this
trip, I forced Gustavo to visit the Seminary, 50 years after
we first arrived in 1967-1968. A peppy young girl stood
behind the reception counter, where Juanito *"Malacara"*
would had been, and greeted us with a wide smile. To our
surprise, we found female students walking in the corridors and working in the administration offices. We talked
to several of them, showed them our black and white pictures of that era that I had brought with me, accompanied
with diplomas and awards signed by priests whose legendary names they recognized as to emphasize that the
Seminary's walls had heard, felt and recorded our existence, with our struggles and successes, that should not
be forgotten in the depth of history.

"Look at that. That is Father Eliezer. He looks so
young. He is buried in the chapel," one of them said.

"This award is signed by Padre Mejorada. He is still
alive. He gives mass in the Temple of Divine Mercy in Puebla. You should visit him. He would love talking to you",
another one said.

The girls opened their black eyes more and more as
they examined the photos and documents, turned their
heads to look at us closely as if looking for the trait that
we still had from our youthful physique.

"Everything is written in Latin," another exclaimed in
admiration.

"How young and beautiful you were. I like those pictures where you are in your soccer team uniforms," said
another one.

Our first stop was the seminarian TV and radio station. The seminarian in charge interviewed us and
scanned my yellowish and stained documents, admiring

the age of each of them. "I will write an article about your visit and post it on our website," he said.

We learned that the Seminary has a mixed student body nowadays, is open to the community and acts as a quasi-university issuing degrees on "Religious Sciences." "If only I knew that these earth-shattering changes were to come, I would never have left the Seminary," Gustavo told the young women at the administration office, eliciting big laughters and some blushes among the group.

We then walked the corridors, which still shone with the glow of light that filtered through the large floor-to-ceiling windows, entered our philosophy classroom and sat at our old wooden desks. I noticed that the desk occupying my spot had part of its veneer surface cracked. I wished I had been brave enough, back then, to have carved my name underneath it and leave my mark in a place that had defined such a large part of my life.

Next, we entered the empty chapel. The Hammond organ stood tantalizingly in the same corner. I couldn't resist. I had learned the Bach *Toccata and Fugue in D Minor* on this organ. Its foot pedals fascinated me. I played its first movement. Gustavo listened, almost in tears, which is very unlike him. Old age turns you soft, I have found.

Then, we moved to the cafeteria, spoke to the nuns making lunch, and commented on how the building was starting to show its age. At the end of our solitary walk, we sat on the bleachers of the soccer field.

"En esta cancha fue donde yo metí el segundo gol que nos dió la victoria en el campeonato. Quedamos campeones en tres años consecutivos," I said.

"Yo fui el que metió el gol," Gustavo interrupted me.

"Noooo. Yo fui. Tal vez tú metiste otro gol, pero no fue en el juego que nos dio el campeonato. Tú siempre has querido ser el mejor, aunque no sea cierto, cabrón," I said with irritation. Our competitive spirit had remained intact.

"Sí, ahora me acuerdo. Tú tienes razón." Gustavo assented.

We sat on the bleachers for what seemed like a very long time, in silence, admiring anew the spectacular landscape, with the snow-covered Popocatepetl in the distance, a view that had never ceased to surprise us since our first freezing winter here in 1967-1968.

Chapter 14: More Climbing

Before "*La Malinche*" volcano in Puebla, Mexico, there was the hike Gustavo and I took with the seminarians at the Juan XXIII Minor Seminary to the summit of the "*Santa Ana*" volcano in El Salvador, led by el padre Chus, our rector.

The failure to climb up to the summit of *La Malinche* ate my insides for the entire school year, especially knowing that Gustavo had become a hero among his newly acquired Mexican friends. He became the strong *novato* from El Salvador. The other Salvadorian, me, was weak. On top of it, he, not me, got to touch and eat unspoiled fresh snow. I was looked down upon as a misfit and a wimp by the group. This was a tough blow to my ego. I knew they got the wrong impression of me. Who knew altitude sickness could be so devastating? I had considered myself to be in great shape. I had made it my purpose, still is to this day, to always be in great shape. I thank the minor Seminary of Santa Ana for imparting this great value on me.

During my high school seminarian years in Santa Ana, I had discovered and faithfully adopted the pleasures of the physical, social, and spiritual benefits of an exercise regimen, thanks to Padre Chus' exercise imports from Louvain. Walking rhythmically --- straight posture, shoulders a little back, chin slightly up, waist tucked, and always exuding a sense of purpose and accomplishment --- was very much applauded and celebrated, especially under el padre Chus' tenure as the rector. Having a slender, sharp, flexible, and well-tuned body meant that one was austere, ate in moderation to avoid gluttony, preferred sacrifice over comfort, demonstrated great deference to others to practice civility and humility, and was ready to adopt the arduous life of a true Christian. No pleasures entered the scheme of this type of life.

Our daily lives were filled with countless duties and responsibilities in the Seminary. We spent many hours outdoors every afternoon playing sports, (seen as duty, not recreation), taking care of the grounds, cleaning windows, floors and toilets, and moving furniture. On weekends, we hiked up any mountain or volcano, small such as the *Monte Santa Lucia,* and the *Tecana,* or large such as the *Volcán de Santa Ana,* visible within 30 miles of the building. So, before the failed climb up *La Malinche* in Puebla, Gustavo and I had ample experiences in the outdoors, of course most of it was done at low altitudes. A total collapse midway to *La Malinche's* summit, therefore, would never have crossed my mind.

✳✳✳

The failure in *La Malinche* made me think of the success in the Santa Ana volcano as a way of soothing my ego. That memorable hike up the dormant volcano happened while at the minor Seminary in El Salvador. El padre Chus organized this trip early November, at the end of the school year and towards the end of the rainy season.

"Each of you will be in charge of carrying your own food, water, snacks, and two thick woolen blankets. If you do not have boots, your tennis shoes will do. I want everybody to sleep well. We're leaving tomorrow at 5:00 a.m. Tonight, we'll go over the songs we'll sing as we march towards the volcano. I will teach you a new song that hikers sing around the Pyrenees. '*Marchemos al compás...ya sean mares, ya sean ríos...*'" Padre Chus, always at the piano, ended up teaching us around five European, mostly German, hiking songs that evening.

Padre Chus was short and thin, but his loud, baritone, and melodic voice, his solid upright posture, and his artistic hand movements that accompanied his speech, just like a classic ancient Roman orator, trapped our attention in an instant. His skills of persuasion became legendary.

On Sundays, the Santa Ana cathedral burst with parishioners at the hour of Padre Chus mass, waiting to be
inspired with increased religious ardor by his sermons.
Padre Chus had spent seven years at Université
Catholique de Louvain and had graduated with the highest academic honors. He spoke five languages, and read
ancient Latin, Greek and Aramaic. He composed songs,
hymns, marches, and anthems for the Seminary. He
played the piano, conducted the chorus, wrote poetry and
plays, and published articles on the philosophical and theological implications of the reforms mandated by the
Concilium Vaticanum II in 1963.

Tears came to my eyes last week when I caught a video
on YouTube of the beatification ceremony of Monseñor
Romero, attended by thousands of Salvadorian Catholics
and other religions and several heads of state, outdoors
next to the monument of *El Salvador del Mundo*, in San
Salvador. All of a sudden, I saw Padre Chus, much older
this time, with his white hair receding to reveal a wider
forehead, reading with his bifocals the Spanish translation
of the Latin document signed by Pope Francis proclaiming
Monseñor Romero a *Beato* of the Catholic Church. I paid
intense attention to the timbre of his voice and intonation
transporting me to my years in the Seminary. His orator
skills had not at all diminished, if anything, they had increased in gravitas. I waited to see if he would pronounce
the letter "c" like a Spaniard, as he insisted we did, explaining that the Spaniards had it right if only on that
letter. Yes, his voice did not change through the years.
"*Justicia*," he read in the video, with the perfect "c" sound,
the "th" sound in English, not like an "s". He was still true
to form. There was nothing Padre Chus could not do. I
wanted to be just like him. He was my hero.

Like every day in early November in Santa Ana, the
humidity and hot temperatures at 5:00 a.m. had dissipated. The cool breeze sweeping down the volcano,
reawakening the city, hit my nostrils to invigorate me with

deep scents of orange flowers, bougainvillea, and eucalyp-
tus. We were nervously fidgeting, like horses in the stables
itching to be saddled for a long ride, in our customary positions in the two-by-two-line formation, divided by grade
levels on the sidewalk, under the early light just outside
the Seminary. The seniors were last, and the ninth graders
were first with a senior as their guide. The seminarian
leader, the prefect, with Padre Chus, led the expedition.
Gustavo avoided me, seeing as we had not yet cemented a
solid friendship at this point, and made sure to line up
next to Torres, two seminarians behind me. He resented
my urbanism, very much alien to his pastoral and farming
backgrounds. For *campesinos* of the northern mountains,
hiking for three or four hours was part of their daily routine. For sure, Gustavo knew how to negotiate a long hike
up the Santa Ana volcano.

We quickly got into our customary walk, which was
brisk, purposeful, and determined, as if we were marching
into heavy opposition. I couldn't ever shake off this walk
in my later life. During my 20 years at The English High
School, in Boston, my colleagues would often comment
that *"I was a man with a mission,"* due to that walk I had
acquired in the Seminary.

Santa Ana citizens knew from a kilometer away when
the Seminarians were coming. This morning, however,
they sensed that something different was afoot. We were
not porting our daily white shirt and khaki pants or our
cassocks, opting instead for t-shirts, and working pants
and shoes. This was the first time seeing el Padre Chus
without his religious habit. The early street vendors who
set up shop for the day would regularly bow and cross
themselves as we passed by on our way to church. Today
they hesitated, as if we had become unholy without our
religious garb. We kept on marching south on *Avenida
Jose Matias Delgado,* up to *Calle José Mariano Mendez,*
taking a right turn and a quick left turn onto *Calle Aldea
San Antonio.*

It took us one hour to reach the outer limits of Santa Ana and enter the narrow dirt road, *Calle Las Cruces*, which would lead us to the hiking trail. As we entered the dirt road, the rich green lush vegetation started to appear and at times, combined with small and large coffee plantations such as *Finca Ayutepeque* and *Los Naranjos*. Very uncharacteristically for early November, dark clouds formed above us and broke into a copious thunderstorm, just as we started ascending, making the trail in some areas very hard and slippery and, in others, muddy and sticky. It seemed like more water was coming down from far up the trail than it was pouring from the sky, forming narrow and deep rivers of mud that rushed over our shoes and soaked our feet. The high canopy of foliage sheltered us from the heavy downpour. The storm seemed to be concentrated on only our side of the dormant volcano, determined to harden our journey. From a distance, I observed Gustavo's steady, long and bouncy stride, making his way into the forest. I wouldn't let him get far away from me by making sure to match his cadence. *He thinks I am not fit enough to keep up with him.*

Far in the distance, one of the *campesinos*, off from tending one of the coffee plantations, called us from his hut and offered us shelter in his *galera.* The precipitous sound of the rain as it hit the red tiles of his *galera*, cascading down to the ground to make small streams that trickled into the trail, hypnotized me. The smell of newly wet, fertile, and dark soil soothed me

The *campesino's* wife offered us tortillas with salt as we wondered if padre Chus was going to make us continue under the storm. Physical weakness was never allowed in the Seminary. One had to suffer, always. Gustavo shamelessly devoured four thick tortillas.

The torrential and dark thunderstorm, as many of them are, proved to be transient, leaving behind deep pools along the side of the trail converting the otherwise deep layer of fertile dark soil into a much more slippery, mushy, sticky, and muddy slope. As we ascended the volcano from the north side, we soon realized that, under the thick canopy of the jungle, the mud gradually disappeared into a deep brown soft layer of dead leaves, trees, ferns, moss, volcanic rock, and all sorts of living things that covered the path like an unsteady carpet. The temperature, little by little dropped from a humid 85 degrees to a refreshing 60 degrees.

We were already halfway up the volcano when Padre Chus suddenly stopped, stepped on top of a mossy log, unexpectedly took a bottle from his backpack, and started distributing a shot of whisky to each of us. We were aghast to see the dark, brown, and thick glass bottle held by his small hand. *"This is going to warm you up and give you strength to last up to the summit,"* he said. Likely, Padre Chus might have remembered the times he hiked the Alps during his summer vacations. Alcohol was rarely seen during our daily lives. For sure, Padre Chus would drink wine during mass, but it never occurred to me to taste it, even though when helping him to officiate the mass, I would alone carry the wine back to the sacristy. I could have drunk it all unnoticed, just to be sinful, but I did not. Here, the sweet and bitter shot of whisky legally permitted by Padre Chus, dried my mouth, and warmed my body as it came down my esophagus, but failed to increase my enthusiasm to keep climbing. I would have loved to gulp two more rapid shots as an experiment. My first experience with hard liquor left me unimpressed.

It was already midafternoon. The rain had totally stopped. Through the dark shadows of the high canopy, we could see the bluest of skies. We had been pounding the trail for almost four hours. We might have waited for the storm to pass at the *campesino's* house longer than our minds registered. "On second thought, I want you to have a couple of tortillas with cheese and water, as well as the whiskey. And keep going up," padre Chus commanded. *"Marchemos al compás...ya sean ríos, ya sean mares..."*

The Santa Ana volcano, called *"Ilamatepec"* by the *"pipil"* Indians, is 2381 meters high and seems to erupt every one hundred years. The last eruption occurred in October 2005. Before this, it erupted in 1904. Both have been small ash eruptions with little human or property casualties. The oligarchy of El Salvador took over the outskirts of the volcano at the beginning of the 20th century, displacing by force indigenous people, to plant mid-altitude bourbon coffee produced mostly for exportation to Holland and Germany. The fertile volcanic soil produces a soothing, earthy, with low acidity, and intensely aromatic coffee bean. This is a natural mutation from the *typical* variety discovered in 1949, found only in El Salvador, and named *Pacas,* after the last name of the coffee magnate whose hacienda produced it. This coffee is described as spicy, malty, clean, very sweet, and delicate by international connoisseurs. Later, around 1958, the Salvadorian coffee producers bred another variety of coffee named *pacamara*, a hybrid of *pacas* and *maragojipe* (another mutation found in Bahia, Brazil, that produces bigger beans). The *pacas* and the *pacamara* varieties of coffee made the Salvadorian oligarchy ultra-rich, including my mother's Castro Meza family, during the first half of the 20th century due to its high European demand. The volcano's forest was preserved to provide the needed shade for those mid-altitude coffee trees. Now, Starbucks regularly promotes the mid-altitude coffee produced from these same trees on the slopes of the Santa Ana volcano.

Our trail snaked around the coffee plantations at the middle of the volcano and later entered the thick forest, then came to an abrupt stop, just before the desolated grey and sandy upper contours of the stratovolcano. A rapid gray blanket of thick sulfuric fog undulated down from the summit. We continued up in a single line until we reached the lip of the crater and stopped to form small groups to survey the scenery, looking for an apt area to camp. The thick fog soon made the ground and the crater invisible. We immediately lost any physical point of reference and some of us started to sway as we walked with a hesitant foot. We didn't know what was up, or what was down. I felt as if I were floating up in the sky among the gray cloud remnants of the recent storm.

We heard each other's voices like in an echo, but couldn't see people's faces, and misjudged the distance between each other. Faces would phantasmagorically appear and disappear through the fog.

After a while of this distressed situation, we suddenly burst into a synchronized nervous laughter. Padre Chus became very concerned and ordered us to hold hands in small groups and sit down where we were to wait for the fog to clear. According to his calculations, the fog would quickly disappear as the night approached and the full moon rose. The temperature fell to around 50 degrees Fahrenheit, freezing temperatures for us in comparison to the comfortable dry 80-degree weather down the valley. I stayed as close to the forest line as possible, with an eye on Gustavo's whereabouts. Other seniors who feared to walk into the abyss of the crater unintentionally decided to join me as well.

Celada, Menjivar, and Hernandez soon started to sing to calm their nerves. We all soon joined and sang, what seemed for hours, to our heart's content. We carried in our heads a collection of around 100 church chants and other classical songs that could be spontaneously sung for different moments and occasions.

Living in the Seminary was just like being in a permanent religious, academic, and sports summer camp, only that the songs were written in a variety of dead and living languages, mostly European. Understandably, most of the songs were in Latin and Spanish, with quite a bit in German, Italian, and French. All taught by padre Chus, and, occasionally, by other recent arrivals from Université

Catholique de Louvain who lived temporarily in the Seminary before being shipped to assigned parishes, as the priest in charge, or as a helper to an older priest.

There were always two or three seminarians studying in Belgium. One of the most memorable recent graduates was el *Chele* Walter Guerra, who graduated three years after el padre Chus and later became the pastor of the *El Palmar,* a church in a middle-class barrio of Santa Ana. When he came back, after five years of intense theological studies, taught in Belgium French, he spoke in "*Frenchanish,*" half French and half Spanish. He became the director of the chorus while waiting for his parish assignment and interjected many French phrases in his teachings. I daydreamed about being sent to Belgium. Gustavo and I were next in line according to all estimates. For that reason, I felt it most appropriate to learn by heart all the French phrases uttered by *El Chele* Walter Guerra. " *Voilà,*" "*Écoutez bien, c'est ne pas comme ça !*" "*Avec sentiment!*" "*Plus fort!*" "*Ralentissez!*"

Last time I visited El Salvador, I had lunch with Ramiro Velasco and spent one Sunday with him and his wife at their country house on the outskirts of the cerro el Naranjo. That same day we drove to the chapel nearby where *El Chele* Walter was officiating mass. I spoke to him in French and made believe I was visiting from Louvain. I shared with him that every time I came to El Salvador I looked for him and never found him. This time I was lucky and wanted to reminisce about the years in the Seminary. *El Chele* Walter did not remember me. He remembered Gustavo. I was very disappointed to realize that in our lives the impact that some people have on us is seldom reciprocated. There was no room for a memory lane dialogue with Walter. I pointed out many common experiences to him, but again, he remembered only that Gustavo was sent to Puebla to study with somebody else and that now he knows that it was I who went with Gustavo.

Sure enough, Padre Chus was right. Gradually the fog dissipated, the dark sky lit with sparkling stars and the full moon rose. We took our cold sandwiches from our backpacks and Padre Chus offered us another shot of whisky. After dinner, from the charcoal-sandy top, we started to make corresponding geographic sense of the clusters of artificial lights seen all over the expansive flat plain. For sure, we could make out the entire territory of El Salvador, the Tom Thumb of the Americas, with a length of 150 miles and a width of around 90 miles.

"The biggest cluster of lights towards the east is the capital, San Salvador, one hundred kilometers away," el Padre Chus said.

"Then, the small cluster of lights to the north of San Salvador must be Quetzaltepeque," Gustavo said.

"No, it is not possible since the lights seem to be flickering at a lesser intensity. It is an optical illusion. Those lights, most likely, are much farther east of San Salvador, even though it looks like they are just north of it. I estimate that it could even be the town of San Miguel," Hernandez, said.

"Don't forget that the small towns do not have a good electrical grid like San Salvador. Maybe the cluster of lights is, after all, just north of San Salvador, but the light bulbs are of lesser wattage making them look further east, but are just north like Gustavo said," Celada counter argued.

"Let's just imagine that the cluster of lights under discussion is just north. In this case, it would have to be the town of Apopa," Lorenzo Amaya announced.

We kept this conversation far into the night, trying to name all the cities and small towns, the clusters of lights, in correspondence to San Salvador, and later to the volcano. There were not many, however.

I was the only seminarian that came from the city proper. The rest came from a variety of villages around the west of El Salvador. Each wanted to know if his village's lights could be seen. This was impossible; there was no electrical power in any of the villages. Only the cities and towns had electricity. In 1966, from the top of the volcano, the black empty areas on the plain were deep and large. The light clusters were very distinct, with well-defined borders, and far apart.

"That must be a ship, those lights that you see south. That immense dark area must be the Pacific Ocean. Can you see the ocean from here?" Israel, the brother of Padre Camilo Girón, asked.

We were tired and sleepy, but went to bed way past our regular bedtime, which was at 9:00 p.m. sharp. From our blankets, inevitably our eyes moved upwards to the sky and our conversation turned to discuss the stars. We were not well versed in the constellations. We named only a few popular star clusters away from the moon light. "Those are *"Las tres Marias"* (Orion's Belt), "That's the *Osa Mayor."*

I did not sleep well that night. I used one of the wool blankets to cover the soft ash mixed with volcanic pulverized rock and covered my body with the second blanket. The temperature dropped to around 55 degrees during the night. We felt unusually cold and warmed our bodies by sleeping in groups next to each other. There was no wind. We did not become aware of how dangerously close we were during our sleep of falling into the crater until we woke up to see the sunrise.

Next morning, after the customary morning prayers and chants, we kneeled on our woolen blankets for our daily half-hour meditation, looking east towards the vast green plateau. The cold stale tortillas and rancid cheese did little to sooth my hunger. The sulfuric tasting water did nothing to settle our stomachs. Soon after breakfast, we found ourselves divided into small groups as we explored the crater, looking down from the edges. Pebbles tumbled down, emitting a clicking sound that gradually faded away. "How far down is the green lake at the bottom?" Castro asked. "I don't know if it is very far or just in front of my eyes." The crater's lips soon became too narrow to safely continue our hike and we decided to turn back to camp. Padre Chus soon after ordered to start our descent down to the valley. "Come on! Start moving down" "Time to go!"

As soon as we entered the forest on our way back, we lost our *"fila India"* formation (single file) and Gustavo, joining forces with Celada, passed me on my left, pushing me hard off the trail. I realized that they were not walking but rather jumping over hurdles and trotting around obstacles. I quickly jerked my neck to look back to assess the scenery behind me. There were no orders coming down from Padre Chus. Beyond the shadows, I noticed Raúl Hernandez and Israel Girón rushing down like lunatics. My instincts told me that an implicit race to the valley had begun and that all civility and obedience to orders or adherence to any honor code were off.

Raúl and Israel flew by me yelling commands and warnings of dangers looming towards them. They jumped jerkily over ferns, logs, overgrown roots and rocks like gazelles fleeing from the lion's claws and quickly disappeared into the jungle. I immediately jumped into pursuit, fearing that the younger seminarians would leave me behind in the dust. For one thing, I couldn't let Gustavo show his superiority by winning the race. I had to take all risks possible to defeat him.

Chapter 15: Race to the Valley

The trail zigzagged and undulated down the steep terrain at a slope that at times became very steep and at others flat. Tall and wide trees, Arrazán and Chicle, Ceibas, Robles, and Caobas, with protruding roots that sprang out from their solid trunks almost like the dorsal fins of a shark, covered this trail. At every encounter with one of those monumental trees, I jumped over the roots and tried to land on the mushy brown soil between them by either speeding up or slowing down, mostly by speeding up. I noticed the trees crying with long vines and soon enough I started to swing like Tarzan. My jumps from the ground to the vines and from vine to vine had to be performed in one smooth movement without losing momentum so that I could approximate the feeling of a free fall.

On our way up, I had paid little attention to the vines and did not use them to my advantage to make walking up the trail easier. After a while of this frantic speed down the volcano, for all I knew, I could have already veered off onto another trail, a shoot off the main one. Looking down hill, the panorama morphed producing an expansive green picture of dense vegetation, the vines becoming irresistible and dangerous. My swings from vine to vine had to be precise and split-second decisions needed to be made between either letting go to land, making sure of landing on a soft spot by avoiding the hard roots, or letting go of the vine to instantly grab another.

The chances of grabbing too weak of a vine to support my weight were high. At that speed and height, a false move would have strewn me to the ground and the odds of a serious head injury by hitting the hard roots or rocks below me were high, but I had to dare. I grabbed all the vines I could to catch up with Gustavo, who must have been doing just the very same thing. Some of the thinner vines would snap just before I grabbed the next one in midair. I was flying under the lush canopy as if a deadly danger such as a jaguar loomed just behind me. The high levels of adrenaline and exhilaration made me feel invincible and indestructible. Suddenly, I caught a glimpse of the two freshmen just ahead of me and in a few seconds overtook them. *That means that the phlegmatic Gustavo, may be just a few seconds ahead.* In the next swing, I flew above Israel and Raúl, landing way ahead of them. *"¡Te vas a romper el coco, Chico!"* Israel yelled. *"¡No te creas Tarzán!"*

The wide-trunk trees started to disappear and with them the vines. I was far from exhaustion, nothing hurt even though my hands were red and covered with scratches and scrapes. A stronger and higher sense of being overtook me and my running and jumping became faster and more reckless. I did not feel the weight of my backpack and had to touch its straps to become aware of its existence. My wool blankets were long gone. They must have gradually slipped out of the backpack straps or gotten caught within the vines. There was no sign of Gustavo. *Shrew and quiet troublemaker Gustavo, he might have taken a shortcut. Run, run, Chico, faster, faster!*

Unexpectedly, I found myself out of the woods and onto a dirt road. I continued running down the hill. It had not rained at all on this road and a foot of dried dirt covered it as if people very seldom transited it. The landscape had changed drastically. My running became slower and I started to get thirsty. Most likely I was lost. The only reassuring sight was that there were no human tracks on the deep dirt, kept hot and dried by the scorching sun. Gustavo must have been behind me or running on a different trail. I started to see coffee plantations and *campesino's* houses. *I must be close to a village.* I gradually turned to a walk and relaxed. Soon I found myself in the center of town with its plaza and white washed church. Ten minutes later Raúl and Israel appeared.

"Here is where we are all supposed to meet. I guess Padre Chus purposely sent us down via a different trail. You did not hear, but he said to wait at "La Majada" church. This is it!, they exclaimed.

"I was expecting Gustavo and Celada to be here before me or come just after me," I said.

"We never ran into Gustavo." They both said with a tint of fear.

Half an hour later, the cerebral and phlegmatic Gustavo and Celada appeared. Looking for a short cut, they had taken a trail off the original one and that led them away from the town and out the woods one kilometer behind where I had exited. I had beaten Gustavo. I had won the race down the volcano, but, anticlimactically, did not feel a sense of victory because Gustavo was not bothered by his arriving half an hour after me. Gustavo, Celada, Israel, Raúl and I embraced into a circle and just giggled for what it seemed like hours reflecting on our epic decent. It took another hour before all seminarians and Padre Chus had arrived at the center of *La Majada*. The sparkling cold water coming out of the small fountain in the middle of the plaza quenched our thirst like a divine elixir.

✳✳✳

In one of my interviews with Gustavo, after a couple of bottles of Concha y Toro, I asked him his opinion about our descent through the volcano.

"You know we love each other as brothers," I began, "and now, as old men, some memories of our adolescent lives darken in the past."

"I'm willing to answer you, but do not corner me with your questions either." Gustavo interrupted me as if anticipating a secret question with no intention of revealing anything.

"No, I will not. I just want you to clarify some of our life events as close classmates in the Seminary. It is for my book," I said, appeasing him.

"Here it goes. Did you feel that we were in constant competition? Were you competing with me or not?" -asked.

He laughed and insisted that he never felt in competition with me, never. I still don't know if he meant it as a slight, or that he genuinely never felt I was a threat to his position as the smarter, better one, and the one voted the most likely to succeed in life by the Seminary. He readily dismissed my question as if to say that I wasn't worth the competition. Maybe I was never a contender in his eyes. I certainly felt he was not being entirely truthful with me. Maybe he lived his adolescence engrossed with his inner thoughts and feelings. In the Myers-Briggs Type Indicator, Gustavo would have come out with an "I" for introvert, a "T" for thinking. This had made him ignore others' sentiments. Maybe he felt ashamed, or maybe he wanted to keep the upper hand to the end. I would never know. He knew I was interviewing him for this book, ever proud and over protector of his image, feared projecting a negative one. I decided to drop the conversation remembering what García Márquez said: "Todo el mundo tiene tres vidas: una vida pública, una vida privada, y una vida secreta."

✲✲✲

The fact that the bishop showed an obvious preference for Gustavo, made me experience my adolescence with a deep need to be in constant competition with Gustavo, hoping that if I ended up on top, the Bishop would focus his attention towards me. The competition might have been one sided, who knows. All through those formative years, I regarded Gustavo as my challenger. I felt the need to topple him from his pedestal. The powerful energy this social dynamic injected on me, motivated me intensely and I measured up my actions aiming at being better than

Gustavo on all aspects: academics, sports, oratory, debates, etc. He was admired by his classmates because of his high academic level. It bothered me that in the heart of the Bishop, Gustavo occupied a deeper place than mine.

In addition, the Bishop's favorite candidates for the priesthood were the ones extracted from very religious *campesino* families and held a biased towards city kids like me. I competed for the Bishop's fatherly love, attention, and approval. I failed.

✳✳✳

I entered the Seminary two years after Gustavo. He was already the darling of the group, the tallest, the smartest, and the whitest. During dinner, two months into my first year, the Bishop asked Padre Barrera, the rector at that time, who I was. Definitely, the Bishop had not been involved in my admission to the Seminary.

I only guessed that one of my rich aunts had intervened with Padre Barrera on my behalf, the most likely being Tía Blanchie, for me to be accepted at the Seminary. Usually the candidates for acceptance at the Seminary had shown early piety and devotion, their families involved in the church, and had been recruited and come recommended by their parish priests, but, if asked, I wouldn't have been able to identify any priest, let alone my parish priest. The Bishop had a good reason to inquire about the unknown me.

That same night I was to discover that I had a talent for reading the Bible aloud, clearly and with great emotion. I had been assigned to be the reader during dinner for that week. We ate in silence as literature classics were read. This time the assigned book was the Bible. The assigned section of the Bible included the 150 Psalms. I had never read them before nor had I ever opened a Bible. My parents did not own one, whereas Gustavo's family recited the psalms by memory, and quoted the Bible multiple times per day as they conducted their chores.

As I started my reading from Psalm #83, suddenly something took hold of me, an inexplicable energy vibrated through me, from the most minuscule muscle and bone, to envelop my entire body. This energy found intense revelation through my voice as I pronounced each word, particularly the word "God". I was talking to God and he was listening, and he was talking through me, sending a powerful message to the listeners. My voice resonated from the adobe walls, the ceramic tiles on the floor, and the clay tiles on the ceiling. I declaimed the psalms from the lantern as I would any other poem, the way I had been taught in elementary school at Colegio La Fé, in Chalchuapa:

¡Oh Dios, no estés en silencio, no estés mudo e inmóvil,
¡Oh Dios! Mira a tus enemigos alborotados,
los que te odian levantan la cabeza.
...Conviértelos, Dios mío, en hojarasca,
en paja que arrebata el viento.
...para que sepan que tu nombre es Yahvé,
Altísimo sobre toda la tierra!

Suddenly, the Bishop dropped his fork over the china plate making a distracting clink. The seminarians stopped eating, looked at the Bishop staring at me, mesmerized, and they also stopped eating and just listened to my reading. I kept reading Psalm after Psalm, oblivious to their reactions. Later, I learned that the monthly academically report cards had also just arrived and I had reached first place in the Colegio San José rankings, beating Gustavo, the darling. The Bishop was stunned by this fact as he read the report at the dinner table. He turned to Padre Barrera and asked who this student was. Padre Barrera subtly pointed at me, as I looked at his table while taking a breather. They both examined me with great surprise and I understood my performance had been totally unexpected. *Maybe this city kid has what it takes to be a priest after all.* Upon admittance, my academic records had shown a mediocre performance the year before, the 7th grade.

Looking briefly towards their table out of the corner of my eye, I knew the Bishop and Padre Barrera were talking about me. *Who was really this new kid from the city?* Reading the psalms for the first time possessed my whole being and transported me to a state of ecstasies which I was to experience again years later during my senior year. *¡Señor, no te quedes callado, Dios mío, no guardes silencio, ¡no permanezcas inmóvil!*

Winning the race down the volcano, reciting those psalms in the dining room during my first year, and obtaining for the first time the first academic place during my first month at the Seminary, gave my identity a complete turnabout. I became a young optimist, sure of myself, and, from that moment on, I hoped to succeed in several other areas in the Seminary and outside it.

For some young people of low esteem like I was, a significant feeling of initial achievement is the only thing needed, at the right time during their development, to give them the feeling that they have the power to become true winners, no more losers, and to put them on a full path of successes in life.

Chapter 16: Tío Héctor Castro Meza

As I finished celebrating my run down the mountain, wiped the salty sweat off my neck, and I became distracted by the roaring sound of a solitary car coming up the cobblestone street. A forest green Willys Jeep M606/CJ3B --the favorite transportation mode in the late 1950's and early 1960's of Salvadorian landowners and a version of World War II US army jeeps-- approached the plaza. It was topless and with its windshield down over the hood. The few *campesinos* gathered around the plaza glanced at the jeep and its driver apathetically as if witnessing an everyday event. The jeep slowed down almost to a complete stop in front of the plaza as its driver shifted to a lower gear before continuing onto the steeper dirt road I had just finished running down.

The driver was a handsome tall thin man, his head snow white, and appeared to be in his middle 60's. A small Panama hat protected his brown tanned face from the penetrating sun. A manicured mustache above full lips adorned a small mouth. I looked at him and resisted the urge to run towards him to greet him by saying, *"Tío Héctor! What a surprise! Which coffee plantation are you visiting today?"* I, immobile, just looked at him. His green jeep turned left and started to climb the dirt road. Tío Héctor, my mother's oldest brother and the one that had inherited, some family members say, taken most of the family wealth, used this road as if it were carved out of the mountain only for him. In a way, it was. My mother's father, Rosendo Castro Meza, had ordered that dirt road to be built when Tío Héctor was just a child (around 1910) to send supplies to his coffee plantation by means of an ox cart. During the late 1800s, El Salvador was experiencing a coffee boom headed by James Hill, from Manchester, England, making coffee growers, such as my grandfather Rosendo, very rich. He became much richer during the collapse of the coffee production in Mexico during its 1910 revolution, shooting up the price of El Salvador's coffee in the European market.

I had encountered the eldest of my mother's brothers, almost 18 years her senior, Tío Héctor Castro Meza, very few times in my life. My mother would see him sporadically during my childhood and sought his approval for her actions and life's decisions. The eldest brother in a Latin family traditionally is the head of the household whenever the parents are absent or when they die. My maternal grandparents, Rosendo and Elena Castro Meza, died before I was born, and Tío Héctor became the sole Estate executor.

I was around 4 years old when my mother took me to Tío Héctor's one-block compound in the city of Ahuachapán. The lush garden in the large square courtyard in the center of the compound was glimmering with orange tones produced by the late afternoon sun, creating darker-than-usual shadows. I looked across the yard to the opposite side of me, and, in the corridor, framed with high ceilings and wooden arches, my tender attention focused on a wooden merry-go-round, imported from the United States, blinding me by its bright lights around its canopy.

This form of entertainment was typical of the ones seen in the middle of central parks during festivities in big cities in El Salvador, only this one was bigger and newer, almost unused, with the horses' pastel colors shinier and brighter than the ones I had ever seen before. I couldn't fathom how such an extravagant toy could be housed inside someone's home. My cousin Elena, the only child in the house, had received it as a Christmas present. I knew then that we were not as rich as Tío Héctor.

Definitely, my mother's fortune was a small fraction of the one Tío Héctor managed to snatch out of the Castro Meza Estate. I was paralyzed with shyness and intimidated by such opulence that despite my strong desire to run to the carousel and take a ride on top of one of those hand-carved wooden horses, I just hid behind my mother's

skirt and closed my eyes. My mother greeted Tío Héctor
with such high deference that I just kept walking hidden
behind my mother's skirt, grabbing it, and pulling it towards my face, refusing to say hello to the old man. The
merry-go-round started to play the Blue Danube. A girl
climbed on top of the most beautiful pink horse with the
longest cream-colored mane and sparkling hooves, turned
towards me, and assumed a posture of intense superiority.
I was a fool to think that she had looked at me to invite me
to join her. Elena, my cousin, was just showing off. Tío
Héctor was enjoying the moment. For a second, I thought
he was about to ask Elena to invite me to the carousel, but
instead he simply sat down on a rattan chair and told the
maid to bring some sodas. I felt that he was insensitive to
my needs as a child. I was not worth his company. I was
not up to his standards. I was not as rich.

My family is full of rumors and stories about how Tío
Héctor managed to steal half of my mother's inheritance.
Tío Héctor was the first to marry and he married one of
the wealthiest daughters of Ahuachapán with a bigger coffee plantation, the Moran's. As soon as he got married, he
received his inheritance. The same was done when my
mother's older siblings, Mamá Lila, Tía Evy, and Tía Cholina, got married.

The problem started when my grandparents died, leaving Tío Héctor in charge. Unscrupulously, tío Héctor
divided the wealth again among all the siblings, giving another inheritance to those already married. He gave
himself the largest share and the best lands around the
Santa Ana volcano to add to the ones inherited by his wife,
Tía Elvira Zalazar Morán around Tacuba and Juayua. The
last unmarried girl was my mother, the second to last
child. After my grandparents died, she was kicked out of
the big house and sent to serve as a babysitter to Mamá
Lila, her oldest sister by 18 years, my mother with no husband to protect her or to fight for her rights. What
precipitated this move was the animosity that her sister

Tía Anitía had developed against my mother during the last years before their parents died.

It all started when Dr. Sierra, new to town and a recent graduate from Medical School in Honduras, visited the big house to call on my mother, whom he had seen one day shopping for vegetables in the market, escorted by two maids. When he asked one of the shopkeepers who that beautiful young woman was, he was told that she was one of the Castro Meza girls.

"They all look alike, walk alike, and speak alike, always very proper, and dress with the best and latest imports from Europe and North America. One thing, the girls are forbidden by their strict mother, Doña Elena, to socialize outside of their mansion. They are always escorted by two maids who talk to us and buy the food and supplies from us," the shopkeeper said. "But this one I think is la Niña Rosita. It also may be la Niña Esperancita. I don't think she is la Niña Anitía. It is very difficult to tell. There are 10 siblings, you know, three boys and seven girls, very close in age, one girl, we don't know who, is adopted. The only reason why I think this is la Niña Rosita is because she is very social and does not always follow her parents' directives."

Dr. Sierra called on the Castro Meza's house the following Sunday. After being announced by the butler, none of the girls dared to go out to the living room to speak to Dr. Sierra. *"I'll go out to the living room,"* my mother said to the others. *"I am not afraid of a handsome foreigner doctor from Honduras, coming to see us."*

That day, my mother spent two hours talking to Doctor Sierra, laughing, joking, and asking about his trip by mule from Honduras. She told him how much she appreciated having a well-educated Doctor in town, since most of the University-trained doctors lived in the capital. She made him understand how she admired his commitment to people's health indicating to him how much she would be willing to ask her father to help him in any manner necessary, so that his stay would be longer and productive. The two-hour conversation, accompanied with homemade pastries and the best-picked coffee from the family plantation, was witnessed by two chaperones, most likely the same maids that went with my mother to the market the day when Dr. Sierra spotted her. The maids sat down in a corner of the living room ready to follow my mother's commands, but never willing to leave her alone with the bachelor. They would later report the full conversation, with all details, back to Doña Elena and older unmarried sisters. The sisters hid behind the living room doors and windows, some up in their rooms, but with an ear tuned to the ins and outs of the living room. The next day, mother summoned Rosita to her bedroom after coffee time in the late afternoon.

"Dr. Sierra came to see me this morning and asked permission to court you every Sunday afternoon, but I refused. Rosita, it is not your turn. It is Anitía's turn to get married. Anitía is older than you are. I told Dr. Sierra that he is free to come every Sunday but that only Anitía will go out into the living room to chat with him, not you. If he pays us a visit this Sunday, you are to stay out in the *traspatio* or in the kitchen helping the cooks, unseen by him. Do I make myself clear?" My grandmother, Elena Castro Meza commanded.

"Yes, mother," my mother responded, running away to cry up in her room that she shared with her sister Evy on the second floor.

From that day forward, my mother did not speak to Dr. Sierra. Tía Anitía, however, fearing that my mother had stolen Dr. Sierra's heart, and feeling second best, made my mother's life in the big house unbearable. This tension between the two sisters increased after my grandmother, Elena, died and became an insupportable wedge in their relationship. The day of Mamá Elena's funeral at the Chalchuapa cemetery, tía Anitía, now freed from all constraints, commanded my mother to never return home.

My mother, defenseless and unwilling to argue with her older sister, and thinking that her dead mother had ordered it before dying, sought refuge in the arms of Mamá Lila, who brought my mother, dressed as she was in her black dress, no suitcase, no change of clothes, to her house in Santa Ana that same afternoon. My mother stopped by the house to say her goodbyes to the workers, to the dogs and exotic birds, and admired one last time the colorful garden and the lush fruit trees holding back her tears and deep sighs. Two maids saw her out up to the front gate, while Tía Anitía, the treasury and accountant of the family, looked down from the second-floor window to confirm that my mother was not taking any jewelry or any other of her personal possessions.

＊＊＊

La Rosita arrived at Santa Ana and entered Mamá Lila's house. She was 23 years old and, as an unmarried woman, under the tutelage of her oldest sister and husband, Don Lorenzo Menéndez Rojas. There, she felt loved and respected by all. Mamá Lila and her children treated her as another daughter and sister. My mother related this story multiple times to us, always ending with a tear in her eyes and a deep broken-up exhale.

My mother was raised to just follow the orders given by her father, and after his death, by her eldest brother, Tío Héctor. Whatever Tío Héctor said was done without question. Only after the insistence of Mamá Lila's husband, Papá Lorenzo, did Tío Héctor give my mother some small part of her inheritance with the condition that the rest was to be given to her were she to divorce my father, Rafael, whom the Castro-Meza clan deemed too low in the social ladder and an opportunist, which many said it was true.

"My father Lorenzo was very strong and not a pusho-
ver," Lorenzo junior, my cousin, told me a couple of
months ago, when I visited El Salvador. "Soon after Tía
Rosita got married while still living with my parents, my
father drove his green 1946 Willys jeep one Sunday afternoon, to Chalchuapa. Do you know how he was dressed?
The same way he did every day of his life: he wore khaki
pants, a long-sleeve white shirt, leather black boots, tall
new straw hat, and, of course, his .45 pistol strapped to
his waist." That was the accepted uniform of all *terratenientes* of El Salvador, in or out of the city, as if they had
attended the same private high school or ordered to use
that uniform by a supreme being. "He entered the *casona*
and asked to talk to Tío Héctor who visited the main house
in Chalchuapa when coming from his residence in Ahuachapán on Sundays."

"You better give Rosita her due inheritance, *cabrón*, as
soon as possible, or there will be serious consequences. I
know you and your brothers, my *cuñados*, have tried to
kill her husband Rafael because you do not find him *a sus
putas alturas*, worthy of the Castro Meza clan, but it is not
up to you to order Rosita to fall in love with whomever you
decide. Give Rosita her inheritance now, *hijueputa*," he
ended discharging a thick spit on the ground as he slowly
placed his right hand over the pistol's handle, insinuating
that he was ready to kill if his request was not met.

Papá Lorenzo was a man of the country with an educated but not as polished Spanish vocabulary, as the
Castro Meza's, with a *machista* attitude towards matters
of women, life and death. One hundred *colonos* lived in his
hacienda. He needed to supervise and command them
with rugged manners. He had a soft spot, however, for my
mother who he saw as one of his daughters, somebody
who needed protection.

Tío Héctor, the University of Chicago educated engineer, couldn't handle Papá Lorenzo's rude farmer's
language and animalistic comportment. Soon after that

confrontation, Tío Héctor resolved to give my mother some of her inheritance, some isolated acres outside Santa Ana. He was never to talk about the rest. He ended up keeping it. The family historic thread of rumors points out that Tío Héctor added some of my mother's inheritance to Tía Esperancita and some part also assigned to Tía Cholina.

A large quantity of gold and cash was left by my grandfather Rosendo in three humongous dark oak armoires, which he had designed and built meticulously by hand, hidden on the second floor of the big house. The armoires with all their riches were given to Tía Anitía, as a dowry for her marriage to Dr. Sierra.

✳✳✳

At my father's wake, I heard some more details of the reasons why my mother's brothers hated my father. While living at the huge, one-level Spanish style house of Papá Lorenzo and Mamá Lila, my father started to court my mother surreptitiously, talking to her through the steel bars on her ground floor bedroom window, a common behavior in the towns of El Salvador. My father left his office at a law firm, where he worked as a legal assistant and accountant, every afternoon around 6:00 pm and walked three blocks to find my mother waiting by the window, straining his eyes to view my mother's face partially blocked, lined by the wooden louvers of the green blinds, and the clouds of the gray smoke spewing out of my mother's cigarette, but clearly hearing her melodious voice. Papá Lorenzo did not approve at first of my mother's conversations with my father threw the window. He used to reprimand my mother saying that a decent girl never speaks to boys out of their social circle and unknown by the family.

One day my father dared my mother to run away with him. My mother was the last of her siblings to get married, knew her chances were dwindling approaching her 26th birthday and took a chance. She must have known about my father's reputation as a bon vivant womanizer and might have wanted to let it be known that she was the one chosen and better than any other one, she might have also felt that her love and money would at the end reform him. My mother dated my father not by going out with him on dates, but only by talking to him after dinner through the iron grates of her bedroom window. She fell in love with a fantasy version of him and with the idealized image of love. She also felt the social pressure to get married before being considered too old and risking becoming a spinster, *una solterona, buena solamente para vestir los santos de la Iglesia."* My father, on the other hand, might have been looking desperately for a salvation and rest from his unbridled life. He was in a spiral of self-destruction for a long time after his first wife Leticia Morales, *una turca*, maybe of Lebanese descent, was murdered. The dynamics with my parents resembled The Flying Dutchman, Wagner's Opera, where Senta vows to be truthful and faithful to rescue the Dutchman from his demise. Somehow, my father convinced Papá Lorenzo, who had become my father's drinking buddy, to give him permission for the wedding, which happened in the Iglesia del Carmen, two blocks down from the house, one early morning on December 28th, the day of the innocent in the catholic calendar, of 1947.

Two days after the wedding, attended only by Papá Lorenzo and Mamá Lila, my mother's brothers came to the house with pistols and rifles looking to kill my father, who sensing danger, had already escaped with my mother to Nicaragua which served as their honey moon. My brother Rafael tells me that Papá Lorenzo, to avoid recrimination from the Castro Meza family, commanded my father to marry my mother or else, after learning that my parents had already been intimate. Mamá Lila, on the other hand, was in total disagreement and refused to give her consent.

She was the one that alerted her brothers to do something to end the affair. Tía Anitía, the most upset of my mother's siblings, would take five more years to communicate with my mother again, at my brother Rafael's birth, to ask my mother to give him in adoption to her and to get a divorce from her husband. There still was time to remake her life with the rest of her inheritance. Sadly, and ironically enough, it turned out that la Tía Anitía would never have children with Dr. Sierra. She was infertile.

My mother, as always when recounting overwhelming memories, with deep sighs and broken up exhales, told us repeatedly the story of that trip, first by bus and then by a small wooden fishing boat to cross the gulf between El Salvador and Nicaragua, *El Golfo de Fonseca*. The dim light of the stars flickered overhead, the reddish sun was about to disappear over the ocean and the moon, at its waxing gibbous, provided with enough light not to confuse shadows with wildlife, and the sky suddenly appeared immense increasing my mother's fear of the unknown. The wise move would have been to pass the night in La Union, El Salvador, to cross the gulf first thing next morning, but my father with the excuse that my mother's brothers were closing in on them decided to hire a private small fishing boat to cross the gulf.

After a couple of hours, the small boat stalled in the middle of the *Golfo de Fonseca,* near Isla *Del Tigre.* The couple waited all night on the bobbing waters until early next morning a passing fishing boat rescued them and brought them to Nicaragua; my mother had stayed awake all night within my father's arms, terrified by the school of hungry sharks that circled the small boat. Her honeymoon was spent in Chinandega. From there several telegrams were sent to Santa Ana asking for the status of my mother's brothers. The couple embarked on the way back days after Papá Lorenzo sent word that the brothers had come back from La Union after they were told the couple had crossed the gulf to Nicaragua. The brothers had returned to their coffee plantations, since December was the busiest month of the coffee harvest, forgetting about my father's affront to the Castro Meza family and hoping for my mother to soon return alone to the *casona*.

My mother was never to return to the family house and never dared to bathe in the ocean in her life, traumatized by her fear of sharks. She, of course, didn't know it then, but a life of the archetype long-suffering wife, as predicted by her brothers, awaited her, but she added a profound loyalty to her husband and dedication to her children, and an unfailing resilience to the obstacles encountered in her life. She faced her role as a mother and wife with self-abnegation and profound stoicism.

Several decades later, Tío Héctor summoned my mother to his deathbed, asking her to come to Ahuachapán as soon as possible. He wanted to set the record straight and give her back what belonged to her. My mother got there minutes before he died, but his daughter Elena, assuming the same air of superiority as she did as a child riding the merry-go-round, refused entrance to my mother, adding more drama to my family's story of how even at the last minute, my mother was swindled out of her rightful inheritance. My mother, a true lady, did not fight her way into his chambers. "Please, just tell my eldest brother I was here to see him and hope he gets well, "she told the concierge as she turned to leave the foyer. The concierge later commented that Tío Héctor had asked his lawyers to draft a bank check of an uncertain amount payable to Rosa Castro Meza. My brother Teto, war survivor, speculates the amount to have been very substantial, a check that no doubt Elena ripped into a thousand pieces just as my mother left the foyer. Elena is aware of her debt to us, debt that will never be paid. I have never spoken to Elena in my life. I would love to hear her memories and impressions on this matter.

Tía Anitía, unlike Tío Héctor, had the chance to beg for forgiveness before she died. She was fortunate to die in peace a few days after my mother's visit to her deathbed and after stating that her coffee *fincas* and her house in Chalchuapa were to be transferred to Rafael, my brother, as a form of payment for any injustice my mother may have suffered.

That late afternoon, after my run down the volcano, Tío Héctor drove his jeep up to his coffee plantation oblivious to my disturbed heartbeat due to the painful memories his image always stirred up inside my soul. The other seminarians kept congratulating themselves for the adventurous hike down the volcano, but not one of them noticed that I had suddenly become quiet, moved away from the group into the shed of an almond tree, with hesitant deep sighs as I kept looking up the road while the green jeep disappeared into the forest.

Chapter 17: Chalchuapa..., Santa Ana..., Guatemala...

Nowadays, I often think of my mother's ancestral home in Chalchuapa. The house, *"La Casona,"* as it is referred to by the residents of Chalchuapa, was built by her father, my Papá Chendo (Rosendo), from a 1908 Sears Catalogue house blueprint, also called "The Wish Book." He chose the print for Modern Home No. 187, modifying it to incorporate his own design. He added a spacious wrap-around, porch and insisted it be built one meter above ground to avoid flooding from the torrential tropical rains. He used wood from the native trees for the second floor, trimming, and the doors, and insisted on cement and clay tiles for the ground floor. Lastly, the shape of the house was made to form the letter "E," as a dedication to his beloved wife, Elena, my grandmother Mamá Nena. The letter "E" story has a prominent place in the history of my family and it was repeated often during my childhood to demonstrate the immense, unlimited love, and respect that the self-taught farmer and builder, empirical Papá Chendo, had for his well-read, artistic, and social-etiquette driven wife. He also added a decorated iron fence with a cement foundation that surrounded the grounds of the property. The side that faced the main dirt road showed an intricate, swirling iron gate. Next to it, Papá Chendo built a pergola, later covered with dense-wide-green leaves of a liana, a woody vine that provided a cozy shelter to unexpected visitors who could sit on a shiny stone bench while waiting to be vetted for entrance to the mansion.

One day, Papá Chendo, walked around his acreage, close to what it is now the Mayan ruins of Tazumal, and found two stone monkey heads that recent copious rains had unearthed. The heads were part of two mid-size basalt statues depicting tropical monkeys in a sitting position. He placed them on top of each of the two posts of the main iron gate. Soon, *la casona* became the sensation of the town and the town's people used to use the mansion as a landmark for giving directions. *"Queda a la entrada de Chalchuapa, ahí por donde está la casona de los dos monos."* I stared at the monkeys with fear and fascination whenever my mother took me to visit Tío Paco, her brother who later inherited the house. Several decades later, I visited the mansion and noticed that the monkeys were missing.

It pained me to hear the rumor that my cousins who inherited the mansion, had sold the monkeys to an American antiquity trafficker for an undisclosed amount. The monkeys, I suspect, carved by the Mayans for the Tazumal, did not end up at any American museum. Most likely they are now decorating a garden or part of an entrance of who knows what American mansion. My cousins gradually sold the antique cars, among them, I am told, a 1924 Chrysler Model B-70 used by my grandparents, and three motorcycles, all 1923 Indian Big Chief, brought by Tío Héctor after finishing his studies in Chicago and used by my mother's brothers, kept for the longest time in the six-car garage. The price of each of those motorcycles at current dollars would be higher than $100,000. The Chrysler now would be priceless.

At its peak, around 20 people, counting the servants, lived in that mansion, which was surrounded by spacious garden beds. My mother and aunts (7 sisters, counting the adopted one) described an idyllic, fairy-tale childhood in an enchanted tropical paradise, surrounded by a great diversity of wildlife and flora. There were the real monkeys, the toucans, the owls, the deer and the snakes, scorpions, and bats. When I visited El Salvador with Carolina, Alejandro and Elena for the first time one summer in 2004, the only aunt still alive was Tía Esperanza, the youngest of my mother's siblings. We sat in her living room and very quickly she started to reminisce. I hadn't seen her for almost 40 years. As soon as she saw me, she asked about my mother. *"Estoy segura de que ya se murió, ¿verdad? Tu cara es idéntica a la de ella."* Thinking about my mother transported her instantly back to the late 1920s, and almost like in a trance, like very old people tend to do, she started to recite her memories. She repeated many times how much she remembered the flowers in the garden and the hundreds of multicolored exotic birds that flew around the patios. *"Chepito, nuestra infancia fue maravillosa. Fue un sueño. Todas esas flores. Todos esos pájaros. Rosita y yo jugábamos juntas todo el tiempo porque éramos las más chiquitas."* By contrast, I don't remember my uncles, Tío Héctor, Tío Chendo and Tío Paco, two of them Chicago University Mechanical Engineer alumni, ever being so effusive when recalling their childhood.

Mamá Nena ran her household sternly and coldly, guided by Catholic dogmas and a strict behavioral code: she demanded meticulous cleanliness and adherence to European etiquette. She sent her daughters to the Sacred Heart nuns in the city for secondary education, but mostly for religious, home economics, and future wife training. The first elementary school in Chalchuapa, *Escuela Simón Bolivar,* was established by Papá Chendo and started by none other than Mamá Nena herself, a graduate from the only *"Escuela Normal"* at that time in Central America, which was based in Guatemala City. Because of this authority, Mamá Nena oversaw primary education for the community.

In *la casona,* the younger children helped the maids maintain the ceramic and clay tiles of the ground floors shiny at all times, the hundreds of flower pots fresh and moist, the exotic birds fed, and their bedrooms tidy and neat. Mamá Nena carried out unannounced inspections weekly. Lorenzo, my cousin, told me recently that he disliked Mamá Nena and resisted visiting *la casona* with his parents because on one of his visits when he was around 7, she didn't let him in the house due to his unshined shoes and dirty nails. *"Esa vieja era brava."* Mamá Nena had years earlier kicked out Papá Lorenzo from la casona when one day he showed up unannounced to visit Mamá Lila, simply because he was still wearing his knee-high equestrian leather boots, his ranchero hat, and his pistol around his waist. *"Aquí Usted no viene a ordeñar vacas, o a amansar garañones. Usted podrá entrar a esta casa a darle visita a mi hija Lilian cuando venga vestido como la gente."*

My mother talked about her father often with watery eyes, ending with a loving sigh, remarking on his slight lisp and loving disposition whenever he talked to her, *"Mi querida Rosita,"* whereas when she talked about her mother, she became serious and would speak of her with admiration coated with an unspoken respect.

The house stood on a 50-acres land with a pond in the middle, *Laguna Cuzcachapa.* Papá Chendo's property was in a very small town, but his power reached to the central government of the nation. When he learned in 1937 that the first blueprint of the Pan-American highway would cut through the middle of his land, he quickly sent a telegram to the dictator at the time, Maximiliano Martinez, asking for an audience which turned out not to be necessary. Because of this letter, the direction of the highway's route was quickly redirected to go around his property, creating after a long stretch of road a lengthy detour with some very dangerous curves. One such dangerous curve was very aptly named *"La curva de la muerte"* and claimed more than a dozen lives. Soon after, one could hear mothers and wives warning drivers about that section of the road. *"Acuérdate, por favor, no vayas muy rápido cuando vayas pasando por Chalchuapa, porque antes de entrar tienes que pasar por la curva de la muerte."*

Not too long after, residents came up with their own legends and stories about those drivers killed negotiating *La Curva de la Muerte.* One told the story about a single gentleman, dressed in an elegant suit, who was late for a big party at the Castro-Meza mansion. When he approached *La curva de la muerte,* he saw the most beautiful woman dressed in a long gown asking for a ride to the party. He picked her up. During the night, the party crowd admired the beauty of this unfamiliar woman with Castro-Meza distinct features: big dark eyes, high cheekbones, voluptuous lips, medium nose, jet black luminous hair, and an oval face. Definitely a relative visiting from abroad, they thought. The gentleman and the unfamiliar woman danced until just before midnight when she abruptly asked the gentleman to take her home, claiming exhaustion. He assumed it to be an invitation to continue the party at her house, which ended up being at the local cemetery. Next morning the gentleman told the story, but nobody believed him. Later, when reading the newspaper, he saw her picture in the obituaries, with her cause of death being an accident at *La Curva de la Muerte* a week before the party. After this encounter, the man literally went crazy and was never heard of again.

The family story about the Pan-American highway and Papá Chendo's letter showed that he had some ties with the Dictator Martinez. My mother told me that when the dictator came to visit Santa Ana, the nuns at the *Colegio La Asunción,* were charged with the festivities on their extensive patio. The nuns designated my vivacious mother to say the welcoming remarks in front of all the national and local dignitaries, after which the brutal dictator, who had years before ordered the massacre of thousands of indigenous people, asked about the identity of the girl. When the nuns told him that it was Rosa Castro Meza, the dictator remarked, *"Con razón, es una de las hijas de Rosendo."* This story also corroborates my suspicion that Papá Chendo had more of a personal connection with the dictator than the family would let on, even though nobody has ever mentioned it.

In 1941, the archeologist Stanley Boggs asked Papá Chendo's permission to excavate a peculiar, cone shaped hill in the area. Boggs had the suspicion that the hill might have been covering a Mayan ruin. He was right. The excavation, between 1942 and 1943, uncovered what is now a national historic monument, the Mayan pyramid of El Tazumal. Papá Chendo died in 1941 and never had the pleasure of seeing the pyramid. General Martinez expropriated the land surrounding the pyramid, reducing Papá Chendo's property by many acres. Soon after, he donated land for a football field, *Estadio El Progreso,* as well as for a basketball court, a church called *El Calvario,* and a school, reducing his property even further. The house is still there today, albeit on much reduced land and needing extensive repairs. My cousins at the present are unable to sell it and unable to make any changes since the government has declared the house to be a national historical monument. Rafael, my brother, called recently to tell me that *la casona* had been finally demolished, ending the last vestiges of the golden age of the Castro Meza family. I cried profusely.

✳✳✳

My brother Rafael, unable to escape this family history has never left what is now a dormant, almost dead town. Many bright souls left town looking for a better life and ended up in the capital of San Salvador or in USA, as it is the case of some of tía Blanchie's children, Dr. Ricardo and Dr. Tito in the USA and Dr. Eduardo in Canada but not my brother Rafael, the engineer. Teto and I tried to pull him out of Chalchuapa by sponsoring his family to relocate to USA as permanent residents.

He moved to Los Angeles with his wife and three kids as Green Card holders, a coveted immigrant status, but he, influenced by his unhappy wife, couldn't take the hard work needed to start a new life in a different country and returned to Chalchuapa after a couple of months. He couldn't let go of the security and rewards provided by his social network that admired and consulted in him. His social status and own identity in Chalchuapa as an engineer, social activist, devout Catholic, and community organizer fulfilled him. To this, one must add the yearning he felt to somehow revive the Castro-Meza legacy. He was not capable of breaking the connection, as I and Teto easily did, to all that once had been.

I, on the other hand, never allowed my soul to develop any attachment toward a place that I only called "the neighborhood where I grew up." I am very proud though, of my ancestors on my mother's side and whenever I have returned to Chalchuapa, I asked my cousins to open all the rooms of *la casona* for me. I would walk around and picture my mother with her siblings running around the patios and Mamá Nena in the kitchen giving orders to the cooks and maids, and that warms my heart. If I walk around the town and I happen to mention that I am a Castro-Meza, interlocutors still immediately look at me with awe. "Do you mean you are a Castro Meza from *¿La Casona a la entrada de Chalchuapa?*" they would ask, wide eyed, as if they were laying eyes on a *bona fide* piece of history.

✳✳✳

The town of Chalchuapa, built on a Mayan settlement, formed a perfect grid, the preferred design by Spanish engineers. At its center stood the colonial whitewashed church built around 1690 dedicated to the Apostle Santiago. Next to it, laid the central park, city hall, and the police station.

At this moment in time, Chalchuapa looks exactly the way it was when I left it, and maybe even worse. When I took my family to El Salvador, my 14-year-old son, Alejandro, described Chalchuapa as a war zone similar to the ones he had seen in his video games. The front walls of houses were riddled with what appeared to be bullet holes, the bottom rail of front doors rotten, roof clay tiles broken, and sidewalks crumbling gave Chalchuapa the look of a war-torn city. The distant Salvadoran Civil War had left a permanent mark, my son thought. He was correct in a way. Many of the *casonas* previously inhabited by the coffee growers of the region had been abandoned, never to see again a hand of fresh paint. The crumbled and almost shredded roads and uneven sidewalks void of trees, combined with walls full of quarter size holes, looked to Alejandro to be the aftermath of hard-fought battles between the military and the revolutionaries, not unlike his favorite war video games. Contrary to Alejandro's initial observation, Chalchuapa had not changed because of the war. The holes were produced by the old plaster turning slowly into dust after decades of total neglect. No battles had been fought on its soil. Instead, a decade long losing battle against the test of time had rendered the city to look the way it did. Chalchuapa looked the same as when I lived there 40 years before, maybe just a little worse for wear.

✳✳✳

In Santa Ana, for a time I was the son of a rich family, and soon, the son of a very poor one, everything came downhill, everything. My father, Rafael Antonio, expelled from the social circles of the city, after not having been able to handle sensibly and grow, as others would have done, the inheritance of my mother, and unable to bear the pressures of social ostracism, he decided to remove the family, with little prior planning, from the city of my early childhood, even though I was a boarder at El Colegio La Fé in Chalchuapa.

Our spacious colonial house, in the rich neighborhood of the city, had already been lost, I ignore the disastrous specific details, I only remember that, overnight, we left

9th *calle Oriente #20*, to live, for a few months, in a narrow and tiny house on *5th avenida sur*. I vividly remember that my father went into hiding without going out during all that time. Many causes of this decline in quality of life are speculated, but all point to my father's crazy behavior. Was my father's obsessive gambling at the casino? The money spent on his multiple lovers, *puterío*, and binge drinking? Was it wanting to run away and hide from the authorities for crimes committed? What could have been? Someone still alive has to know. Maybe Tío Jorge from El Salvador or my cousin Martita Menéndez, the closest to my mother.

It turns out that after that little house, we ended up in Guatemala City. My father aspired to a new and clean start in Guatemala. Teto, the knife-throwing command, tells me that another reason for our rapid transfer to Guatemala was that my father was running away from justice: one night, shortly before our sudden departure, Raphael Antonio, in the middle After one of his longest episodes of drunkenness, decided, with one of her distant cousins and helped by a blowtorch, to break into the house of Mama Chagua, her great-aunt and benefactor, to rob her precious jewels, valued at hundreds of dollars.

There were court proceedings during his absence that resulted in the court confiscating the house. According to Teto, the house had really been my father's wedding gift from Mama Chagua, not part of my mother's inheritance. The house was then transferred back to Mamá Chagua as payment for her stolen jewelry, or perhaps as punishment. Fifteen years later, during my time with Norma, Mamá Chagua, from her deathbed, was to order her lawyer to transfer the house to my mother. My father had already paid enough for his wrongdoing.

Honestly, my father never ceased to amaze me with his secrets. It took me almost 60 years to learn from Teto the truth behind our trip to Guatemala. Our trip to Guatemala turned out to be an escape from his shame before society, as well as from the authorities.

We arrived in Guatemala City late at night early November of 1955 in a tiny 1952 Austin Mini Cooper that my father drove. Pirri, 9 months old, slept on my mother's lap, while Teto, 2 years old, slept in the back seat on my left, and Rafael, 4 years old, slept on my right. I, normally hyperactive and over excited, stood in the middle of the car floor, with my arms spread across the backs of my father and mother's seats, looking through the front windshield.

"Papá, Mamá, ¿verdad que yo soy el rey? Yo nunca me duermo como hacen mis hermanos," I remember saying. *"Sí mi rey,"* my mother repeated. If only I had understood the gravity of the situation, then maybe I would have remained silent.

My poor mother, the eternal obedient wife, did not have a say in the matter. Her sole sense of relief would have been the knowledge that my father's frequent young mistresses would remain in El Salvador, and the reassurance of finally being out of reach of the judgmental eyes of her brothers and of the community of Santa Ana.

There was a time, once, however, when my mother reached a high level of frustration and anger before Teto or Pirri had been born. In one occasion, the maids, doing errands around town, saw my father entering an unfamiliar house with another woman and ran home to alert my mother. This time she reached the limits of her patience, found one of my father's pistols and walked to the house of the mistress with the clear intention of killing her or killing my father, or both. My father remembered my mother standing in front of him looking at him in his underwear, in bed with the other woman. My mother pulled the trigger and the gun did not shoot. She tried it again without success. My father trembled while my mother spewed loud maledictions at the woman. Gradually my father, composing himself, convinced her to let go of the pistol. Crying, exhausted, already pregnant with my brother Teto, the street fighter, she slowly walked back home with an injured pride and an honor betrayed. My father ended up impregnating that mistress with a baby girl. I met her the day of Pirri's high school graduation. She and her mother passed by the school as my father, Teto, Pirri and I came out of the building. Her name was Blanca.

Teto, the war survivor, and I, nowadays, admire my mother's unshakable commitment to her marriage. One reason for this was her Castro-Meza resolve of never giving up, *"nunca hay que dar el brazo a torcer"* she would say, and another reason being the proud desire to prove her brothers wrong. The alternative to remaining steadfast was not as palatable. This would have required her to surrender with her head down and return to the cozy living of her ancestral home with the added degrading burden of the stigma against divorcees.

Nowadays, Teto often shares with me his belief in cosmological justice. According to him, there are forces in the universe that conspire to make wrongs right and punish those who have inflicted unimaginable pain on others, especially on the defenseless. Such forces act sort of like the vigilantes portrayed in Hollywood movies who take justice into their own hands. Teto believes strongly in this mystical cycle of justice. I don't. My mother, he states, is the only one among her sisters who lived happily with her husband during the last 20 years of her life, after my father joined Alcoholics Anonymous.

They did everything together during those years, often walking on the streets holding hands to the surprise and envy of her other sisters. All their husbands had died prematurely, leaving them behind to endure painfully lonely years as widows. There are horrible stories regarding death in my aunts' families. One husband committed suicide, another died of liver cancer, one niece also committed suicide, the husband of another, recently married, died while driving *la curva de la muerte,* and another sister died young from a stroke. My father died almost 20 years after my mother, left alone to live with the constant remorse and deep culpability of the damage he inflicted on his family. Teto says he feels at peace knowing that somehow our mother was redeemed. The universe punished those who kept great part of my mother's inheritance, and my father for squandering what remained.

✳✳✳
✳

I was born among all the benefits associated with wealth, especially in a country like El Salvador, where economic inequalities in the 1950's were absurd. Around fourteen families, landowners of coffee plantations, ruled the country as the top 1%. Mine was not one of them, but it came very close to it. Before my mother's inheritance disappeared, we owned a profitably sized coffee *finca*. So, during the first seven years of my life, I had no need to venture outside the Ruiz-Castro compound. Five maids took care of all our necessities. It took my father a mere seven years to destroy it all.

When we moved to Guatemala City, we lived in three different houses over the span of three years. Our last residence was a small, newly constructed house that was part of a new development of cement row houses named *Colonia 20 de Octubre*. This development was built by president Ydigoras Fuentes for the lower classed on a huge parcel of land next to the Guatemalan *Campo Marte*, an immense training field for the Guatemalan army. Our house stood at a frequently transited corner, one block from the bus stop, at the intersection between the 24th avenue and 28th street.

Unpaved streets led to a huge green field, *el Campo de Marte*, where I often took my younger brothers to kick around a soccer ball. My father had thrown this ball to us from the street over the *patio's* wall one late afternoon as he approached the house coming from some kind of work. Teto recently told me that at that time my father was smuggling guns from Guatemala to El Salvador. My father even showed up in one of the Guatemalan national newspapers once. He was pictured being interviewed by a reporter asking him what he thought about the recently deposed Salvadoran president, oblivious of his dealings with arms smuggling.

The evening we received the soccer ball, my father, as he approached our house, heard our voices and giggles coming from the patio and decided to surprise us. This new soccer ball made of shiny dark brown leather, with long transversal fine seams and oval sections, bounced over our heads, suddenly interrupting our playing. We grabbed it in awed silence. Most likely, the group of children that played soccer every afternoon after school on the street adjacent to our house had accidentally kicked it over when trying to shoot a goal. We would never have guessed it was a gift from our father.

We gathered around the patio's farthest corner and kept silent. Our mother, unaware of the event, kept cooking dinner, waiting for my father to come home. Before long, somebody knocked loudly at the wooden front door. We pleaded with our mother not to open it because we thought the other children were coming to get their ball. My mother waited, but the knocks soon became too persistent to ignore.

When she opened the door, there stood our father, so we ran to greet him and tell him all about how the children who had lost their soccer ball never came to collect it. Maybe they didn't know where the ball had landed and thought it was lost. I remember my father's mischievous smile when he finally told us that the ball was his present to us. He had bought the ball, or acquired it somehow, from a vendor at the *portales* in front of the *parque central.* Regardless of how he had gotten it, we were excited to have a new ball. I seldom wanted to bring Teto with me to play with the soccer ball at the *Campo Marte*. He would usually start to scream if I didn't bring him, which would drive my father crazy. Teto's temper tantrums would bring my father out of his alcoholic stupors and make him get up with his leather belt in hand ready to strike me, unless I changed my mind. Teto always, with a wide smile, almost mocking us, ended up coming with us to the park. Anyone with younger siblings knows how difficult it is to shake them off.

We loved our soccer ball and took good care of it by spreading wax or animal fat on its kenaf or fine hemp yarn seams and over its entire leather surface every week. One day, however, I kicked it very hard to Rafael, who was the goalie, and he couldn't stop it. A thick line of bushes stood behind him. A dirt road, that cars used to enter the *colonia,* came after, and beyond the woods. I remember the ball disappearing through the bushes. Rafael and I were sure the ball had been stopped by the snake vine underneath the bushes. Teto sat behind me impatiently waiting for his turn to kick the ball.

We looked for the ball until after the sunset, went home, and asked our father to come to look for the ball. The next day, we returned to the field after school to look for it, and the day after. We did this for many weeks. We never found the soccer ball. We all fell into a deep sadness. That soccer ball had brought us, three brothers, together by providing us with a fun daily activity; we were not ready to accept its loss. Now, we think that an unscrupulous driver picked up the ball that most likely rolled through the bushes to land in the middle of the dirt road and decided not to return it to the sad children that were desperately looking for it.

During our stay in Guatemala, my parents often left me alone in charge of my younger brothers. Every afternoon, missing our parents, Rafael and I climbed to the flat roof of the second house we lived in on *27 Calle, Zona* 5 to wait for them. We used one of the downspouts in the patio as a ladder, carefully stepping up on its metal braces, then grabbing on the soffit and swinging upwards to position our elbows on the edge of the roof to finally push our bodies up onto it. A false move would have been fatal. Once on the roof, we walked to its edge and sat for a long time, watching the cars pass by below us until the street became dark. I don't remember what Teto, three years old, left alone on the ground, did during that time, most likely crying uncontrollably. One early evening, suddenly, we saw a taxi parked across the street in front of the house and a couple carrying a baby got out and started to walk towards the house. Teto tells me now that he actually went up to the roof too, aided by Rafael, who couldn't stand his crying any longer.

"Ahí está mi Papá y mi Mamá con Pirri, bajémonos rápido antes de que abran la puerta," I told Rafael. We ran across the roof already scared, anticipating a belting from my father, swung from the soffit to the downspout, and rapidly descended to the patio as my parents entered the house. On our rush to get down, the downspout became disconnected from the gutter and leaned awkwardly towards one side. "¿Qué pasó aquí?," my father asked. "No sabemos qué pasó," I said. My father believed our story and we never again climbed to the roof. It is very probable that Teto went up the roof with us, if not that night he would have run to my parents to spill the beans and we would have received another of my father's beltings.

That winter, we discovered what cold temperatures did to the body. Our bodies were used to hot weather conditions of Santa Ana, but it was a shock to us when the weather plummeted to the low 40s in Guatemala City. We shivered and trembled, and complained every night and day about the cold. My father bought us several thick colorful blankets with quetzal designs made by K'iché indigenous people in Momostenango at the portales next to the parque central. I remember spending several days in our beds under those blankets in the room I shared with Rafael and Teto.

Nights presented a problem for me. At night, Rafael and Teto woke me up at different times asking me to turn on the light bulb before walking to the bathroom. *"Chepito, prenda la luz. Quiero hacer pipí."* I had to get up from bed, walk to the center of the room, pull the light string, and stand waiting for my brothers to come back to their beds. Soon, my mother noticed my permanent sleepy head during the day and asked my father for a solution. A long string appeared in my bed the next night, one end attached to the header of my bed and the other at the porcelain ceiling light fixture. When my brothers woke me up in the middle of the night, half-awake I had to simply extend my arm and pull down the string to turn the ceiling light on. However, this was only a temporary solution, for I would always fall back asleep before my brothers would come back from the bathroom, only to be woken up soon after by the bright light. I would turn it off, but the same sequence would just be repeated several times at night.

That same year, my father bought a car with what must have been the remains of my mother's partial inheritance, made it into a taxi, and stationed it in a prime spot at the *Parque Central.* From his strategic position, he was regularly hired for long trips by tourists, mostly boring Americans, who paid well and tipped big. My father would pretend to know English by only memorizing necessary phrases to gain more fares.

At that time, Rafael and I were at the end of our school vacation, three months, from November to February. The days cooled down, the skies became clear and blue. Rafael and I developed the independent habit of walking alone 25 blocks to the *Parque Central* to see our father and, especially, to circle the smooth cement sidewalks of the *parque* with our old-fashioned heavy metal *patines,* a Christmas present. We ignored the deep lines on the insteps of our feet created by the brown thick leather straps and enjoyed stopping by my father's stand for him to readjust the length and the width of the roller skates that would inevitably loosen by our aggressive skating. We became extremely agile at the sport, showing off our circling technique to avoid people, obstacles, or to stop.

Tired, but happy, on our way back, we distracted ourselves by pretending we spoke English. We would imitate the sounds we heard coming out of the mouths of the Three Stooges, whose movies we saw at *El Cine Olympia* on *Avenida 14 y 27 calle*, every Sunday matinee. We also emphasized the accents we heard in the voices of Gary Cooper; Glenn Ford, Richard Widmark, and Stewart Granger. Westerns were our favorites. We walked for countless blocks speaking gibberish, nonsensical words, that we believed sounded exactly like English. Adults looked at us attentively trying to understand our language. We believed we had them fooled. When we tired of that game, we started to read all the street signs we saw on the way. Rafael learned how to read before me. I read short words; Rafael read the longer posters, titles, and subtitles. *"Tienda La Barata. ¡Mejor Mejora Mejoral!"* He would read excitedly.

I learned little at school while living in Guatemala City. During those three years, I attended three different schools, two private and one public. They were a sharp contrast from the upscale private/boarding school of Santa Ana. Our displacement from El Salvador was drastic and perturbing, impossible for us to understand. The first boarding school, *El Asilo Santa María*, functioned more like an orphanage than a private parochial boarding school. The few memories I have from that institution are associated with desolation, abandonment, fear, and insecurity. Rafael was put in the same school. I was six and he was four. The nuns and priests, almost to a pathological degree, were stern, dark, and diabolic: no kind words, no loving remarks, no understanding of the soul and mind of a small child. My parents, still with a deep trust of

Catholic institutions, might have thought they were providing a good education for us. They were utterly wrong. I have only dark memories from that school: a long, barracks-style dormitory, where a priest stood in the shadows of the entrance, ordering us to go to sleep because there was this ghost who came at night to steal children who were still awake; a chaotic long line to get hot oatmeal mush, the only dish for breakfast; my sickly brother, with his yet to be discovered lactose intolerance, crying and calling me often to help him with his soiled underwear; a bully hitting me repeatedly during recess while I receded to the confines of an isolated corner; and a long line under the scorching sun waiting to enter the church on Sundays.

Presently, I have a recurrent nightmare attributed to that dormitory. I wake up kicking with all my force this shadow that tries to pick me up from behind. I say, *"Te voy a matar hijueputa. Te voy a matar."* I always wake up my wife, Carolina, by my loud mumbling and she softly pats me back to sleep. I wouldn't be surprised that, knowing what I know now about the abuses of priests against children, that this was occurring at that school. The only solace I have is that the nightmare of living in that school lasted only for one year: my second grade, and Rafael's kindergarten. I asked my parents during one of their frequent visits to Boston, why they had put us in the *Asilo Santa María* that year because we had suffered a lot. They did not reply, just stood silent facing me with utter visible pain.

We lived in Guatemala for three years. My father moved us back again to El Salvador after having utterly failed to remake his life in Guatemala. With empty pockets, we landed at my paternal grandfather's small adobe house in Chalchuapa. Here, my three brothers and I shared one large rectangular, musty, and moldy room with my parents next to the garden.

Our street, like all streets in Chalchuapa, and most of the pueblos founded by the Spaniard colonists in Latin America, was built very narrow, with enough space to allow transit for horse carriages and oxen carts. The narrow streets let the tropical sun cast its direct light only at high noon. One could always find a sidewalk with shade at any other time. The sidewalks of Chalchuapa were unusually high to allow the daily heavy rainfalls coming from the *Volcán de Santa Ana* down *la loma* to flow down the streets, which would become canals carrying tributaries to the river just out of town, and to let people walk easily out of their houses without getting their feet wet. At the corner of streets, however, residents had no alternative but to jump into the muddy streams, risking stepping over toads and the occasional water snake.

There were times when the residents built wooden platforms at each corner to cross the streets during heavy and lengthy storms that would last for weeks. Nevertheless, for us kids, it was inevitable that we would trip off the wooden platforms and bridges to land into the putrid chocolate colored water. With our cheap leather shoes, soaked with dark water and mud, we would squelch back home, spraying passersby with mud and water that seeped out of the seams in the soles of our feet.

The flooded streets deterred all vehicles from passing. You could count the number of vehicles in Chalchuapa with one hand during those times, mostly green jeep Willis' and some new Toyotas, which the very wealthy, like my Castro Meza uncles, garaged in their houses. Chalchuapa, situated behind the *Volcán de Santa Ana*, was captive to legendary rainstorms and the occasional pacific hurricane.

My mother told us that one time during her childhood, in the 1920's, one of those storms, probably a Pacific hurricane, reached such unparalleled strength that a family of monkeys was carried from the Volcán to her family's *traspatio* and that a cow had dropped from the sky in one of her coffee plantations. She and her sisters woke up the next morning surrounded by monkeys screeching in the traspatio, eating their mangos.

The sidewalks and the streets of Chalchuapa were made of loosely cemented cobble stones brought from the nearby quarry and placed directly on the ground. Houses were built with very thick, around two feet deep, adobe walls, not cement, and with red clay tiles for their roofs. All main entrances to the houses were made of thick carved wood.

In this house of my paternal grandfather, Papá Rafa, in Chalchuapa is when I was most afraid before going to sleep, all thanks to my father's scary bed stories. There was *la Carreta Bruja* (the bewitched cart) driven by ghosts after midnight to steal children who refused to fall asleep. Most likely my father had watched the silent Swedish film "The Phantom Carriage," where the legend of the Death Driver or the Cart of Death is told. In it, the last person to die each year, if he is a sinner, must drive the Cart of Death for the following year. There were several nights that I heard *la Carreta* passing loudly in front of our house. Later, I found out that it was a real *carreta* pulled by oxen used by the town to collect garbage. I heard the squeaking and rattling as its metallic wheels made their way over the uneven cobblestones. I imagined this thin transparent ghost poking the oxen, hoping that he would not sense my awakened presence.

There was the story of *la mano peluda* (the hairy hand). My father loved going to the movies. He must have gotten the idea of scaring us from several 1940-50s movies, with a severed hairy hand ready to harm us when reluctant to fall asleep. There is a long list of Hollywood movies depicting a scary hand: *The Beast with Five Fingers, The Creature from the Black Lagoon, Mad Love,* and *The Hand of Orlac.* Late at night, hearing that we were still awake, my father went out to the corridor to scratch the wooden planks of the two doors of our bedroom, producing the exact sound we imagined the severed hairy hand would create. Trembling with fear, we covered our faces with our sheets, frozen, and started to pray to scare it away before it decided to strangle us. My father went to the extreme of constructing a *mano peluda* using an old construction glove glued to a broomstick which he would slowly insert through the cracks of our wooden bedroom window.

To make things worse, there was also this windowless dark room in the back of the house, towards the end of a long corridor, which we were forbidden to enter. My father called it *el cuarto de la monja sin cabeza,* the room of the headless nun. Teto tells me that there was this legend about a nun that fell in love with the town priest at the turn of the 19th century. The nun lived hidden in that room that was connected by a long tunnel to the living quarters of the church located directly half a block away behind the house. The nun used the tunnel every night to see her priest lover. One day, the nun was found decapitated in her room, allegedly killed by zealous extremists, like Opus Dei operatives would have done, had they existed then. Tío Jorge, my father's younger brother, brought his wife and kids to live in that windowless room for a while and we stopped calling it the room of la *monja sin cabeza.*

✳✳✳

My parents were not especially religious. I do not remember regularly attending church with my family, but I often would venture to the park after mass if we ever did end up going. It occupied the area of one street block. Blocks, as measured by the Spaniards, were around 100 square meters. El Parque Central, with a fountain at its center, nurtured dense oak, teak, and cedar trees, with some coconut palms that lined alongside the walking paths around its perimeter.

During this time, there was a promenade every Sunday evening after mass in *el Parque Central*. Nowadays, the park has been newly renovated by my brother Rafael, the civil engineer of the family. The prominent and powerful families of the town participated, old and young, in these traditional promenades. The only rule of the promenade was that the eligible bachelors and debutants walk leisurely around the park, the girls clockwise in an inner circular path, and the boys counterclockwise in an outer one.

I remember watching my older rich male cousins, Tito, Ricardo and Mauricio Urrutia, performing this social dance between the sexes. The girls and the boys would walk in packs of pre-arranged dense groups of no more than five or six members, the boys with their arms around each other's shoulders, and the girls locked arm in arm.

This flirtatious dance started usually with a specific boy looking intensely at a female and saying aloud a *"piropo."* The boy would have known beforehand that the girl liked him thanks to messages sent to him via her close friends. Next, both the girls' group and the boys' group would conspire for the two to escape unnoticed by the parents to meet surreptitiously in the dark behind the thick tree trunks. It was difficult for parents to notice these escapes. The packs would continue walking around and around, giggling, at times loudly, pretending to play the game knowing that the couple was passionately kissing somewhere in the dark, hidden away from the disapproving gazes of the adults. This would repeat every Saturday and Sunday after the evening mass with different couples, for some it would be their first encounter with the opposite sex, for others the precursor of a long marriage.

Only the wealthy youth promenaded their youth around the park. The poor, the campesinos that came to town to sell their fruits and vegetables on Sundays, and the maids and laborers, watched the promenade at a distance from below the raised sidewalks, admiring the newest European and American dress fashion worn by the rich boys and girls.

At the time, I was only 10 and too young to join in the fun. My amusement on Sundays consisted of walking five miles with my brothers early in the morning up to the *trapiche*, a natural spring converted into a swimming pool. On our way back, we would stop at our step-paternal grandmother's stand at el Mercado, looking to eat some *"Yuca con chicharrón,"* with *"curtido"* and spicy tomato sauce. If we were lucky, in the evening our *Papá Rafa* would send us to the corner *tienda* to get the special turkey sandwiches made by Doña Maria, our neighbor. These sandwiches were made with fresh French bread spread with mildly spicy tomato sauce, lots of water cress, cucumbers, hot green peppers, some sour cream, Dijon mustard, some kind of wine, lots of garlic, more tomato sauce, black olives, onions, some cilantro, and with a big piece of white turkey meat in the middle. These sandwiches, *'panes con chumpe,'* were legendary in the community and people lined up early in the afternoon just to get a taste.

Doña Maria started before sunrise on Sunday mornings by ordering her workers to slit the throat of ten to 15 turkeys, which had been roaming around her backyard during the week. Next, they boiled them in huge pots over a wood burning stove. Often, on my way to the trapiche, I would glimpse the workers plucking the feathers off dozens of half-boiled turkeys. I hated the smell of cooked feathers and couldn't believe that those turkeys were alive just a few hours before. Her special hot sauce and her stew sent their spicy aroma permeating all over the block on Sundays. It was criminal not to eat one of those panes on these days, but we did not eat them often, only on special holidays.

Nowadays, driving around Boston, I run into wild turkeys, stop, let them cross the street, and at these moments it is impossible for me not to flash back to Doña Maria's *"pan con chumpe."*

During our stay in Chalchuapa, my mother struggled to find something to feed us for dinner and had to resort often to the charity of her well-off sisters. The family had reached dirt bottom. She had to bite her pride, knowing that the entire family repudiated her for having remained with my father. The Castro-Meza clan, led by Tío Héctor, kept offering incentives for her to get a divorce, pointing out at every instance the devastating future that awaited her children. Teto, the knife-thrower-commando, tells me that Tío Héctor offered to give my mother back some land, were she to divorce my father, land that belonged to my mother in the first place. My mother never acquiesced.

To avoid the awkward moments of asking for help, my mother wrote notes to her sisters asking for specific items. It was our job to deliver those notes. *"Quiero que uno de ustedes vaya a la casa de tía Blanchie y le de este papelito,"* my mother told us one night before dinner. I never volunteered. I disliked the chore of begging for food. Besides, I was terrified of the aggressive dogs that guarded the houses of my aunts. *"Yo voy,"* my brother Rafael always volunteered. He felt proud and accomplished whenever he came back with food for dinner, but not always. *"Este papelito dice que necesito una docena de huevos para darles a ustedes de comer esta noche,"* my mother told Rafael. We were hungry and desperate and decided to look out for Rafael's return outside on the sidewalk from where we could catch sight of him as soon as he turned the corner on our street.

Half an hour later, we saw Rafael entering our street with his quick and bouncing gate, carrying a brown paper bag in the palm of his right hand. His right arm was bent upward, and the palm of his hand rested over his shoulder. We couldn't wait for those eggs to reach our bellies. As he approached us, we heard a "splash-cracking" noise and then a splat on the sidewalk just behind him. We saw it. One egg had somehow fallen from the bag and landed behind Rafael. My mother ran to help him. We all ran to see. *"Mi hijo. Déme la bolsa antes que bote todos los huevos,"* my mother said. She took the bag from him, opened it and started to cry. *"Oh, mi chichí siempre está en otro mundo,"* my mother uttered through her sobs. We all looked into the bag. There was only one egg left. Rafael had dropped 11 eggs on his walk back from tía Blanchie's house without noticing it. One of the eggs in the bottom of the bag had cracked, as tía Blanchi piled them up one on top of the other, without noticing, spilling its yoke. Soaked with egg, the bottom of the brown paper bag had created a hole in the bag which had started to disintegrate half way. One by one the eggs started to fall as Rafael had walked back. We had witnessed the fall of the penultimate egg. I remember clearly his radiant face, smiling, full of excitement, fulfilled, half a block away, oblivious to the sound of cracking eggs. He was bringing food home. That night Rafael did not eat, seized with embarrassment and the failing sense of having disappointed mother's expectations. I don't remember how or what we ate that night.

Our rich cousins never came to visit or play with us, not by fault of their own, but because they were the products of a society strongly led by social norms that governed interactions between the rich and poor. It wouldn't have ever occurred to them. If it did, they sensed our social status as being far below theirs. Our only link was a blood relationship, which was kept intact by the deep adoration they had for my mother that lasted until she died. They cherished my mother because she imparted unconditional, tender love upon them, constantly celebrating their educational achievements on her weekly visits to her sisters and brothers living in Chalchuapa.

We, looking to play with the latest toys and, if we were lucky, to eat some good food, took turns visiting our cousins of the same age. Teto for a time became the "adopted" child of the Urrutias, visiting their Chalchuapa home daily to play and eat dinner with their younger son Quique, one mouth less to feed for my mother. Much later, Ricardo Urrutia was very kind to my parents. I found out after my father died that he regularly had sent money to my parents while they lived in LA, something that he was not in any obligation to do. His unselfish gesture surprised me and touched my heart deeply.

This was the time when I would also often visit Eduardo Urrutia, Tía Blanchie's son of my same age, even though I had to compete for his attention because he was always with a clique of other affluent friends. I was often at the mercy of Eduardo and his friends' plans and what they would regard as having fun. I never dared to make suggestions of my own. Maybe I felt oppressed by my family's poverty and thought that those of lower economic status did not have a say.

On one of those days, the group decided to spend the afternoon pretending to be alpinists. They ransacked the house garage, grabbed a couple of long ropes used to corral horses, and trekked out of the city to a place called *la quebrada*, a sort of deep canyon, with *el Galeano* river running along its bottom. We soon found a trail descending to the river and once arriving at the bottom, we chose the highest and steepest river bank to climb back up. Tall trees stood at the top of the canyon, gradually decreasing in size as the vegetation made its way down to the river. The tallest and strongest of the group climbed first, using his hands and legs, imitating the way a monkey would move in the jungle trees. He swung from branch to branch with much disregard for the height, stepping on protruding rocks, zigzagging his weight slowly all the way up while carrying the ropes transversely around his shoulders. Once on top of the river bank, he tied both ropes around a mango tree and descended with the ease and grace of a professional climber to meet us at the bottom; no need for helmets, gloves, carabiners, or harnesses. We wouldn't have known such equipment existed.

It had rained the night before, but the waters had not yet completely flooded the river's embankments. Small puddles of water had formed, dispersed alongside the river, some obscured by a layer of natural debris and green leaves snatched from the trees by torrential rains the previous night. *"¿Quién se anima subir primero?"* The tallest boy asked. Eduardo grabbed the rope first and I jumped to grab it after him, feeling protected by the invisible shield of my blood relation. The other boys fell in line behind us. We used the same rope, at the same time, leaving some vertical space between us, while the second rope was left dangling next to us. We lacked any awareness of the safest way to climb rocks or steep, muddy, lush, tropical, unstable mountain walls. Inexperience and adolescent overconfidence: the perfect formula for disaster.

Just before Eduardo reached the top, he lost his footing and recovered it quickly, but not without initiating a small, muddy avalanche that suddenly pelted my face and filled my eyes. As an instinctual reaction, I let go of the rope to wipe the mud of my face, and subsequently tumbled down towards the rocky river bed. As I fell, I saw the other boys with their heads down, leaning very closely to the wall, almost attached to it, protecting themselves from the barrage of mud and pebbles Eduardo had loosened. I saw tree branches passing by my side with some of their leaves brushing my shoulders. The fall felt never-ending. After what seemed like a very long time plummeting towards my imminent death, I landed in a small pool of muddy water. I had fallen into it, breaking through the layer of leaves, and avoided hitting, by mere millimeters, the heavy rocks that surrounded it. I felt nothing, no pain. I had landed softly on my back, the heavy impact absorbed by water, mud, and leaves.

The tall boy came to my rescue, expecting me bloody, with a cracked skull and twisted limbs. Eduardo yelled from his perch, *"¿Qué pasó, por qué tantos gritos?"* I jumped out of the pool, my body shaking uncontrollably.

My left shoulder was bleeding, some branches had scraped it on my way down, but that was the only damage. We soon dismantled the operation and walked back to town, swearing we would never speak again about this day. My mother attended to my scraped shoulder. I don't remember what lie I told her to explain such an injury. I was 12. I could have died that day, but by some twist of fate, I did not. I have interpreted this near miss and several others in my life, as the product of divine intervention.

❋❋❋

While in Chalchuapa, one day when I got home from school, I found my father and his father, Papá Rafa, talking to a Salesian priest from Guatemala. The priest had been making the rounds in the town recruiting boys for entrance to religious life in their last year of primary school. He showed me pictures of the Seminary and its expansive grounds: two soccer fields, a basketball court, and an outdoor olympic swimming pool. The entire house became excited about the idea of my becoming a priest, a thing that had never occurred to me. My mother's statue of San José, her miraculous saint that helped her during the 30 hours of my delivery, and the reason for my first name, stood prominently against one of the walls in the corridor. That statue constituted the extent of my religious knowledge. I don't remember ever going to church with my mother. Sunday Church attendance was not part of our lives, but the illusion of studying in a high school with such rich facilities attracted my attention. Who cared if the place was called Seminary! My decision was a resounding yes.

A week later the priest came back to ask about my decision and there it all broke down. He asked for a monthly tuition that sounded that only the very rich in town, like my cousins, could afford. I don't know what the priest was thinking. He might have assumed that Papá Rafa, not rich, but with means, would pay for my education. I was devastated. There was no future for me. I had to find a job as an apprentice somewhere to learn "*un oficio*". I had done especially well in the sixth grade and my teachers at the *Colegio La Fe* expected me to go to the city of Santa Ana, as all my cousins had, for high school and later to the capital of San Salvador for a university career. I cried, becoming depressed and unhappy.

Papá Rafa made his living as a clothing door-to-door salesman on credit. His territory covered the municipality of Chalchuapa. Most of his clients were campesinos that had recently moved closer to the town and lived on its outskirts. He decided to hire me as his helper on Sundays. My task was to carry a valise full of new clothes samples on my back. We walked door-to-door from 7:00 am to 6:00 pm. At each house, he took his ledger out, and asked the client for the weekly payment of his previous purchase.

The secret of the business, not unlike today's credit card companies, was to require only the minimum of payments, whatever the client could afford weekly. A cotton new shirt or pants would end up costing the poor client four or five times its original price. Papá Rafa had to be persistent with each client and not lose sight of any change of address. As soon as the client was done paying an item, Papá Rafa would sell them another one supposedly of the latest style. They would always buy something new, and the cycle continued. He took me to a good eatery for lunch and I ate all I wanted. The coins he gave me at the end of the day I passed on to my mother. That was a start. Maybe I could have learned how to become a salesman. Teto told me that he inherited my job when I left for the Seminary and that Papá Rafa gave him 10 cents from each payment collected.

My mother soon told her sisters about my failed attempt to enter the Guatemalan Seminary. Tía Blanchi came up with the suggestion to try the Minor Seminary in

Santa Ana. This Seminary didn't yet have a building and it was temporarily being housed in the Palacio Episcopal, Bishop Barrera's house. A half-a-block-wide Spanish colonial, it was a far cry from the Guatemalan site. It did not even have any sports facilities. Seminarians had to walk every day from the house to attend classes at the Salesian Colegio San José, integrated with the larger student population.

How my family managed to find the funds necessary to send me there, I cannot be sure, but I think my mother's devout sisters, Mamá Lila and Tía Blanchie, paid for my tuition. I entered the Santa Ana minor Seminary on February 27, 1963, escaping, what Teto now tells me, the stress caused by never having enough to eat, the traumatic pain from seeing my mother's suffering because of my alcoholic father, continued social small-town shame caused by wearing our cousins' hand-me-downs, and a general sense of complete family dysfunction.

The oversized pants, hand-me-downs from Tia Blanchie's children, Mauricio, Eduardo and Ricardo, made Teto, the knife-thrower commando and street fighter, look like a miniature clown and subjected him to ridicule by his peers. This was the time when he started to fight daily at school and be sent home bloody, starting a series of school expulsions that lasted up to his high school years. "*A mí me expulsaron de todas las escuelas habidas y por haber,*" Teto now-a-days says. My mother, a competent seamstress, did her best to tailor the pants to Teto's size, shortening their hems, painstakingly unseaming their oversized waist and restitching them to Teto's measurement, but no amount of alterations could mask the fact that they were clearly second-hand. Being ridiculed by his classmates at school because of being poor affected Teto the most.

There were incidents later in high school that totally devastated him. One was when the Salesian teachers asked him to be part of the basketball traveling team because he was the best player they had seen in years during recess, but the requirement of buying the school sports uniform was impossible for my parents to meet. Only the affluent boys whose parents made big contributions to the *Colegio* and were able to buy the uniforms were asked to participate regardless of their skill level. Teto still affected, tells me this story often with tears in his eyes. He tells me how he, all dejected, left school the day he was told he couldn't be a member of the basketball team and walked back home crying.

Feeling obfuscated and deeply angered, he cursed as he walked finding some relief in hitting the solid front walls of all the houses in his path with his fist as he made his way back to the Multis, incapable of understanding such a flagrant injustice. The irony is that often the people who professed to be just and proclaim that their job in life is to develop just human beings like the priests did in *el Colegio* were the ones who were more oblivious to their own acts of injustice. "*Si solamente mi papá y los curas del Colegio me hubieran dado todo el apoyo que yo necesitaba en aquel tiempo!*" Teto often says.

This was around the same time in Chalchuapa when my father's asthma worsened. He had asthma attacks every night. Many were the nights when he reached the edge of death. On these occasions, the entire barrio of Chalchuapa became alarmed and the preparations for his imminent death were jump-started. The priest was called to give my father the last rites, the ladies of the house would start to mumble the rosary, Dr. Sierra would inject him with adrenaline as a last-ditch effort to save him, and my mother would sit next to him, staring blankly into the distance and clutching his hand as my father struggled to breathe. There was no treatment available for asthma in the late 1950's, leaving the patient with only household remedies and folkloric treatments to stave off the tightening pressure in their swollen bronchioles.

During one of his asthma attacks, my father would sit on a chair next to a table where a bowl of steaming water was placed. He would cover his head with a towel and breathe in the steam. Then there was the injection that he would promptly insert into the side of his thigh. Next, he would light a special cigarette filled with medicinal powder and take some puffs. I never knew what treatment worked for him. Nobody would sleep during these nights. The women of the house would walk in circles back and forth from the kitchen to the bedrooms, from the living room to the bathroom, and back again to where my father was, lost without any new options for treatment, just waiting for my father to die.

One night my father was the most on the verge of dying he had ever been. I kneeled on the ceramic tile floor in front of the small statue of San José my mother believed had granted her multiple miracles in her life and who she never left behind in our moves from house to house. I clasped my hands, and prayed, "*San José, por favor, te lo pido, no dejes que mi Papá se muera,*" chanting repeatedly while the women rushed behind me already moaning with grief and murmuring prayers for the dead. Teto inherited the statue of San José and at the present has it in his house in Cambridge, visible behind the glass of one of his china cabinets. My mother insisted during her later years that the statue was Teto's, not mine. Teto needed guidance and protection from *San José* the most. She was sure he would grant her a final miracle and bring Teto out of his drug addiction and alcoholism. All her praying must have worked because he has been sober now for almost twenty-five years.

The day after yet another near-death episode, Dr. Sierra came to examine my father and asked my mother to look for allergy-causing agents around the house. My mother promptly found a large flower with drooping petals blooming in the garden that covered the middle of the patio. I had admired the glowing orange of the large flower from the patio door of our room that day in the morning, before walking to school. I almost felt sorry when my mother clipped the flower off its stalk, but that day I understood that flowers that bring beauty in nature could also silently poison people like my father.

Asthma defined and limited my father through his life. It carried a heavy social stigma in those days. He was looked at differently by other kids at school when he was growing up. They never invited him to join in their soccer games after school before going home, climb the *jocote* and mango trees abundant just outside the *Colegio San José* campus, and during weekends, go swimming at the municipal pool in *apanteos,* just outside of town or run away after attempting to extract the honey from hanging beehives. My father, to satisfy his need of adolescent social belonging, used his verbal abilities to sooth the occasional physical threats, and silently accepted his classmates' views of him as a sickly, terribly thin, good for nothing classmate.

He became a recluse, excelling academically more than socially, but found that girls, maybe out of pity, or because they found him harmless, loved his talent for telling jokes and funny stories. They were inspired by his singing of contemporary love songs by Carlos Gardel and Agustin Lara and couldn't resist listening attentively to his love poems. Girls were attracted to him and gathered around him in recess and after school, making the active soccer players jealous. Later, the other boys had no choice but to become my father's close friends or else he would have all the girls to himself.

My father loved the seashore and thought that swimming in the ocean ameliorated his asthma. He heard that swimming was good for his condition and became a great swimmer. His body was well formed, short, with a protruding chest. He became obsessed with the exercises developed by Charles Atlas, believing that his capacity for air-intake during asthma attacks would improve. He did them before swimming. I was 14 when he introduced me to this program. He asked me to do them soon after waking up and before taking a shower. He was proud of my following his exercise regime. I followed it well into my adulthood. By that time my father had become a drunkard and expected to die very young from asthma, delirium tremens, or stomach cancer, but he believed I would live a long time, thanks to the exercises.

One theory is that he became an alcoholic due to the insecurities formed by his illness and the hope that alcohol might act as a cure. After a couple of whisky shots, he would come out of his otherwise timid state to become the life of the party, a troubadour, a skillful tango, mambo, and chachacha dancer, and a sort of a clown, to compensate for his insecurities. At the *Colegio* he became the center of attention, his wit had no challenge, his charm attracted the boys to gather around him because they wanted a share of the girls, who ended up truly falling in love with him, not out of pity. Later, after marrying my mother, Papá Lorenzo called him Cantinflas, after the Mexican comedian popular at that time around the world, who my father accurately imitated in many ways.

One day, an international doctor came to El Salvador promoting a new asthma treatment that included surgery and started recruiting patients. My father enlisted, not before signing several contracts and consent forms that eliminated the doctor's liability in case of death. The treatment consisted of a sort of ganglionectomy or re-nerving around the carotid vein. I think it was a gland that was removed from his neck. The operation was extremely successful and since that day, my father's attacks decreased in intensity, which was promptly seen as a Godsend by my mother and the other women of the house who were relieved to leave those sleepless nights by his deathbed behind.

My father died at the age 96, 15 years after my mother, but not from asthma, just from natural causes, whatever that means. Throughout his later years, he never suffered from organ failure or blood pressure problems. He didn't even begin to lose his mental faculties until past his early nineties. Make no mistake, however. It may have been a miracle that my father's liver was intact and his body in fine condition towards the end of his life, but no one should have to watch a parent slowly lose his mind. When I travelled to Los Angeles to settle my father's affairs and escort him back to El Salvador to live out his final days, he no longer recognized me and would slip in and out of relative lucidity. My son, Alejandro, who had driven from Utah to help me, had to remind my father constantly of my identity. Strangely, he seemed to know who Alejandro was in relation to himself but could no longer remember his own son.

After hearing the news of our father's death, Teto and I flew down to El Salvador for his burial after my brother Rafael finished with the arrangements. My father ironically now rests in peace in the Castro-Meza mausoleum in the cemetery of Chalchuapa. I do not have any idea how my brother Rafael obtained possession of the plot. As soon as I entered the town, my mind filled with flickering images of my mother and father's family histories, fighting for emotional space, jumping and shuffling unorganized in my brain, producing in me deep sorrow and nostalgia that made me run away from that place as fast as I could. Even though I lived part of my childhood in Chalchuapa, in a family nucleus with constant traumatic experiences, poverty, and hunger, it pains me to consider it to be the town where I grew up. Instead, I prefer to say that my childhood home was Central America, because making the concept more general sometimes makes the pain more bearable.

My maternal grandparents Héctor Rosendo and Elena Castro
Meza. c 1920.

Mamá Lila 22th birthday 1930

Papá Chendo 1940

My mother Rosa Castro Meza (bottom right) 15th birthday with classmates Carmen Afane, Elida Sagastume and Carmen Pinzón 1936

My parents' wedding, with Papá Lorenzo and Mamá Lila Iglesia
del Carmen, Santa Ana 12/28/1947

Separate Wedding Reception. Castro Meza family: Mamá Lila,
Tía Blanchie, Tía Esperanza, Lorencito, Tito Urrutia, Papá Lorenzo,
Ricardo Castro, el "cabezón".1947

Separate wedding reception. My father with his family Ruiz Camacho. Papá Rafa, Mamá Angelita, Tía Nena, Tío Chepe, Tía Bita, Tío Efraín. Tío Michel took this picture. My mother did not attend.

My father High school 1936

My mother, 1946

My parents civil wedding, one month before their catholic one.
November 11, 1947.

Next to me Alicita and Elsa Menéndez Castro.
Río Lempa, Hacienda Los Apoyos, 1960

With Neto (Standing), and Alicita, (with hat)
Playa el Cuco. La Unión.
A month after Papá Lorenzo's death, December 1959.

With my mother
Jan,1949 and
Jan, 1951.

With my father and Buck. April, 1949

With my parents, my brother Rafael, Santa Ana Feb. 1953

Family picture the year we left for Guatemala City. November 1956

With my mother and three brothers: Rafael, (el Chichi) Héctor, (Teto) and Vidal. (Pirri) While in Guatemala City. 1958

With my brother Rafael on top of my father's green and blue 1952 Chevy Pickup truck.

With classmates. Seminario Juan XXIII. Feb 1963.

Virgin Mary procession. Seminario Juan XXIII. May 1965

Monseñor Barrera1965

With my little brother Vidal (Pirri) Las Multis, 1966

Delivering the valedictorian speech. Graduation ceremony. Colegio San José / Seminario Juan XXIII. 1966

My classmates. Seminario Palafoxiano Puebla, México, 1968.
Gustavo third, top row. I, fifth, top row, from left.

With Gustavo and Costa Rican seminarians. Mexico City, 1968

With Gustavo and Gilberto, the goal keeper of our soccer team's, "El Milán", Seminario Palafoxiano, Puebla, México. 1970.

With Gustavo, forth from left, top row, and the soccer team. Seminario Palafoxiano, 1970

My ID Seminario Palafoxiano. 1967-68.

Gustavo Orellana and
Elsa Rivadeneyra
Puebla, México. 1970

Gustavo with Elsa and I with her sister Gloria.
Puerto de Veracruz. 1970.

Declaiming my favorite poem *"Más Allá"*.
Seminario Palafoxiano. 1969.

With Gustavo. Seminario Palafoxiano, 1970.

Luncheon Speech. Seminario Palafoxiano. Puebla 1970

Playing Bach's Toccata .
Seminario Palafoxiano Chapel. Puebla. January, 1970

Seminario Palafoxiano with the Popocatepetl volcano in the background. 1967, the year of our arrival.

With Alejandro Arenas, who later became the Seminario Palafoxiano's father Confessor, and community children. Puebla, Mexico. 1970.

With Norma Henríquez,
Fiesta del Simón Bolívar, Club Atlético. Santa Ana 1972.

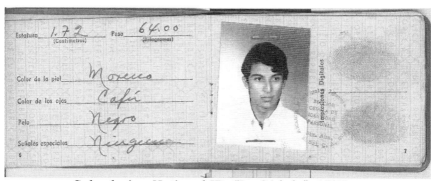

Salvadorian National ID, "La Cédula", 1970

My brothers Rafael and Teto with my mother, Martita Menéndez de Molina, Alicita Menéndez, and Martita's son Eduardo, 1976.

On my way north. Stopped to be a student at Gustavo's institute. Puebla, September 1972.

US Visa. October 1972.

With Sharon Ford García and her 7-year-old daughter, Natalie García.
Jorge García, Sharon's husband took this picture. Christmas Eve, 1972.

ATLANTIC 7-0473

9451 EAST BROADWAY

ST. LUKE'S CATHOLIC CHURCH
P.O. BOX 798
TEMPLE CITY, CALIFORNIA 91780

10/20/72

To whom it may concern:—

Introducing Francisco Ruiz who has been in this country for about ten days, from his native San Salvador. Though he speaks no English he is a willing, conscientious worker and very intelligent. He has been helping our maintenance man all this week and has done very well with gardening, window washing and similar tasks. We cannot afford to employ him beyond the end of this month. He will do any kind of work.

(Rev.) John J. Birch, Pastor

100 a. mth.
2-3 h. p. day

My first job ever at St. Luke's Catholic Church. Father Birch's letter of recommendation, Temple City, California. 1972.

EL MONTE UNION HIGH SCHOOL DISTRICT
ADULT SCHOOL
Student Service Fee 50¢

E. F. PLATZ
ASSISTANT SUPERINTENDENT
INSTRUCTION

NAME Francisco Ruiz

ADDRESS 9766 Hermosa

CITY Temple City Calif.

1973-74
Form 9-8-6   91780   № 41127

El Monte Union High School Adult School. January 1973

Boston

American Airlines
endless summer

TRAVEL ORGANIZER

1973 — American
air
Ernesto
lines
Gálvez and
Francisco Ruiz
at Pasadena —

.The American Airlines pamphlet that attracted my attention, out of many others, at the airline's ticket office in Pasadena, prompting my friend Ernesto and me to buy a one-way ticket to Boston. June, 1973.

Ernesto and his fiancée, Sandra, 1974

Chapter 18: Mi Primo Neto y La Hacienda Los Apoyos

The afternoon was falling and a stormy day was fading into an evening full of olive and silver colors. The solar king was almost hidden over the horizon. One could still see it hidden between some peaks, red as a bronze disk. Clouds of pink, navy, and light blue were forming in the sky; adorning the colorful heavenly light, presaging days of wonderful bliss. Soon the night would fill the Earth with darkness. The breeze that reigned in the mountain carried the sweet songs of distant *chiltotas* and *tortolitas* fluttering as they hid within the green and dense branches of the vibrant trees of the rocky peaks.

In the bowels of the mountain, we were traveling in a green Jeep Willys, which, despite the roughness of the rocky road, advanced quickly, rattling and swaying from side to side. Bouncing and jouncing, we went. We had left the city two hours ago and at that moment, no one spoke. We were looking a little bored and our faces were white and our hair a light tan because of the deep layers of dust covering the road that billowed up in a cloud and blew into the uncovered jeep. There were sections of the narrow road, before disappearing in the forest, where it felt soft, and the jeep didn't jolt around because of the half-meter of fine dust that covered the path. The jeep looked like it was swimming in the dust.

In the backseat sat a lady, already in her fifties, with a basket on her lap. A white handkerchief adorned with yellow flowers covered her head, whose thick hair had begun to whiten. Of white complexion, but now a little yellowish because of the dust, this was Doña Lilian Castro de Menéndez, Mamá Lila, as my mother, Rosita, tía Chocha to my cousins, asked us to call her. Mamá Lila was the mother of seven children: two boys and five girls.

On the right side of Doña Lilian sat her youngest daughter, Alicita, dressed in blue trousers, a long pink and blue plaid cotton shirt, a hat thrown a little to the right, and a silk scarf around her neck that fluttered with sudden bursts due to the uneven wind. Alicita had been my babysitter for the longest time. This is the reason why, decades later, it felt normal for me to stay at her house when first arriving to LA.

After a long time of silence, Neto spoke to his father, saying:

"Papá, what time will we get to the hacienda?"

"We will arrive around seven at night, we just crossed the *presque se seca* brook," replied his father who had just thrown a cigarette butt out onto the narrow and rocky road that looked more like a sidewalk.

"I can't wait to get there. After this long school year, I want to spend the three months of vacation at the hacienda doing nothing. Chepito and I are going to have a lot of fun with the horses and the trips to the Lempa River to swim, not to mention that the .22 caliber rifle is just for me. I want to see if I can hunt some turtle doves, opossums, and iguanas to eat," Neto enthusiastically announced.

"*¡Puta!* Watch out with that rifle. Lorenzo, your brother, almost killed one of the campesinos the other day. When he fired at an iguana, somehow, the rifle moved, and the bullet went straight to the feet of the campesino who had just pointed out the location of the *garrobo*," Don Lorenzo Menéndez, Neto's father, grunted in warning and punctuated it with a coarse thick green spit expectorated into the dust.

"Ay! Lorenzo! You never learn to civilize yourself. Next time, please warn me before your nasty spits so that I can close my eyes and my ears," Mamá Lila scolded him. Papá Lorenzo, as my mother urged us to call him, smirked mischievously, and felt the sudden need to gulp a third shot of whisky.

Soon we turned to silence, and there was only the unceasing purr of the jeep that continued shaking its passengers back and forth, the rocking growing stronger whenever Papá Lorenzo changed gears, which was often.

Neto, as he was affectionately called--my mother frequently called him Netillo-- was 12 years old, and I was 10. He wore blue jeans with black leather boots and a straw hat: the uniform every wealthy city boy wore when going to visit the family farm. Neto's hair was dark brown, and he had a slight straight nose, brown eyes, and was growing taller than the rest of his siblings. He was not so thin of chest, and his muscles were already a little developed. He enjoyed great health and a mind that found pleasure in his studies. He was of few words and of few friends at school, although he occupied the top academic ranks.

He loved nature and was fascinated by the arts, especially music and drawing. He had recently won a drawing competition of a human skull in biology class. To draw the skull, he placed the large poster board on the ping-pong table and rested the textbook with a black and white picture of a skull against the net, as I observed his hand movements from behind him. After a couple of hours of erasing and sharpening, Neto was not pleased with his work and placed another poster board on the table to start all over again.

At this moment, Alfredo March, married to Neto's sister Elenita and the architect in the family, noticed Neto was in distress and offered assistance. Alfredo sharpened the pencil, and from a longer distance to better observe and capture the image of the skull, began to move his body with slow oscillations, back and forth, side to side, almost without looking at the poster, as he started to draw. He would pause to switch the pencil from one hand to the other. He drew with the left, he drew with the right, as we, mesmerized, slowly saw a perfect drawing of a human skull magically appear. Neto and I observed for the first time an artist at work and learned what talent looked like. Neto spent the rest of the day trying to emulate Alfredo's drawing with great success. I watched the process and did not dare to touch anything.

I was born and raised alongside Neto. We had slept in the same crib, sucked from the same bottle, and ate from the same dish. He had gone to the Marist School of Santa Ana; *El Colegio San Luis,* I to the Colegio La Fe de Chalchuapa. We had gone to the family farm on every end-of-the-year three-month vacation, but this holiday had cruel and maddening events in store for us.

This great friendship with Neto was due, in addition to being cousins and loving each other as brothers, to the close sisterly love that existed between his mother, Mamá Lila, and my mother. They were very close even though Mamá Lila was almost 14 years older than my mother and their relationship was more of a mother to daughter than just sisters. My mother did not hesitate, after Tía Anitía kicked her out, to leave her maternal home, to go help her older sister with her younger children. And, when my mother married my father, she bought a house a half block from the Menendez house. I was soon born, and from my first hour of existence, our two families had been inseparable.

Papá Lorenzo was 58 years old, was of medium height, and had a protruding abdomen and dense blond hair on his arms. His eyes seemed to flash greenish light. His official uniform was khaki trousers and shirt: the uniform of the landowners of El Salvador. He was a smoking chimney, partial to the *embajadores* brand of cigarettes, and never interrupted the routine of taking more than a few drinks of the *aguardiente Tic Tac* every afternoon and evening, and often as soon as he got up in the morning. He was born and raised in the hacienda called *Los Apoyos,* which had been inherited by his father from his Spaniard father, covering an area of 150 caballerias (5,000 acres) in the days before the turn of the twentieth century. It was divided after his father's death among three siblings. The 50 caballerias (1600 acres) of Papá Lorenzo were the most fertile; irrigated constantly by the floods produced by the *Río Lempa.*

The jeep led us through some switchback curves into the forest, and several times Papá Lorenzo had to use the high-pitched jeep horn to alert the children of the mountain peasants of our approach. Their job was to open the wooden slam gates that marked the different properties that we had to cross. Their reward was a nickel coin. The children ran with enthusiasm to open the fences that sometimes were made of simply a tangle of sticks bound with barbed wire. Sometimes we would meet a group of three or four children, some with large tummies full of worms and others completely naked and barefoot. They would emerge suddenly out of the forest like little curious elves without a home. The forest was so dense in some parts that no houses were visible from the road.

Soon after, we arrived at a famous ravine that during the winter was almost impassable. On the other side rose a steep rise that we called *La Cuesta del Conejo,* because the mountain looked like a rabbit's back haunches or it might have been the spot where rabbits roamed. Here we routinely got off the jeep to rest our stiff bones and numb muscles from sitting for hours on end.

Papá Lorenzo took the opportunity to have another drink followed by an *embajador,* sans filter. Alicita and Mamá Lila remained sitting in the jeep rearranging their scarves and dusting off their *cutis.* At this traditionally scheduled stop, Neto and I enjoyed running down to the brook at the bottom of the ravine to explore its waters. We would observe at the bottom of the crystal water, still visible by the dimmed light of the yet to disappear sunset. There under the pebbles, there were nervous little fish that swam in little dark clouds we liked to poke with a stick to watch them frantically disperse as if birds disrupted out of a tree. This rest also allowed the driver to engage the jeep's 4x4-transmission by shifting two small floor gear sticks without which the jeep could not climb *La Cuesta del Conejo.*

Already too dark, Papá Lorenzo bellowed at us to come back to the jeep. To finally ready the jeep, he asked us to complete the last task before leaving. Neto and I had to walk to the front of the jeep to manually inspect the front tires and remove any obstacle on the path we could muster with our thin arms. Even with the aid of the double transmission and the mountain pinion, at times, when the jeep was too heavy full of supplies that Mamá Lila brought to her shop at the hacienda, the jeep couldn't go up. Neto, Alicita, and I would have to cross the brook, knee deep, and hike up the steep hill to lighten the load.

At the other side of the mountains with its two peaks that we call the *cubiletes*, we were awestruck by the view of the enchanted valley as we started the descent down the other side of the ravine. The night was already thick and the screeching of the crickets and cicadas and other innumerable fauna sounds in this summer night made it clear that the city was now well behind us. The landscape, even though already obscure, sparkled with a few yellowish lights that fluttered from the great valley called *e Jícaro,* and reflected on the waters of *el río Lempa.* Some lights emanated from campesinos' oil lamps and wax candles, others, much stronger but still yellowish, came from the low-voltage light bulbs powered by a gasoline generator. These bulbs were the ones that illuminated the family compound of the hacienda.

The generator only worked for about two hours during the night, almost always at dinnertime. Today it had been working much longer waiting for the patrons. The campesinos enjoyed looking up to the *cubiletes* from the *jícaro* valley to watch the bright headlights of the jeep and the cone of shadows and reflections in its wake. The beams of light would zigzag in the switchback curves, totally disappearing in the dense forest only to reappear later farther down the descent. The *cubiletes* became alive with its incandescence that projected its power and protection to the inhabitants of the compound. The jeep's gradual downward spiraling oscillation through the mountain alerted the entire population of the valley that the *patrón* was about to enter through the main hacienda's gate.

The jeep's headlights lit the trees in front of us, producing long shadows and black images that could scare the bravest child in these black nights. At present, those passengers with a weak stomach vomited what they had eaten or drunk at the stop next to the ravine before climbing the *La Cuesta del Conejo*. Later, tired and anxious, when the barking and howling of the dogs that abounded in the houses of the campesinos increased and became less distant, and the road softened, we knew that it was a short time before we'd reach the main gate of the house.

Just before crossing it, we heard the cheers of the forest children who jumped off their perches to meet the jeep, no matter the time of night, and ran in a stampede racing to see who'd make the five cents after opening the main large mahogany gate first. The gate, a little bit eaten away by beetles, opened to the magnificent driveway lined with native fig trees, leading up to the mansion. At the foot of the front porch, four young campesinos waited and later rushed to meet us with their sombreros in their hands and started unloading the *tanates* from our laps and from between our feet. Now that I remember, I think I sat down on one of those *tanates* all the way from the city. They began taking the rest of the store supplies, hardware parts, suitcases, and one tank of gasoline, making a pile on the front steps of the mansion as one of the porters approached Papá Lorenzo.

"Good evening, Don Lorenzo," the porter said, taking off his hat and bowing slightly.

"Good evening, Magdaleno," exclaimed Papá Lorenzo, getting out of the jeep, "How are things around?"

"Well, they're going well, but yesterday the train killed two cows and we didn't have time to castrate the three Zebu bulls you told us to do," answered Magdaleno in a tone of concern as if he had committed some crime.

"Well, let's see what we can do about that train, and as for the other unfinished tasks, you have to complete what I have told you to do. You are the manager of the hacienda and you have to manage it well when I am not here," growled Papá Lorenzo, ending with a spit over the railing of the front steps.

"Forgive me, Don Lorenzo. I will not let things be un-fulfilled. Now, the campesinos have been waiting for you since midday for their monthly salary. Some are already half-drunk, others have been sleeping under the fig tree," Magdaleno added nervously adjusting the belt of his *corvo* and his *cuma* so the two blades settled evenly on his hip.

"Let's go to the window, and tell Juanito to prepare the monthly *pisto* for the men."

While they paid the campesinos, we finally entered the house, cutting through the long lines, and received a sea of greetings as the campesinos lifted their hats in our di-rection. The house was rectangular, with two long corridors; one on the north and the other on the south side of the house, each bordered by a green, waist-high, wooden fence, with a gate in the middle. The south corri-dor faced the stables, the north one the large lush patio, with a stone pathway in the middle that one had to walk through at night to reach the spacious outhouse. This pa-tio was covered with tall tropical fruit trees which opened, just beyond the outer barbed-wire fence, to a large vegeta-ble garden.

We dreaded going to the outhouse in the middle of the night. We had to carry a flickering oil lamp, the small flame always on the verge of extinction under the pressure of the slightest breeze. The fluctuation created an eerie puppet light show of moving, frightening shadows, which we thought to be ghosts ready to squeeze our necks.

One night, Alicita, scared of the dark, woke me late at night to accompany her to the outhouse. As we approached the gate to the patio, I heard the *lechuza's* eerie raspy screech. Instead of a quite hoot, the barn owls of the hacienda sounded more like a woman screaming in the dark about to be brutally murdered. It seemed also that the *masacuata* that lived between the ceiling and the roof rattled its tail more fervently, and that the crickets increased their deafening chirping. We opened the gate and walked down the five steps that led to the patio. Here, Alicita, terrified by the sounds of the night, grabbed me intensely and closely with her right arm, while her left hand carried the oil lamp as we started our slow walk towards the outhouse. At times, she let go of me to block the sudden gusts of wind from surrounding the wick that threatened to go out.

Our first destination was the aboveground *pila de agua*. This had a tiled roof and a middle high partition wall, that started just above the surface, to separate us from the other half used as a drinking trough for our horses and oxen and hid us from the campesinos that frequently walked by the fig tree just outside the outhouse.

On our side, servants used the cold pool's water to do the washing, and Neto and I used it for our daily shower with a metal *huacal* full of soapy water. The outhouse was attached to one end of the rectangular pool. We kept walking slowly. I noticed that Alicita had tightened her grip around my shoulders. I felt suffocated but did not dare to pull away. Rather, I decided to increase the speed of my steps until we finally reached the pool. As we reached the door of the outhouse a smoky gray formation with a human face appeared to manifest out from the middle of the pool, and, in unison, Alicita and I produced the most hair-raising scream that could have woken the dead. We saw the spirit dancing with abrupt upswing movements before speedily moving towards us and it soon enveloped us, ready to suck our souls to the bottom of the pool and the underworld. A sulfuric odor soaked our nostrils. Uncontrollably shaking, Alicita and I, with increasingly louder screams, turned around and started running on the stone pathway back to the house.

Papá Lorenzo stood on the north corridor with his pistol drawn, ready to kill. Neto hid behind him expecting an intruder to suddenly appear through the immense elephant ears foliage of the Colocasia plant that bordered the pathway. The servants had already run from their quarters, which stood next to the stables. They reached the east corridor by going around the house, to avoid crossing the main dormitories, and huddled in a corner by the entrance of the dining room. Alicita and I had dropped the oil lamp, already extinguished, into the pool before fleeing and in the darkness had decided to run towards a bright light that suddenly had appeared at the east corridor's gate.

"Stop and don't move or I'll shoot you dead right where you stand!" Papá Lorenzo bellowed as we came running.

¡Somos nosotros; no dispare! Alicita and I yelled, assuring Papá Lorenzo that it was none other than his daughter and nephew.

Everybody gathered around us to hear the story of the malevolent spirit, but before we could barely finish, Papá Lorenzo ordered everybody to go back to bed immediately. That night we went pipi in the chamber pot.

The logical explanation was that we had become so scared of the shadows of the night that when the oil lamp's fumes were carried by the breeze over the water's surface, we mistook them as a face, a spirit, coming out of the water. This was a perfect example of panic caused by fear that was based on an illusion, not on real danger. A perfect psychological feedback loop: a fear spread from Alicita to me and vice-versa. Such loops have been well documented in birds, mice, cats, and rhesus monkeys.

No matter the realistic explanation, from that night on, Alicita never walked to the outhouse, using her small chamber pot instead. I decided to just walk to the fence to pee through its railings, and during that school vacation, I never went to the bathroom again during the night, although Alicita begged me sometimes to accompany her.

Our panic that night could also be understood as an extension of the hacienda's cultural context, where the supernatural explains the unexplainable. At night, the sound of an oval rock rolling across the floor tiles would wake us up. As big as a medium-sized watermelon, they had brought it from the river years ago to use as a doorstop to keep the door to the master bedroom open during the day. The rock would roll in the dark from beside the closed door, gradually gaining momentum, until it reached the center of the room. From there, it would roll back toward the front of the room until, with a great, resounding blow, it would slam into the wooden door and stop. What does the spirit that moves that rock want to tell us? We would ask ourselves that question the next day. Maybe there is treasure hidden under this house.

It occurred to Lorencito one day that he wanted to speak to that spirit. He stayed up all night waiting to hear the rock roll. As soon as he heard it, he turned his flashlight on, grabbed the gun from the nightstand just in case, focused the light on the source of the noise, and saw that the stone had stopped in the middle of the bedroom as if sensing that it had been discovered. With a sense of dread, he silently turned off the flashlight. The moment the room went dark, Lorencito heard the rock resume its path back toward the door, again producing its sinister knock, and he rushed back to bed. The next day, to check, he observed that the rock was in its usual place against the closed door. The supernatural, the spirits, the ghosts, the apparitions, the belief that there is a parallel world that we do not see, but sometimes we feel, played fundamental

roles, not only in the hacienda, but throughout my childhood.

The south corridor of the house looked more like a
large porch and faced a large patio with no vegetation,
used by horses, cows, carts with oxen, and open to the
campesinos. This patio was always dusty and hot because
it lacked trees, and we considered it to be the backyard of
the house. The horses were always prepared and saddled,
tied to the posts adjacent to the porch. Our daily riding
trips started from this corridor.

The main house had no modern implements. There
was only an external pipe that fed the kitchen and one
corridor with a faucet of fresh water brought from the tank
built at the base of *los cubiletes* that collected water from
a natural spring. All its furnishings -the huge armoires of
each room, the bureaus, the night tables, the trunks, the
chairs, the credenzas, -seemed to have been hand-made
by family ancestors from the same sawn wood, the same
mahogany trees that grew in the *cubiletes*. The three-foot-
thick walls of the house were built of adobe in 1860, Papá
Lorenzo had told us.

That night, as was the custom for all first nights at the
hacienda, the dinner was especially succulent. Multiple
dishes were served with an abundant supply of cheeses
and cream, fried beans, a tray of sauce dishes, olive oil,
and a basket full of warm tortillas. The beans were regularly eaten with Salvadorian cream and hard cheese; the
sauces were used for the salad and meats. The hacienda
diet did not include exotic spices or chilies. Food flavor
came from the garden herbs, mostly cilantro and parsley,
combined with plenty of onions and a great deal of garlic.
Neto and I ate an average of five thick, soft, warm tortillas
per meal. After dinner, the dining room table was cleared
and the *terratenientes* of neighboring haciendas, like Alfredo Pacas, sometimes including their wives and children,
arrived in their Land Rovers to join us, especially to play
poker for hours on end.

After dinner, Neto and I ran down the corridor to claim one of the new hammocks. While the adults played poker, we were entrusted with the RCA Victrola that needed to be wound by hand. The bottom draw of the Victrola contained 1930s, 1940s, and some 1950s hard and thick graphite 78-rpm RCA records, mostly in Spanish, but some in English. There was an ample supply of thick needles that we needed to change often because the heavy records would be played continuously all night wearing down the points.

Papá Lorenzo had brought 20 new records this time. The list was full of *rancheras,* some tangos, and some *boleros,* but the audience in the hacienda couldn't get enough of *rancheras,* or rather, the Mexican country songs. The records featured Pedro Infante, Jorge Negrete, Los Tres Reyes, Los Panchos, Los Dandies, and Alicita's favorite, Lola Beltrán and one year later Neto would bring one of Elvis Presley's records, the 1960 hit "It's *now or never"* and Paul Anka's 1959 hit, "Lonely Boy."

From the dining room, the poker players would shout out their requests, and Neto and I would skip to their desired record and, later into the night, some requesters, already very tipsy, would forget about their dealt hand, and would start singing, until soon all would join in. Papá Lorenzo's favorites were Hace un Año: Hace *un año que yo tuve una ilusión, hace un año que se cumple en este día, me recuerda que en tus brazos me dormía y que inocente muy confiado te entregué mi corazón,* Papá Lorenzo would sing, provoking heated jealous murmurs by Mamá Lila who knew he was remembering one of his several mistresses. Later in the night, a heavy discussion would ensue about whose turn it was next. Lorencito, Neto's older brother by 10 years and in love with Merceditas, played the guitar and sat next to us to sing along with the love *boleros* of Los Panchos:

"Cerca del mar yo me enamoré y como la luna, la brisa y la espuma también te besé..."

"Sin ti no podré vivir jamás y pensar que nunca más estarás junto a mí..."

"Ódiame por piedad, yo te lo pido, ódiame sin medida ni clemencia, odio quiero más que indiferencia porque el rencor hiere menos que el olvido..."

"¡Ay! Amor ya no me quieras tanto, ya no sufras más por mí..."

"Usted es la culpable de todas mis angustias y todos mis quebrantos"

"...Sí alma mía, la gloria eres tú."

✳✳✳

Several years later, after having taken my vows, publicly announced my vocation as a servant to God, and assumed the black cossack tied at the waist with a banded blue fascia, ---the blue color indicating that I was still a seminarian and not an ordained parish priest --- as my daily uniform, I came back one Sunday to the hacienda as a member of the Bishop's entourage. But this time the festive atmosphere was accented by religious music, commotion, and plenty of food, and not by boleros and rum. Mamá Lila directed all the maids and cooks to arrange long tables with spring flowers and long white table cloth in the corridor to accommodate such a large group. She was very proud of me.

Neto came to the Bishop's palace to pick us up in a new Willys Jeep to drive us to the hacienda following the same rode we had taken so many times before as children. He examined my attire with great surprise and hugged me without uttering a sound out of respect to the cossack and fear of triggering an improper conversation, risking the offense of my religious sensitivities.

I sat in the back and the bishop sat next to Neto in front. The other members of the Bishop's entourage took the train to the *Laguneta* station that served the hacienda. That Sunday we celebrated mass in the chapel Mamá Lila had built years before next to the elementary school for the campesinos. I helped the Bishop baptize 100 children of the same campesinos that had seen me grow up. I found myself assuming a more dignified posture as I helped in the religious ceremony with extra devotion, as to assure the people, who had known me as a child, understood I was seriously committed to becoming a priest. That day they could not relate to me as they once did. I was up there, untouchable, so close, and yet, so distant as a messenger of God; most of them probably thinking, *"ese es el niño Chepito, el hijo de la niña Rosita, se va a hacer cura. ¿Quién lo hubiera podido pensar?"*

✳✳✳

The following morning, Magdaleno, using a metal rod, hit the train rail that hung from a ceiling beam in the south corridor exactly at 4:00 am every day, producing a loud clanging that reverberated throughout the Hacienda waking up even the heaviest of sleepers. Neto and I got up and walked to the corral after washing our faces in the ceramic sink Papá Lorenzo had recently installed in the hallway of the north corridor. The corral expanded behind the stables. Its entrance stood to the side of them. A wall made of large boulders, that had been brought years before from the *cubiletes,* surrounded it. Here, barbed wire would have been useless because the *toro* that lived in the corral would have ripped through it easily in moments of passion or anger. Once there was a *toro* that broke even through the rock wall, forcing Papá Lorenzo to thicken the wall with more rocks. We loved to go every morning before breakfast to sit on the stones of the wall to watch the milking of cows, and at times, a campesino would ask us for help. We were terrified of the *toro* and would ask them to secure it far away from us before helping.

The campesinos taught us to tie the calf to the mother's hind legs so it couldn't reach her udders during the milking. There were 250 cows to milk by hand. It would take two hours, from 4:00 am to 6:00 am, to milk the cows. As a reward for our labors, we would drink a couple of glasses of warm milk fresh from the cow. The rest of the milk was promptly poured into 100-liter metal canisters to be transported by oxen carts to the train station of *La Laguneta*: destination Santa Ana. The milk was sold to the *Lopez y Lopez* distributor, the largest of the nation. I don't remember the milk being refrigerated on its transport to the city, unless the train had a refrigerated wagon, which I doubt. Nobody, however, got sick from drinking it just the way it was.

During the first full day of our summer vacation on the family *hacienda* this year, we lingered around the corral until a maid appeared behind us to announce that breakfast was being served. We headed to the dining room crossing the courtyard of the stables and noticed that the horses were already saddled and tied to the hitching rail. There were two hitching rails outside the south corridor. We crossed the corridor, opened the main door of the dormitories, making sure we did not trip over the rock, and without making much noise because Alicita always slept late, opened the door that led to the north corridor on the other side of the house. The dining room was long and stood at the north end, forming one of the corners of the rectangle. There was another narrow and long corridor at the shorter side of the rectangle that connected the dining room to an antique, large kitchen where meals were cooked in an enormous firewood stove.

To serve the hot meals, the servers had to walk from the kitchen and down this corridor with a floor of uneven and unpolished red thick clay tiles that could easily make anybody stumble. These porous tiles kept the temperature of the corridor very cool. It also had a permanent smell of dairy because Mamá Lila used this corridor to curd the milk when making the cheeses. The dining room, in a corner of the triangular house, had two doors, one facing the

narrow corridor that led to the kitchen and the other facing the north corridor. Each of the other two walls of the
dining room had a wide window with a metal screen, one
facing the lush patio and the other the barn and the workers quarters. The doors were also protected by metal
screens.

A cool breeze always blew from the corridors through
the doors and out the windows. I do not know if this
stream of fresh air was designed on purpose by the ma-
sons who made the house, or if the breeze just appeared
by chance, but the truth was that the dining room contained the freshest cool air in the house. That is why, on
hot summer nights, men would play poker in the dining
room.

This morning, when we reached the dining room, Papá
Lorenzo was already sitting at the head of the table. The
criada was also already coming across the narrow corridor
with steaming trays of scrambled egg dishes, fried black
beans, cheeses and cream, a basket of tortillas, ripe bana-
nas, hot coffee, and milk.

"Good morning, boys," said Papá Lorenzo. He glanced
up in our direction while pouring hot, frothed milk into a
cup of steaming coffee that the chef had prepared by pouring boiling water through a cloth filter containing ground
coffee that had just been toasted over the *comal.*

"Good morning," we replied.

"I think that Toño already saddled us several horses.
You know that Ciclón is mine. You work it out amongst
yourselves about who rides *Celaje* and *la Gallina*. Please,
leave *Satélite* alone. That horse almost killed Toño the
other day on one of his runaways. Toño thought it was the
end of his days on this earth. What stopped *Satélite* was
when he decided to gallop through the corn fields. Hitting
the husks slowed him down."

Consulting a list written in a notebook, he continued.

"We have to go and see how the work on the *pista* is
going, since that *zarza* has to be pulled out as soon as

possible to be able to plant rice, which is our new grain crop. It's the new productive method that your brother Lorenzo learned during his studies in Honduras. Right now, he is driving the tractor. He is very into it. He has been already working from six in the morning".

Papá Lorenzo took a sip of coffee before continuing.

"After that, we will go to see the sugar cane fields because the workers have already begun to cut it and I don't know if we'll have enough oxen carts to take the canes to the *molienda*. They may have to make multiple trips. Then, we must go to the river and take a look at the spot where the train killed the cows. I want to see how that happened. I don't want the damn train to keep killing my cattle. Finally, we will have lunch next to the river in the same place as always, under the Ceiba, at the *matalté* pool. I already told Magdaleno to send a rider with our lunch to the river by noon. Remember that soon we have to do a bovine, ovine and equine census. Let's start with the horses, many have been born this year and they walk in wild herds throughout the hacienda. We will have to go out on horseback to drive them to the corral. For that I will need the help of many *colonos*.

Finally, after taking a bite of a soft, warm tortilla, he finished his overview of the day's agenda telling us,

"Go wake up Alicita and ask her if she wants to come with us. We may have to saddle another horse. At the end of the day, when we get back, you must go help Magdaleno geld the bulls, we need more oxen to pull our carts."

"*Si, Señor*," we replied, knowing very well that Papá Lorenzo's word was always final.

At the end of breakfast, I walked up to the stables to talk to Toño, the *corralero*.

"I see that you saddled three horses. We're leaving soon", I said."

"Which one did you want, *niño* Chepito?" he said. "I prepared *Celaje* for you with no saddle. One thing, this time you have to be more careful than ever, because

Celaje, being a thoroughbred, likes to run a lot and nowadays he has become more unfriendly. I hope you didn't forget how to ride a horse. They don't teach that in el Colegio," he said, chuckling amiably.

"Well, okay, I hope Neto is not bothered by riding *La Gallina.* He is moody and gets stuck in the mud easily. He may want to snatch Celaje away from me. I would ride *Satélite,* but Papá Lorenzo put him out of commission," I commented adjusting the small hunting knife I had already tied to my belt. Neto had decided to take the Winchester .22-caliber rifle that he never let me borrow.

Papá Lorenzo always had to ride a very tall muscular Quarter horse, with its head held high, standing at attention, and with hair grayer than white. *Ciclón,* his new horse, was the only one who could support the 250 pounds of his rider. Papá Lorenzo's other horses were also thoroughbreds: *Emperador* and *Principe,* but they both were already too old to ride. Before giving *Ciclón* a free rein, Papá Lorenzo took a regal look around as if waiting for the campesinos to bow upon his passage. Using his western style cowboy spurs, he jabbed *Ciclón* into a fast trot. Alicita didn't come.

Mamá Lila, who had come out on the railing of the south corridor to say goodbye, yelled to her husband: *Tengan cuidado. ¡Qué Dios los bendiga!*

In no time, we were all three already riding our horses, each of us with our hats and spurs. We were born to ride. At first, we rode in the arms of our older cousins as infants, then on the horse's haunches behind them with a small burlap sack as padding, next, on our own horse, bareback, as many campesino children do.

With no saddle, the horse's sweat and ours, after a few hours, mixed into our trousers. When we dismounted at the river, Neto and I realized that our pants were heavy and sticky. We didn't have any other clothes to change into. The sweat soon dried up, as if somebody had ironed them using starch. The stiffness of our trousers scraped the tender skin of our buttocks and groin. Avoiding contact with the stiff fabric, we walked slightly bow-legged once off the saddle. We undressed completely, no need to be modest in la *hacienda,* and ran to dive straight down into the deep pool, called *Matalté* by the natives, a spectacular lush section of the *río Lempa,* covered by an immense *ceiba* tree. The cold *Lempa* waters had the same delicious impact on our hot bodies as those ice coffee lattes have in a humid summer day in Boston. Neto and I were not yet ready for the monumental rite of passage of owning our own saddle that would be made to our measurements and specifications. This would come later, signaling the first step towards young adulthood and beyond childhood. When this rite was passed, we would be considered young men who deserved respect and admiration from the campesinos of the hacienda and their daughters.

Later, Teto, war survivor, would tell me that the tradition of going to the hacienda for three months during school vacation continued in my absence years later after I left to join the Seminary. During those years, Teto, Rafael, and Pirri took turns with the horses and the one who most excelled in riding them was Rafael. Over the course of one of those summers, he became very adept at imitating the Apache move of the western movies when the Indian continues firing his rifle at high speed while riding his horse sideways, hidden from the view of the white cowboys. Rafael also spent hours practicing his jump from the high rail of the south corridor directly onto the saddle, imitating a cowboy escaping from the saloon, by pushing the swinging cantina doors open and with one jump, landing on top of his saddle and riding away. *Celaje* was by then old and not easily startled.

In our time, we were not allowed to carry pistols, but we were content with the hunting knives and the Winchester rifle that Neto held with his right hand, resting its stock on his right leg. We also knew that we rode the best horses of the stable. Papá Lorenzo told us that *Celaje* was of Peruvian breed, and that La *Gallina* was Arabian.

We started our workday with a trot, making the horses dance. *Celaje*, with his whisky-colored hair, danced sideways. I firmly restrained him by tightening the reins around his neck, if not, he would suddenly jump into a gallop. *La Gallina*, on the other hand, danced with less elegance. The wind shook our white shirts, made of fresh cotton and long sleeves, and from time to time threatened to snatch away our hats and extinguish the match in Papá Lorenzo's hand for the third time as he tried to light a smoke.

Alongside the *pista*, as the path became flat, we heard the loud motor of the tractor and saw at a distance Lorencito pulling a tall, thorny shrub, a thick chaparral, out of the soil. A crew of muscled, shirtless campesinos was unraveling a thick, heavy, steel chain from the shrub's trunk. After, the crew moved quickly to chain another shrub. The young men cut the branches into short pieces with their machetes and threw them into an ox cart, which made trips to unload them in the middle of a field where they would dry in the sun for a few months. Later, the campesinos would use them as firewood for cooking in their straw huts.

Sometimes the roots of a thorny large shrub went deeper than expected and the tractor's front wheel would tip backwards to dangerous levels, forcing Lorencito to switch to a lower gear. Lorencito worked 10 hours daily removing the thorny bushes from the *pista,* and by the end of the school vacation it was ready for planting rice at the start of the rainy season in May.

The thick layer of fine dust softened the path we were riding on, the horses' racing instincts heightened, and already frustrated from being restrained, made strong intermittent sudden impulses to start a gallop. We heeded this body language and gave them free rein. "Let's see who gets to the creek faster at the end of the *pista*," Neto shouted. At this moment, we raised our chins and took a deep breath, dazzled by the yellowish grassland that ended at the ravine towards the south side of the river Lempa, and towards the north, at the train tracks. To gallop at full speed, I took my hat off with my left hand and used it to hit *Celaje's* back haunches repeatedly to incite his speed further. We never used crops to whip our horses. Neto, encumbered with the rifle, let his hat flop from around his neck, using his left hand for the reins and his spurs to encourage *La Gallina.*

After climbing a short hill, one could see, in the foreground, another extensive meadow, and cornfields, crisscrossed by streams and narrow trails. These cornfields were bordered by a large plain, with brown spots scattered across its golden surface: cattle grazing on the other side of the *pista.* Far, almost at the end of it all, on the other side of the river, there was an area of very low hills and bald sierras that didn't belong to the hacienda, but to *el Obrajuelo,* the hacienda de *los Chemises,* Papá Lorenzo's nephews. Farther beyond into the horizon, lofty mountains, with large green patches and gloomy canyons, could be seen, and, finally, still further ahead, bluish peaks, and a diaphanous horizon that stretched into Guatemala and marked the border with El Salvador.

We experienced the most ecstatic moments of our early youth when we were galloping on our horses. The closest to it, I imagine, would be flying like an eagle. Some days *Celaje* won, and on others, *La Gallina.* Just before reaching the ravine, half-dried at this time of year, we had to bring the horses to a slow canter to calm them down. Soon, they started to snort, with their mouths foaming and their sides caked with sweat. We found a leafy tree to protect us from the sun and waited for Papá Lorenzo to catch up.

We dismounted and took advantage of these moments for Neto to find game to hunt. No snooty *chiltota,* haughty dove, and sleepy iguana that could have been on the branch of some nearby Ceiba, escaped his rifle bullets. Despite his young age, he had excellent marksmanship. Where he rested his eyes, there he sent his .22 caliber bullets. Sometimes, he mounted his horse to shoot, to give him better height and view. The horse stood still, and Neto synced his breathing with his, firing just before inhaling. At other times, he had to wait for the horse to calm down for a long time, after our fast gallop, before shooting, only to have the horse spoil the shot in the last moment when he decided to adjust his legs just as he pulled the trigger.

Most of the hacienda encompassed the great valley of the Lempa River: about 30 *caballerías*. The *cubiletes* and other mountains bordered it to the south. The grassland was the most fertile and 250 cows, 10 bulls, and 100 horses grazed on it. The grassland was constantly irrigated by the Río Lempa and multiple brooks that fed into it from the *cubiletes*. At the start of the grassland, there was an oasis with a spring of crystal-clear water surrounded by coconut, palm, orange, lemon, and banana trees that we called *La Finquita*. The humidity level and the high air quality of this spot I haven't found anywhere else except in botanical gardens around the US. On the way back, we stopped here, as was our routine, so the horses could rest and eat as we explored the area. Our high cowboy boots, made of leather, protected us from the dangers of the deadly *Coral* snake, also known as the most poisonous snake in Central America.

In short, *Los Apoyos* was the most fertile, rich and beautiful hacienda of the region. It produced all kinds of crops: maize (500 loads), beans, peanuts, rice, sorghum, and, of course, coffee. The sugar cane field was immense and kept the sugar mill, *la molienda,* grinding day and night during the month of December and January. Thousands of *atados de panela*, many 100-liter aluminum milk containers, and other agricultural products were taken every day at six in the morning to the train station, *La Laguneta*, in the direction of Santa Ana, where buyers bought them. This was how Papá Lorenzo made his fortune, which gave him ample resources to keep his daughters studying in the USA and Europe, and his eldest son, Lorencito, in Honduras at the school Zamorano of agronomy. There were still no plans for Neto or me, but Papá Lorenzo used to say that we both would go to Argentina, as his brother Gonzalo had done, to study agronomy and learn about cattle ranching in the immensity of the pampas down there. These summers spent in the Hacienda become happier every time I remember them.

One day on our way back from the river, Neto and I got into a fight over the rifle. I felt like punching him on the face, but Papá Lorenzo was trotting just behind us, so I decided to leave him behind instead. I got up, quickly mounted Celaje, and I galloped toward the house. Celaje was tireless and sensing that the moment of returning to the stables was near, he put much more energy into his gallop and became a runaway horse traversing the *pista*.

I used the maximum of my strength to restrain him without success. He ignored my commands. I began to pray to God to make *Celaje* realize that he needed to stop before arriving at the house. There is no greater danger for a rider than a runaway horse because almost always the rider goes flying over the horse's head onto the ground in the end. If he is lucky, he doesn't hit his head on the rocks, but instead falls gently onto a flat area covered by several inches of dust, but I had no idea if luck was smiling upon me that day. I hung on tightly to the mane of *Celaje*, pressing my legs against his chest and lowering my head and neck onto his neck.

I glued my body against his and disappeared from view. A casual bystander would have seen a lone horse galloping at full speed across the *pista*. I wanted to make my body another part of *Celaje* so that he wouldn't buck and suddenly throw me. We jumped many fences and walls dividing different regions of the hacienda, as if we were in an Olympic obstacle course. I was not a jumping expert, and I didn't do anything. I just grabbed his mane with my two hands and hung on for dear life. I don't remember what I did with the reins.

For a moment, I saw a vision of myself tangled all bloody within the barbed wire fences. I prayed to God that wouldn't be my fate. There was a brief moment when a band of wild horses with their dominant mares joined in the fun and the rumble and their cloud of dust scared me even more. My legs began to tremble. *I am going to die*, I thought. One hundred meters before arriving at the house, *Celaje* decided to crazily increase his speed even further; he knew that plenty of hay was waiting for him. Now I was in a state of panic. But no, the thick stone wall of the corral frightened Celaje and at the last moment he decided not to jump it, and with a quick turn to the right he avoided it and ran alongside it, and then I sat up, arched my back, and pulled the reins again to restrain him. This worked, little by little, until *Celaje* came to a full stop.

I had heard stories of horses dropping dead after an incident such as this, but *Celaje* kept snorting, foaming, breathing unnaturally heavy for a few long minutes. I did not ride *Celaje* after that for a very long time. Nobody did.

❋❋❋

One day, that same summer, the muffled sounds of a .45 caliber pistol attracted the attention of a group of campesinos working on the outhouse patio, but they didn't make anything of it. The sounds of gunshots were not unusual around the compound at this early hour since Lorencito often stepped outside of the vegetable garden to practice his skills. This was the same vegetable garden where, 6 years earlier, I had fired my first shot. My father, most likely drunk at that time, stood behind me, helped me hold the pistol with my two hands, and with his help I pulled the trigger. Before walking to the *pista* to start driving the tractor, Lorencito would insert thin sticks at a 100-

meter distance, upright on the ground, and shoot at them while kneeling with one leg bent up and resting the Colt Python double-action .357 Magnum revolver six-shooter pistol on his right knee. He had become famous throughout the county for his shooting stunts and winning bets against his Menendez cousins. They couldn't fathom how Lorencito would magically put a bullet through the thinnest of sticks and keep the wood intact, without knocking them over, and leave the tiniest of bullet holes.

Neto and I were eating breakfast when we heard the distinct gunshot, but doubted that it had come out of a pistol and concluded that it had to have come from the crackling firewood of the kitchen stove. We continued eating our refried black beans with cream on top.

Just as I swallowed a sweet piece of fried, ripe plantain, we heard the haunting scream of a maid that had gone to the *pila* to start the daily wash. She ran, traversed the stone path in no time, stopped at the steps leading to the north corridor, and screamed. We heard her cry coming through the dining room windows, which were always kept open. "Don Lorenzo! Don Lorenzo! Don Lorenzo!" She kept repeating.

We stood up and ran to the middle of the corridor only to encounter a dozen people already congregated there and some running towards the outhouse. Alicita was the first to arrive to find Papá Lorenzo still breathing lying on the outhouse floor. He died seconds later. He had shot his gun against his chest, right through the heart. Later we learned that his doctor had diagnosed him with terminal cirrhosis just before leaving the city and had given him three months of life. Neto and I couldn't comprehend the finality of his act. Neto told me many years later that he recalls going into a state of shock and couldn't hear people's screams of pain, and that he felt like he was walking on a cloud or a floor covered with a thick carpet of cotton balls upon hearing that his Papá was dead. I reacted with deep silence to the entire event and to the pain of the family. I only remember standing next to Neto without uttering any words, but sensing he needed me next to him all the time. I don't remember ever seeing Papá Lorenzo's dead body.

That school vacation ended abruptly. The jeep made its last trip of the season back to the city with Papá Lorenzo's body. The family took the train back to the city. It was the week before our 1959 Christmas celebration. The family, in deep mourning, decided to celebrate absolutely nothing. I got off the train and took the bus to Chalchuapa to Papá Rafa's house, where my father had brought us when we first returned from Guatemala. My mother took only Rafael, my brother, to Papá Lorenzo's funeral because he was feeling sick as usual and started to cry as my mother was about to leave. If not, my mother wouldn't have taken any of us. Funerals were not for children.

I went to Santa Ana three days later to spend time with Neto. The Menendez-Castro family had decided to mourn Papá Lorenzo's death in solitude in a private island off the eastern coast of El Salvador, in el *Cuco*. There, we ate iguana's eggs, and tons of turtles' eggs, and watermelons, and kept hunting, and swam in the ocean, and traveled by *Cayucos* around different small islands. One night, I burned my right arm with a Coleman lamp that tipped over while traveling in one of those *Cayucos*. Alicita showered me with undue attention to heal my burn as if to do something good, as if good acts would help her make sense of Papá Lorenzo's death. Neto, the youngest and the most pampered, cried at night, deeply affected with a sense of abandonment. Papá Lorenzo did not get a chance to read Neto's excellent school report card, his reward would have been a jeep, his first one. Alicita and her single sisters got drunk, as did Lorencito every night. Mamá Lila was inconsolable and shut herself away in the innermost room of the island house the entire month, dressed totally in black, *luto entero,* in permanent praying. Papá Lorenzo's death unleashed a downhill gravitational force that pull down the family in all facets of its life. His clear vision of life accompanied with the strongest of personalities and determined authority could never be replicated by any other member of the family, not even by the ones traditionally assigned to the task, the males of the house: Lorenzo and Neto.

During the year of mourning dictated by the Catholic Church, the Menendez-Castro family plunged aimlessly into constant despair and absolute dysfunction. The fact that Papá Lorenzo did not leave a written testament contributed greatly to the disarray. The family expected Lorencito to carry the baton, but he, either due to his inexperienced youth and not having been properly formed by his father to take such a magnus undertaking -- the administration of a thriving multi-million *hacienda*-- or to Papa Lorenzo's overpowering personality, which did not ever permit Lorencito to have the chance to assume serious responsibilities at the hacienda, found alcohol to be the perfect escape from it all, terrified by the knowledge that he couldn't ever fit in his father's shoes. *"Qué putas sabía yo en aquel tiempo, yo tenía apenas 24 años,"* Lorencito told me last year when I asked him about that time.

The single sisters, Alicita, Martita, and Elsita found solace with a spiritist charlatan who came to town announcing that he could speak to the spirit of Papá Lorenzo to ask him about his wishes after his death, and to other roaming spirits and entities in the house, and that he could foretell the future. Elenita and Martita, who I met recently in Santa Ana, told me that they wanted to know through the *espiritista* if Papá Lorenzo was blackmailed by enemies to end his life. Elsita particularly became fascinated with secret societies like the *Rosacruces*. Nightly séances were conducted at the Menéndez-Castro house that ended with Ouija sessions. Mamá Lila, grief-stricken, became overprotected of Lorencito, who took the role of the man of the house, greatly ignored her daughters who soon started also to engage in risky behavior with young men and use high dosage of alcohol. All this was a perfect formula for disaster. This is the way the year 1959 ended and the 1960 started. It took less than 30 years for the Menéndez-Castro fortune to dwindle to almost nothing. Neto endured the pain and with great efforts and frequent interruptions became a lawyer. Such a tragic sequence of events is not uncommon. Families can lose great fortunes in a blink of an eye, as mine did.

Chapter 19: Puebla II

The same year Gustavo and I met Elsita and Gloria, we asked the rector of the Seminary in Puebla for permission to enroll in night courses at the Colegio Benavente to obtain a teaching license. This was encouraged by the Catholic Church to staff their numerous catholic schools with highly qualified seminarians, were they to decide to take a year off from their studies to perform community service, and also it was thought to help seminarians to emulate Jesus, the *maestro par excellence*. Gustavo and I, enticed by the newly discovered outside world and its pagan pleasures, left the Seminary compound twice per week with permission by the rector to take pedagogy and psychology courses in coed classes at the exclusive private Colegio Benavente run by Lasallian Catholic Brothers.

This was our first time sitting next to high society girls, proud about their bodies and dressed in the latest European fashion. Their faces were artfully decorated with the most expensive French cosmetic products, imitating Brigitte Bardot and Simone Signoret. Their wide, intense, and expectant eyes searched for independence, adventure, and desired a peaceful, happy, and abundant future. The students were overwhelmingly female, some nuns in the mix. The girls had recently graduated from high school, having grown up in wealthy *gachupín* families in Puebla, and had decided to question their parents' expectations of garnering a law or medical degree, opting instead for a service career as elementary-school teachers.

Gustavo and I, without trying, living up to our spiritual roles, soon became the go-to people for psychological and religious orientation and personal advice. Here, I discovered how the power of a pious, honest, and religious life, with no dubious agendas, could exert on others, especially the youth. Within the Latin Catholic tradition, the expectations that believers put on the soon to become priests are enormous and their deep faith projected unto seminarians almost magical powers, or so I believed. Those girls believed that spiritual and practical solutions of their most intimate young adult conflicts, struggles, and desires came about only thru conversations with God's messengers, we, the priests and seminarians.

This represented a new heavy burden for me. I absolutely did not have any answers to these worldly girls' innermost ethical, emotional, and religious conflicts. Gustavo and I, however, soon became the stars of the student body. The girls only needed an enthusiastic good listener at that moment in their lives and our status of foreign students put them at ease. This also gave an added out-of-the-box perspective and an exotic tint to our encounters with them. At the end, they came out with their own solution, thanking us profusely. Listening to others in silence is powerful.

"Just tell me what I have to do, please," *Eloisa* asked me one day worriedly under the shadows of a thick pillar, of the many that surrounded the school's large patio, after having pulled me aside between classes to pour her heart out to me.

"I need to understand your situation much better, please keep talking, and consider all good possibilities so I can help you," I said in a reassuring murmur.

"I think I know what you are suggesting. You want me to stop seeing him because he wants only one thing from me. You know what I mean. I think you are right. I will break up with him. Thank you for your advice."

Soon after, multiple dinner invitations started to come our way. We refused most of them. Our praying schedule at the Seminary did not permit us to indulge in pleasurable downtime with rich families. The more we refused their invitations, the more they increased in number. It was inevitable. Soon we submitted to those desires and started missing the evening prayers, hoping that on our late return to the building, climbing the Seminary's wide stoned wall wouldn't represent a dangerous risk, and if this turned out to be futile, that the octogenarian care-taker, Juanito Malacara, would take pity on us, keep quiet, and open the steel heavy wide doors after a slight knock. Soon, during those opulent dinner events, we found ourselves having religious and philosophical after-dinner discussions with the girls and their mothers, with a hot cup of coffee spiked with a generous amount of a strong cordial.

It didn't take long before we became a challenge for the girls who were evidently enticed by the forbidden fruit. There was nothing more passionate in this pursuit than the prospect of tasting and acquiring the forbidden object of desire, especially when the pursuer was a pious virgin Catholic girl and the avoider a virgin seminarian. The al-lure of the possibility of breaking us and having us as their faithful, super intelligent, and forever-honest fiancées consumed their intense souls. Their parents would have been more than happy with the prospect of their daugh-ters marrying one of us.

Gustavo and I kept chaste during wide immense temp-tations. This is what the Monsignor back home would have wanted. During my last visit to Puebla, to see Gustavo, he confessed to me that by that time he already had made the decision to desert the Seminary and that he was more dar-ing with the girls. Monsignor Barrera used to tell us stories of how chaste vows grew stronger in some young seminar-ians destined for greatness under intense testing similar to our situation during that year at the Colegio Benavente. All our transgressions were almost abruptly initiated by the girls that gave us long hugs and kisses in the dark areas of their spacious homes when their mothers were not looking.

I still remember their faces and names. Maria Luisa was chubby with long brown hair, vivacious and talkative. Mercedes was short, round faced, with big green eyes with shades of gray. Eloisa, the young novice, almost a nun, transformed her intense physical attraction into a spiritual relationship with me. The day of my twenty first birthday in 1970, Eloisa planned a party in my honor and invited the class to her multi-room *casa colonial* near the center of the city. After singing *"Las Mañanitas,"* Eloisa presented me with a dense compendium containing the newest translations of the entire literary works of Shakespeare, the 1967 blue cover Aguilar edition, which was years later stolen from my bookshelf in the *multis* apartment by one of my cousins who gave it as a present to his girlfriend. I have been looking ever since for a copy just as the one Eloisa gave me. I used her book as my solace and read Shakespeare's tragedies and sonnets during the long months I cloistered myself in my room full of ennui, after having left the Seminary. That book meant a great deal to me. It had pulled me through the darkest period of my life. After a long internet search, I found a copy of the same book in Buenos Aires, Argentina. I entrusted to Teto the task of buying it for me on one of his trips to that city with his Argentinian wife and two sons. In my hands, this copy, however, does not touch my heart as intensely as the original, without Eloisa's lovingly written dedication to me on the inside-cover.

Also, there was the blue-eyed, blond, and very well endowed, Dominique, who expressed a pointed desire and unrestrained passion for the pleasures of life with the slightest movement of her body. Poblano male drivers, routinely in a big hurry to get home to see their wives or mistresses, stopped their sputtering vehicles whenever Dominique crossed the *Avenida 25 Poniente* on late afternoons to enter the Benavente College for her evening psychology classes. We watched her in surprise from the other side of the street while waiting at the main entrance with a modest degree of male pride as the drivers sent jealous darts our way. She was working on a psychology degree and used to engage in long intimate conversations about the difference between a confessor and a psychologist. Her undulating walk slowed down almost to a halt, not unlike a snake hesitantly crossing the trail aware of danger, but with an intense awareness that all eyes were on her. Gustavo recently told me that Dominique's gregarious, innocent, and sensual interactions with life got her killed two years after I left Puebla. I was shocked. Her innocent character proved to be too much for one of her jealous boyfriends. Her murder was never solved, not unusual, due to the lack of efficiency in corrupt Mexico. Gustavo also told me that Eloisa became a nun and missionary and now lives in Senegal.

During the subsequent months, Gustavo and I fought over my Shakespeare compendium with Eloisa's loving dedication to me on the first page. We had just finished *Don Quijote* and Gustavo was determined to read my book next. I detest to this day, my cousin thief for not understanding the deep attachments that one develops with books, especially one with a love dedication on the first page. It pains me to know that I won't ever be able to read it with Eloisa's dedication again.

In one of our end-of-the-year educational field trips at the Colegio Benavente, we ended up going to the Mexican capital, the Distrito Federal. Here at one of the most popular of Mexico City's amusement parks, *Los Juegos Mecánicos de Chapultepec,* all personal barriers were broken. We took turns with different girls at the *Montaña Rusa*, the *Chalupas*, the *Carros Eléctricos,* and El *Tren del Amor.* In these times, extending your arms around a girl's shoulders was a serious declaration of love. I desired to ride at least one time with Mercedes, but it never happened. Gustavo usurped her from me and ended up kissing her. As always, the phlegmatic Gustavo took the lead on many of these love experiences. On our way back, I did not speak to Gustavo and my silent treatment lasted for over a week. Every time I ran into him in the hallways, I restrained the impulse to break his rabbit looking front teeth. I felt ugly and undesirable and felt that the Mexican poblana girls admired and were in love with the image of a tall, blue eyed, European-physique perfectly exemplified by Gustavo. A Ladino looking guy like me was too common in Puebla. Last year when I visited Gustavo, he brought that incident up.

"What did you want me to do? Mercedes was easy, everybody knew it, but you were so, so, so insecure and afraid of rejection that prevented you from seeing her true instincts. You would have never kissed her. The proof is that you never kissed or embraced any of those girls. I did plenty of that."

I went to see Mercedes the day before I left Puebla at the end of June of 1970. We spent two hours talking and 20 minutes saying goodbye standing very close to one another with our noses almost touching. Her wide green eyes kept looking at my mouth. Now I understand her obvious desire. However, that day I chickened out and remained chaste for a long while longer. Gustavo was right. The truth was that I was terrified of my inability to kiss and more importantly of the profound shame and humiliation that a rejection could have caused me. Besides, the strength of my vocation at that time was still strong. I was conflicted. I did not want to offend God engaging in physical contact with a girl. I took my timidity as a divine sign.

Next day, in the early morning of a sunny spring day, I found her waiting for me at the bus station to say goodbye and to offer me another long friendly hug with the same results as the night before. I said that I was coming back soon to see her again. That was a pure lie. I never saw her again. When I visited Gustavo last year in Puebla, he told me that Mercedes moved to Europe soon after I left and was not heard of or ever seen again by her family or friends. I still have a couple of pictures she gave me the day of my departure. In one, she stands in the middle of *La Piazza San Marco di Venezia* with hundreds of pigeons flying low behind her as a white-bearded man with a cane spread seeds in his wake. The other is a passport picture. Both have remained in my personal photo album since that day.

I was proud to have withstood all sorts of strong temptations with the most beautiful girls imaginable. I felt clean with my vocation intact as I sat on the comfortable seat of the *Flecha Roja* bus, destination Tapachula, the border town with Guatemala, thinking about my near theological future in Louvain and my meeting with Bishop Barrera, the day after my arrival. Later, back in El Salvador, all these prospects and frustrations would be long forgotten when I met a woman named Norma.

Chapter 20: Norma II

From that day, after our descent together from *El Cerro Santa Lucía,* I visited Norma every night after dinner, sat on the same lime green sofa next to the TV in her living room, and stayed until around 11pm. It took me only three minutes to walk from my house to her front door. From my third-floor-apartment, I had only to look down from my bedroom window to her ground floor apartment directly across *las multis* courtyard, to notice when she had exactly sat down on the sofa to wait for me.

The regimented rituals of seminarian life prepared me for a life of adherence to routines, which led to the formation of both, good and bad habits. Today, a familiar sense of accomplishment engulfed me as I walked to Norma's apartment. Through the open doorway the seamstress of the first floor sent her rhythmic tapping of her Singer sewing machine's needle, the *finca de café* that bordered *las multis,* now in full blossom, squirted out fragrant whiffs of a mix of honey and jasmine, and the barrio boys, Teto, the street fighter, included, gathered at the corner grocery store, spread through the alleys of the *multis* their boisterous laughter.

As I walked, I softened my steps as not to hear the tapping sound of my shiny black shoes as they hit the cement sidewalk. I was no longer the unwanted, the left behind, Gustavo's sidekick, the one who was not good enough to be sent to Louvain. I had a real purpose in my life: to discover what was forbidden, now that I felt unrestrained by religious norms and dogmas. *"La única diferencia entre el animal y el humano es que nosotros podemos controlar nuestras pasiones, te conviertes en un animal cuando no lo haces."* The Seminary had let me down, it has taught me lies. Seminarian codes and truths became suspect, unreal and totally inapplicable to the dynamics of my new social circle, whose members, I sensed, lived for the moment and considered the acquisition of instant pleasure to be their supreme moral law.

Norma pretended to be absorbed by a non-descriptive TV program as she waited for me, perfumed, radiant, just out of the shower, with her nails painted red, wearing a light blue thin-polyester blouse combined with a pair of tight dark blue jeans that accentuated her plump rear and showed the thinnest of waists. If I took longer than usual to arrive, she would walk out of her house impatiently to the corner grocery store to buy gum or any other treat.

At the corner stood a daily congregation of unemployed and truant barrio boys who, when noticing Norma crossing the dirt street, started to make way for her in anticipation of an enjoyable scene. Norma, sensing their desires, increased her sensual hip swing and the angle of her supple breasts. The boys, as she walked through the group, received her with deep sighs, accompanied by lustful eyes, ending with a variety of respectful but direct *piropos* regretting that she was already taken by *el picaro padrecito*. *"Qué daría yo por ser el padrecito!"* *"Tanta carne y yo comiendo frijoles en la casa."* She loved those hormone-intense moments and came back to her house super excited. As I entered it, she jumped on me, kissed me and hugged me with great ardor as if she had just been injected with an elixir of passion. She and I kissed and hugged for an eternity, not unlike any other puppy, adolescent love, and watched soap operas produced in Mexico and Peru followed by some dubbed American TV shows. *Simplemente María* was the Peruvian version of an extremely popular Latin-American soap opera, and *Sombras Tenebrosas* (Dark Shadows), the American TV show.

The first one brought tears to Norma's eyes. *María*, an almost illiterate maid who worked for rich families in Lima, is seduced and abandoned by her aristocratic boyfriend. Our relationship mirrored the one in the TV. I was poor, but in Norma's eyes well above her in social status. I assured her that I was not at all like Maria's boyfriend. The second show induced great fear in Norma's heart. The ghosts and vampires, looking like normal people at night, were ever-present in the gothic mansion in Maine. Norma didn't mind this rollercoaster of emotions because she found solace and security in my arms every night. She started to feel less alone and abandoned.

I soon discovered that her father, Don Chico, worked as a bartender afternoons and nights at the Casino Santaneco housed in a Spanish colonial mansion in the center of town located on the opposite corner of the central park. Recently, in one of my trips back to El Salvador, I stood in front of the casino to look at its whitewashed walls, reminiscing about those years with a tender heart, imagining its splendor in the late 60's and early 70's. I contemplated its entrance with nostalgia and saw anew the Santa Ana aristocracy of the 1950's making its way to the interior ballrooms, surrounded by imported Spanish tapestries and under Italian chandleries, full of anticipation and glitter, to celebrate weddings, graduations, *quinceañeras*, and a successful coffee harvest. Now, as I stood in front of it, absorbed by my deepest nostalgic memories, attracting the attention of some passers-by, I couldn't believe that I was looking at a well-kept mansion, untouched by the effects of the bloody Salvadorian civil war, when many others like it on the same street had not been so lucky and were now all decrepit, decayed, and abandoned.

Even though most of my extended family, the Castro-Mezas and the Menendez-Castro's, had been part of this scene, my alcoholic father and downtrodden mother never attended a function at the casino together. My father, the dandy of the town, went to the casino with his rich friends when he was in high school before marrying my mother. Much later, occasionally, my mother would pass by the casino with no intentions of entering, only to be noticed by her old rich classmates, the Afanes and Sagastumes, who would then invite her for a cup of coffee to reminisce her *colegio* years. Maybe ashamed, she wouldn't say a word about her poverty and sufferings. Much later, Teto was the only of us who attended parties there, invited by our rich cousins.

Back when I was obsessed with Norma, one time, wanting to get a closer look at her father, Don Chico, I passed by the casino to look through the tall glass windows and observe him, so I could figure him out. I had never met him in person, only having seen him from a distance as I checked outside my apartment window, waiting for him to leave for work so I could visit Norma. Don Chico served whisky to the landowners of coffee plantations, and he did it with great deference, grace and conviviality. He did not look to me like somebody who could kick me out of his house once he found out I was spending most nights with his precious, young daughter. He joked with his bosses, ordered the waitresses around, and moved promptly and efficiently behind the bar counter. All in all, an agreeable bartender and loved by his superiors. From what I could observe, it did not seem extremely ridiculous or foolish of me to think that this man would let Norma and Yolanda, who were almost 18, have total control of their lives, enjoy a free range of the house, spend their days in leisure activities, skip school daily, and dedicate only some short moments of the day for grocery shopping, preparation of meals, and housekeeping. My new social circle, it appeared, lived without rules and discipline. Maybe this is the way to achieve happiness in life, I thought. Why should I torture myself with following strict rules of conduct?

"Where is your mother," I asked Norma one day.

"My mother, Berta, left me to go north when I was around 12 years old. I have lived alone with my father since then. After my mother left, my father brought Yolanda from *el mercado* to help me with my house chores. My mother said that her life had become unbearable, a life without a real future, and that my father was a weak man, too nice, maybe too decent. In her eyes, he had no ambition and was fully content with his low-level job as a bartender at the casino. She needed action, adventure and excitement," Norma said, the pain in her voice making her lisp more prominent.

Later, soon after I arrived in Los Angeles in October 1972, I learned that Norma's mother came to Los Angeles in 1966 and had since remarried. Her new husband was a Chicano with an almost unintelligible accented Spanish who owned the sleaziest cantina: a dank dive bar, quasi-Mexican bordello, on the outskirts of Riverside. In the mid-sixties, the US economy was booming. Mexican migrant workers and undocumented immigrants were crossing the border by the thousands, and he was desperate for a female companion to help run the cantina. Berta, with her oval green eyes and shiny white skin, and with a keen business sense developed in the cutthroat environment of the Santa Ana's *mercado central,* quickly conquered the Chicano's heart. This gave her a great opportunity to get her resident papers in order and wait until the day when she could petition at the immigration offices for Norma to legally immigrate to Riverside. It did not matter that in the meantime her job at the cantina may have included sleeping with sexually deprived migrant workers whenever the Chicano desired it in the name of good business practice.

Berta very soon saved enough money for the steep immigration lawyer fees and plane tickets for Norma. Berta saw her present questionable life as a small price to pay. A mother must do all she can to have her children near and safe. She did not ignore the fact that young and desirable Norma could add an extra pair of hands, and if required, more than that, to the Chicano's business. Life was much tougher back in the Santa Ana central market where Berta barely eked out a living selling fresh and not so fresh meat, and where some of the women and girls, married and unmarried, lived a life of promiscuity, in and out of the *mercado.* Thievery and petty crime were the norm in the *Mercado Central,* as is the case in many Latin

American *mercados, El Tepito* market of Mexico City being the perfect example. Life in these *mercados* was punctuated by serious criminal activity such as knife-fights and murders originating from historic feuds among shopkeepers whose ancestral families had owned or rented their spots since before the turn of the 20th century. Luis Buñuel, the renowned Spanish film director, depicted painfully well what life was like in a Mexican *mercado* in his quasi documental 1950 drama *Los Olvidados.*

Life at the cantina in Riverside was not that different, but the Chicano had guts, from my short encounters with the couple, I could surmise that the Chicano pleased Berta, and gave her all she needed. The Chicano drove the latest car model that GM could produce, which would prove to be not only the envy of any rich Salvadorian *terrateniente,* but the entire shop keepers of *el mercado.* If they could only see her in the passenger seat as the Chicano cruised slowly in his big automatic, air-conditioned ride on the way to his cantina. Don Chico had become a distant memory by then. Berta felt accomplished. Money in Riverside was never an issue. She had become a lady.

Norma's mother had escaped *el mercado,* but the life of *el mercado* followed her, like an oil stain that would not wash out, and became evident in her new life in Los Angeles. Norma was also a product of *el mercado,* and *el mercado* stayed with her, even though its effects on her lessened, as usually happens to second generations. Puppy love is blind. If only I had not been so inexperienced and naive. But, maybe, deep down, I understood that it was better this way because it made it easier for me to continue exploring without risking my life as a bachelor.

That night, with a slow and happy step, I began my short walk back, knowing that my mother had been awake waiting for me, perhaps praying to San José that I recover my senses, reconsider and break with Norma. Saint Joseph did not hear her this time.

Chapter 21: El Mercado Central

I entered the *Mercado Central* of Santa Ana only once as a child to visit my father's aunt, Mamá Chagua, who made a lot of money selling bread and being as an astute real estate speculator. After her death, she left behind quite a real estate fortune. My father, after being brought to El Salvador from Guatemala by my grandfather, was soon deposited at Mamá Chagua's house. She raised him. In a way, my father was also a product of *el mercado central.* The *Mercado's* social activities were unknown to me, but I had a sense of the tough lives carried by the mostly poor merchants. Mamá Chagua owned her own stand, placing her at the highest status in *el mercado.* Most of the merchants lived on the outskirts of the city and leased permanent spots inside the Mercado. Many descended to the city daily from the countryside to sell their fruits and vegetable. Lacking a permanent spot inside the building, these merchants had no other option but to set up shop outside on the narrow sidewalks and obstruct the flow of pedestrians. Soon their merchandise overflowed onto the pavement surrounding the *Mercado* with exposed baskets and sacs in the middle of the narrow streets.

Recently, when walking around this city, I was amazed to discover that the entire center of Santa Ana had morphed into a huge chaotic mercado and I imagine that the lives of the merchants have not experienced much improvement since the mid-twentieth century. There is no way at this moment of telling where the center of the city starts and the mercado ends, not unlike many other Latin American cities at present.

When Teto and I flew to El Salvador for my father's funeral, I dared him to walk through *el mercado* with me. I wanted to feel the chaos and the danger, and maybe far away in my subconscious, connect with the social roots of part of my proud father's family. Teto was reluctant, but I insisted. "*Si algo pasa yo no lo estoy salvando,*" he finally gave in. He took the opportunity to look for his old *amigos mariguaneros.* We marched, not walked, through the market. Teto, the street fighter, knew where to stop and look for his old friends. Sure enough, he ran into one, *La Chencha* and they reminisced about their lives of crime together for a few minutes. I sensed Teto felt uncomfortable thinking about his old alcoholic, drug addiction, crime ridden decades. This is a coping mechanism that I have seen him use often to not to succumb to the temptation of tasting that life again, even if it is just for a quick moment. "*Yo soy un alcohólico y drogadicto,*" he often says, "*mi condición nunca se cura.*" We got out of *el mercado* in a hurry. I wished to stay much longer, but I couldn't remain in the middle of *el mercado* without soon being noticed as a total outsider and a possible target.

The market, crowded and overflowed, forced customers to walk slowly, bumping into each other, always alert, looking back and sideways, with half of them almost falling on the beans and tomatoes when it was time to give way to the bus number 50. Daily shoppers were pestered during their slow walk by a cacophony of jeers and shouts in an incessant drone of sale pitches as they bumped, pulled, and poked each other to make way through piles of red and yellow mangos, homemade soaps made from pig's intestines, and live nervous poultry, not unlike the Shuk of Jerusalem, the Mahane Yehuda market, only probably much more dangerous and dirtier. In the middle of all this, the shoppers still found the energy to yell back to bargain their prices. This ignominious, theatrical, cultural display was easily tolerated only by the poorer housewives. Upper class ladies wouldn't be caught dead inside it. The *Mercado Central* was visited daily mostly by the maids of rich landowners that demanded a fresh *almuerzo* for their families every day.

Looking for some excitement, on vacation after being cloistered at their boarding schools run by the nuns of El

Sagrado Corazón, La Asunción, La *Medalla Milagrosa,* o *La Esperanza,* sometimes rich *muchachas,* with their expensive imported dresses and accessories, would tag along with their maids to do the daily grocery shopping. This sight always created a commotion in *el Mercado.* Unlike many other countries, the shopkeepers inside *el mercado central* of Santa Ana were almost 100% women. Their husbands and sons took care of the heavy lifting and transportation of the goods. Many of these men pulled heavy wooden carts filled with vegetables and fruits to distribute them among the shopkeepers. Other men owned small pickup trucks and hired laborers to carry 100-pound sacks of grains, mostly corn, rice and beans on their bare backs.

These men inevitably would stop their chores, puffed up their breasts and tightened their biceps to whistle and throw piropos at the rich *muchachas,* inhaling deeply as to get a whiff of their exotic perfumes, to the annoyance of their employers and the jealous looks of *las Viejas del Mercado.* There was no other place in the city where the distance between rich and poor, the educated and the illiterate, the powerful and the destitute was more palpable than in *el mercado.* Drunkards, drug addicts, pickpockets, prostitutes, drug dealers, traffickers, and murderers roamed within alongside with the honest, dedicated, hard-working women, while bankers, heiresses, rich landowners, and wealthy businessmen ruled the world on the outside.

The rich landowners lived in the spacious Spanish colonial houses clustered between the Santa Ana Cathedral and the Church of the Calvario, on the *Segunda Calle Poniente* and *Calle Libertad* in the center of the city, where the *Casino Santaneco* and the club of government workers were located. During the bloody Salvadorian civil war, most abandoned these houses to live in exile in the USA and others retreated to the countryside, never to return. Last year when walking on these streets of Santa Ana with my brother Rafael, I noticed that several of these once glorious colonial houses, mostly built in the late 1800s, had been declared historic landmarks and were crumbling away, still abandoned. Some of them had been already razed to the ground to allow the building of ugly, disordered and disparate cement structures now housing small stores. A few of the abandoned houses had been converted into Evangelist churches. One of these historic landmarks now houses the Santa Ana *Casa de la Cultura,* others small day care centers. Maybe these houses should be connected and converted into a safer mercado for the ones doing business on the sidewalks, I thought.

The hard workers of all Mercados Centrales, big and small, including the informal economy, deserve only respect from me. The economic development of such small country like El Salvador has depended greatly on the indefatigable work ethics brewed within its subculture of savvy entrepreneurship, despite all odds and oppression.

Chapter 22: Norma III

My mother knew only too well the shocking low level of education and social decorum rampant in el *mercado*. My grandmother Mamá Nena prohibited her daughters from tagging along with her maids in their daily grocery shopping for the family of 10 children. Logically, my mother saw Norma as a product of that environment and watched in horror as I gradually succumbed to the enticing allures of such low level and murky social norms and dynamics. She believed, true or false, that *"La Puta de la* Norma," (*Norma, the slut*), well-schooled in the art of sexual advances and black witchery by her mother Berta, had concocted a love potion with a formula known only by people in the countryside and *el mercado*. For sure, Norma had slipped me some in a drink without my knowledge. There was no other explanation. What else could explain the profound fall from grace of an ex-priest-to-be? I recently asked my street expert brother, Teto, if he knew about some Salvadorian cultural aspects related to love potions. What exactly was my mother talking about?

"*Las putas* that I knew, counting the loose girls of el mercado, told me frequently about their love potions. Such potion, a repugnant one, had as its main ingredient '*agua de calzón*' with *ruda. Las muchachas del mercado,* would boil their bloody, used underwear with generous amounts of this green herb, the ruda. Eventually, the boyfriend was offered a cold or hot drink of this liquid. This potion is also called '*té de mico*'," Teto continued.

"Nights before offering this love potion to the boyfriend, girls *del mercado* engaged in '*la prueba del puro*'. At night, the girls built a small altar with many candles. In the middle of the table surrounded by candles, the girls placed a stolen or borrowed photo of the boyfriend next to a figurine of San Simón. There was always a glass full of '*agua de ruda*' on the table that the girls would have to sip until finished. Then the girls started an invented chant as they smoke the cigar, something akin to a sorcerer's chants before conjuring spells. *'Puro te conjuro que Chepito solo se enamore de mí. Puro te conjuro que Chepito nunca vuelva a ver a otra mujer. Puro te conjuro que Chepito se acueste conmigo y que me embarace. Puro ten conjuro que Chepito...'* Teto couldn't contain his loud hearty laugh while telling me this story.

He continued, "The women *del mercado* had another ritual to bewitch their lovers. This included the burying of a glass bottle full of hard liquor in the house backyard garden, tied to amulets pierced with long needles to turn their lovers' attention to them instead of the liquor found *en las casas de las putas.*"

The history of these rituals I think could be traced to a combination of Aztec beliefs, Cuban *Santería,* Spanish gypsy cults, and Catholic religion. For example, to this date, Teto believes that my brother Rafael has been forever *embrujado* by his wife Lorena and that is one of the reasons why he stays in Chalchuapa under total submission, despite being a civil engineer with a masters from Spain on bridge construction and earthquake-proof structures and has lived in extreme poverty for the past 15 years.

According to my mother, the only explanation of my obsessive, crazy love was that Norma had given me this potion cold, after one of those sweaty, hot evenings, making me lose my mind and fall idiotically in love with her. My mother believed that this potion helped Norma keep me blind to what she really was, while at the same time extending a very short leash to my social activities with family and female friends. How could a seminarian, almost a saint, a son of God, fall from so high down into the bowels of hell? Teto tells me that my mother during that time cried every night and threw curses to Norma through the kitchen window when she happened to see me with her, sitting on the lime green sofa. My mother did not dare to open my eyes to Norma's pedigree, fearing a devastating blow to my supposedly innocent heart, which at that time was growing ever more malicious. During this time my poet brother, Rafael, would recite anew his long poem, dedicated to me months before, titled "*Mi héroe caído.*"

✳✳✳

When I arrived back from Puebla to the *Multis* after a 4-year absence, I was totally unaware of its social make up and the personal histories of its dwellers and it took me a long time to understand the social culture of the barrio. Later, I learned of the neighbors' shocking susurrations about the private escapades of Norma and Yolanda. I treated these girls as I only knew how, as expected by a seminarian, with idealized romantic respect and deference, and as God's children. Not unlike the way Don Quijote speaks about his darling Dulcinea. During my entire life, I have been very deficient in understanding hidden agendas and people's nasty motivations and in seeing the cruel realities of life. I think in many ways the Seminary made me, or maybe I was born, a naive half-wit, oblivious to the messages between the lines. Or, a case could be made that some capacities in my brain function have been long atrophied. Or, it could be that I was damaged by the constant traumatic childhood experiences resulting from living with an alcoholic father that made me incapable of seeing far beyond into people's eyes, blind to their mean intentions. Or, it has been my perfect psychological defense mechanism to avoid pain, using the "don't-think-about-it" technique. In the final analysis, I have generally taken life at face value for better or for worse.

My wife Carolina and my brother Teto, and many of my friends, have repeatedly told me during the years that I am too naïve and that my high degree of education has done little to remedy this condition; they say that in a sense, instead it has made me even more overly trusting. Teto always tells me that I, with all my intellectual and esoteric reasoning, don't understand anything. He sometimes gets outraged with my innocent intentions because he reads them as tricks loaded with hidden agendas and the subtle purpose of mocking and humiliating him. He is a product of the streets, and as such, understands life and people the way they really are, with all their instinctual, almost impossible to break, desires, always looking to take advantage of others as a means of survival. He even goes further to tell me that politically the Republicans in the United States are the only ones who know how to *babosear* (dupe) *al pueblo* because they use simple, unadulterated, language that speaks to people's instincts in a way that is easy for their voters to understand, whereas the democrats, with their law degrees and government lingo, speak in a way understood only by the highly-educated elite. *"Gente como usted no sabe hablar con el pueblo,"* Teto has told me repeatedly.

It was not long after sensing my mother's disapproval of my relationship with Norma that an irrational, obsessive jealousy started to control my emotions and conduct. I became very suspicious of Norma's loyalty and my mind was invaded by images of Norma cheating on me with those rich kids, radiating French cologne aromas, out of *el barrio.* In the *Multis,* the first apartment buildings in Santa Ana, I could always watch what Norma was doing in her apartment at any time of day, especially when my jealousy was heightened by my mother's repeated insinuations. I walked to my room and remained in the dark, glued to the window looking down to Norma's place through the Persian blinds for hours. During my night visits, I started to interrogate her about her day, asking for the minutest of details and movements, with my eyes fixed on hers on the lookout for any unusual nonverbal gesture, to discern if she lied to me.

She was at a disadvantage for if she wanted to do the same, she couldn't spy on me from her apartment because her vantage point did not allow her to monitor my movements. No matter how much she wanted to, especially in those times when she received word that many of the female university students were after me, she could not spy on my life as much as I could on hers. One-time, full of doubt, Norma went so far as to send Yolanda to spy on me at the university. She was suspicious of me. I was not double-timing her. She should have known better.

Gradually, I became desperate and fearful of abandonment. My constant spying on Norma reassured me but increased my mother's need to look for a logical reason of my obsessive love and found it: for sure, no doubt about it, Norma had bewitched me with a love potion. One day my mother decided to break her silence.

"*Chepito. No entiendo por qué usted tiene que salir con esa mujer, ¿no sabe que ella ha tenido tantos novios? Usted necesita una muchacha decente, educada, así como Ud.*"

I stared at my mother and said nothing.

"*Mañana viene a la casa una amiga con su hija Marta. Quiero que la conozca.*"

Again, I said nothing. By this time, I had already decided that I didn't want to be the first boyfriend of a decent girl and for sure the object of *una gran enculada.* Besides, decent girls were deeply religious and prudish, too much dancing around to get to the point, which they eventually did. But I would have to repress my desires for the longest time or get married with a girl like that.

※※※

The feeling of being left alone, unwanted, unloved, abandoned, can create long, sustained, and terrifying periods of unhappiness, self-doubt, and insecurity. The feeling of not being good enough is devastating. One root of this trauma can be traced to the time my parents decided to enroll me in a boarding school, *Colegio La Fé,* for kindergarten. I had just turned five, it was early March 1954. "*¡Mire qué bonitos son esos patitos! vaya a jugar con* *ellos,"* my mother said to me. I walked to the center of the patio of *el Colegio* to immerse my right hand in the cold water of the fountain. Soon, four small ducks approached me expecting some food. This was the perfect distraction.

"¿Y mi mamá dónde está?" I asked with fear in my voice when I turned around to find my parents were gone.

"Tuvieron que salir. Ya van a venir," the director Mercedes Avilés Colón said.

My parents did not return for a while to make sure I became used to my new home. That's the way I was left in the boarding school: cold and with no emotional preparation for the separation from my mother. She came back a month later on a Sunday to see me during visiting hours.

My parents never gave me a good reason for their decision to put me in a boarding school at such an early age. My parents spoke to each other in a low whisper whenever we were present, or when asked tough questions, as if protecting us from evil. Their secret conversations appeared to me as hiding the truth from us.

They even brought my own crib, pillows and toys from home. I clearly remember not being able to sleep at night staying awake staring at the ceiling counting its tiles made of natural palm of *petate*, one tile at the farthest corner stained with rainwater and another with its threads ripped. There were 110 tiles, I remember.

I, already an adult, asked my parents repeatedly the true reasons for my abandonment in one of those times they visited me in Boston. They didn't answer. With saddened faces, they remained silent. I obviously had brought up painful memories for them. Teto speculates that my mother wanted to keep me away from the horrors of my father's alcoholism and its impact on her. My father told Teto one day that when I was 4, I used to kick him out of the house as soon as he entered. I would scream at the top of my lungs, *"Esta no es su casa. Esta es mi casa y la de mi mamá. Váyase de aquí."*

A second cause of my fear of abandonment was the refusal of the Bishop to come to rescue me, to look for me, to guide me in my moments of isolation and desperation after I had decided not to return to the Seminary. I hoped he would come. He never did. A third cause of this fear I attribute to the time in Chalchuapa, in Papa Rafa's house, when I was 12, having had a big argument with my father, and decided to run away from home. I made my suitcase and walked with my shoulders hunched to the bus stop, crying profusely as my father watched me from the front door. While I waited for the bus, I expected my father, the one at fault, to come fetch me and ask for forgiveness, to hug me, to tell me how much he loved me. I peeked back and still saw him standing at the front door unsure of whether I was bluffing. He never came. He just let me go. I wasn't worth his attention and love.

Another cause of this fear I attribute to the time my first wife Claudia left me soon after our marriage several times, only to come back after my pleading with her. The last time, she never came back and left me alone with our son, Eric. One of my recurrent nightmares from which I wake up trembling, or crying, and frightened to death, is about Carolina, who without any previous warning, leaves me, abandons me, proving that I was, and have always been, unworthy of love.

Finally, the worst experience of deep sadness and mental pain, one that had a profound traumatic effect not only on me but on my brothers, Teto and Rafael, happened in February 1962. That year, my parents decided to go back to Guatemala alone with Pirri, our younger brother. I had just turned 13, Rafael 11, and Teto 9. It might have been because of economic reasons, or shame, or because the family had reached dirt bottom. My parents distributed their eldest sons among different affluent relatives, all from my mother's side of the family. I ended up with Neto, Mamá Lila's younger son. This time my mother didn't play a trick on me like she did when she left me at boarding school. This time, she took me to Neto's house and had a meeting with Neto's sisters and mother -- Papá Lorenzo had already been dead three years -- while I waited inside Lorencito's room. Neto had all the latest imported toys, the idea of playing with them lessened the deep sorrow and fear my mother's departure created in me. *"Toda la familia está muy contenta de que usted va a vivir aquí por un año,"* my mother told me with a smile that did little to hide her pain from breaking the family apart. *"Está bien, mamá,"* I responded, holding back my tears.

My cousin Neto was self-absorbed and spoiled, receiving the constant adoration of his mother, Mamá Lila, and five older sisters. Lorencito, the other man of the family, lived full time at the hacienda. Since, consciously or subconsciously, Neto probably felt like there could only be one dominant male, I became his sidekick, relegated to the status of a *mantenido* worthy only of Neto's leftovers. This literally included food leftovers. That year I was hungry every day, resorting to breaking into the refrigerator at midnight to steal a glass of milk. There is no worse feeling in life than that of not feeling at home in somebody else's house. That year, I understood that I was only a second thought and that I was tolerated only because I was keeping company with the king of the house, Neto.

When the school year started, nobody came to say goodbye and wish me a good year. Neto walked to the most expensive private school in town, the school for the rich, *El Colegio Marista,* and I walked to the second best, *El Colegio San José.* I was starting the 7th grade, Neto the 9th. Soon after, maybe because of malnutrition, the 20-block walk to school became unbearable. What felt like a heavy physical weight pressed on my heart and shortened my breathing, causing the need to rest, to sit down someplace. I remember making several stops to rest at people's front door steps before reaching *El Colegio San José.* One day I decided to make my first rest stop at Tío Michel's *yuquería.* He noticed my lack of physical strength and gave me a large glass of *horchata* while I rested. That became a daily routine for me.

As a consequence of my emotional and physical instability that year at *el colegio* I became a discipline problem for the Salesian priests and brothers. I talked non-stop in class, became very hyperactive, and was sent often to Padre Catedral's office, the director's office, to sit through his lectures on my classroom disruptions. I remember his fiery eyes full of anger. He would have belted me if he got the chance. Strict physical discipline was the only answer for reforming unruly boys. This same priest, years later, would hit Teto's head repeatedly with a textbook as he read it aloud making his way down the rows of desks in the classroom when Teto was a student at *El Colegio San José*. Teto wouldn't have it. One day, when Padre Catedral came behind Teto to strike his blow, Teto stood up and grabbed the sleeve of the priest's cossack, ready to break his nose with his karate punch. After that day, the priest became fearful of Teto and stopped his physical abuse, althhough Teto was expelled before the year ended.

My history teacher, also Padre Catedral, had had enough of my disruptions one day and violently threw his long stick of white chalk at my head, startling me. I suddenly became painfully aware that there was a teacher at the front of the classroom. I remember clearly Gustavo snickering at me with his hand over his mouth, trying to contain his laughter. I had spent months just talking to whoever sat next to me in every class without stopping, as if I had been inside an impermeable plastic bubble all this time, popping it only when a new teacher would enter to give a demonstration. Such diversions from the typical lecture structure of each class were very seldom, like when the math teacher peeled an orange and separated the slices one by one to teach us about fractions, or when our music teacher played Verdi's Aida's march with his trumpet to illustrate the 4/4-time signature.

Gustavo always sat in a row behind me and to the right, where all the seminarians sat, one behind the other. The seminarians were the best students in the classroom and excelled academically due to their extremely regimented lives that helped them become calm and focused. The regular students, which included me at this time, ignored the seminarians, finding them too reserved, somber and gloomy. The minor Seminary, not having its own school building, sent the seminarians, blessed by the Bishop, to the *Colegio San José*, a private school for the middle class, to get educated mixed among the sons of the general population. The seminarians, all of them from remote villages of the country, as was the case for Gustavo, saw being enrolled in a high-quality Catholic school, the *Colegio San José*, as the highest honor and privilege.

I learned nothing that year at *El Colegio*. On the other hand, Neto was on the honor roll at *el colegio Marista*, the private school for the *terratenientes*. It was unimaginable at this time that after the end-of-the-year vacation of 1962, to the amazement of the entire school, I would change membership from one group to the other. I would go from being one of the most disruptive, low-performing, non-religious-student, to joining the group of reserved seminarians, totally transformed into a disciplined and focused student. This was a miracle that the *Padre Catedral* couldn't believe. There was no need any longer to throw white chalk sticks at me to make me pay attention to his lectures. Teto often tells me, *"dichoso Usted, se escapó de la locura de mi papá. Yo nunca tuve esa oportunidad."*

One day, during the time I lived with Neto, around the middle of the school year, I got up in the morning with a heavy headache and walked to the bathroom to wash my face to get ready for school. I didn't make it. Halfway to the bathroom I plummeted to the floor in front of the maids and Lorencito, convulsing in a seizure and disturbing the early morning silence of the Menendez-Castro family. Later, Dr. Sierra preliminary diagnoses were questionable epilepsy. This incident saved me from my depressing life as a forgotten afterthought. My mother was sent a telegram demanding her immediate return from Guatemala to come fetch me. My parents understood their folly of breaking up our family. My brothers were then picked up from their respective family homes: Teto from Tío Paco's and Rafael from Tía Anitía's. We moved back to Papá Rafa's house in Chalchuapa for a second time, where we had lived three years earlier upon our arrival back from Guatemala.

※※※

At the *multis,* I gradually started to notice that Norma and Yolanda, intimidated by my seminarian misplaced snootiness, behaved in my presence at their very best, refraining from all uneducated, street level, *mercado* comportment. They still treated me as if I had never left the Seminary, paying careful attention to avoid actions, words, and comments that could have horrify my pious sensitivities and turning them undesirable under my eyes, or so they thought. They were not perfect. Yolanda often excused herself and asked for forgiveness whenever she broke decorum with me, especially when she used obscene words, sat on the green sofa with her sensuous pinkish legs fully opened, reclined her back, and let her red transparent panties show under her miniskirt-- a comportment, I guess, popular in the *Mercado Central.* Despite their apparent promiscuous behavior, I had, since meeting Norma and Yolanda, even though my mother would strongly disapprove, seen truly only love and innocence in their eyes.

After the long lethargic months, I spent cloistered in my room, Norma, Yolanda and their network of friends, contradictory to anything I believed, aided me in a new awakening into the real world, Teto's world, the world of the streets. The girls made it acceptable to unleash my desire to intensely search and experience the unknowns the

Seminary had trained me or domesticated me to keep hidden, or at least underdeveloped, lest I succumbed to the devilish path towards hell.

I jumped from a world of depression, fear, and easy boring contentment towards one of defiance and exhilarating attraction to the hidden pleasures of the unknown. At 21, my rebellious adolescence had just started. I envied and wanted to catch up with what Teto had already long experienced. It was a sort of death wish that took over me with no regard for the consequences of my actions. Teto had started to drink alcohol when he was 12 and date girls when he was 13, graduating from drinking to smoking marihuana, taking LSD, and ingesting speed at 16. This was the same year my father reached a level of desperation about Teto's uncontrollable behavior. As a solution, he forced Teto to enter the military unit of Santa Ana even though he was underage. The general in charge, Benavides, was at that time dating my father's daughter, our half-sister Anabelita, and took Teto in.

When I came home from Puebla for a short vacation, I became incensed by my father's callousness. After a week of constant arguing where I resorted to my few concepts of sociology and psychology to prove the devastating damage that forcing Teto into the army at such a tender age could have on his mental state, my father relented. He never forgave me and often would refer to this incident as the biggest regret of his life. The military, he thought, would have saved Teto from himself and channeled all his anger and violence towards a purpose. Teto tells me that he thinks that had he stayed in, most likely he would have become an assassin during the Salvadorian Civil war and ended up dying young at the hands of an enemy.

At 21, long after my brother Teto had had his formative years living on the streets, I too started to live fast with total absorption and uncontrollably immense emotions. I had a long time to catch up. Why should these pleasures be considered mortal sins? Norma provided the stage, the choreography, and the content. The almost illiterate Norma and Yolanda presented me with quick actions, overflowing passions, and desires void of intellectualism, reflection, social constraints, or pressures, and a general conduct unrestrained by a moral compass.

Teto had often pushed me, before my relationship with Norma became crazily intense, to accompany him to his adventures and often invited me to try marijuana with our cousin Freddy Ruiz. I refused every time.

One night however, I acquiesced to their pressure. "*Esta es la mejor mariguana del mundo. Me la traen desde Guatemala,*" my cousin Freddy said showing me a brown paper bag full of thick green leaves while we sat inside his pickup truck parked next to the *cafetal* behind the *multis.* He went ahead and rolled the leaves with a thin white paper and made what appeared to be a humongous thick Cuban cigar, only this one contained entire rolled leaves. "*Tenés que contener tu respiración, y trata fuerte de no toser,*" he said.

Soon, as if I had woken up from my present reality, I found myself entering what seemed to be another one, only more tangible where the senses responded to stimuli with augmented sensations. All sounds, from the faintest to the loudest, distant and close, idling cars, music coming out of the *multis'* balconies, Freddy's voice, and heel steps on the sidewalks, including the light from the corner post, became part of a harmonic symphony that oscillated constantly between the musical ppp's and the fff's, conducted by an invisible baton.

This visual and auditory distortion produced an unknown panic in me. "*A Chepito le está dando una gran pálida,*" Freddy ran to tell Teto who had left me alone with Freddy, gone up to the apartment, and couldn't wait to see me stoned. I on the other hand, wanted the effect to end immediately. I begged Teto to find a solution for my panic attack. I wanted the comfort of sane normalcy now. "*Ya le va a pasar. Así pasa la primera vez que uno fuma, vuélese la paja para distraerse,"* Teto said. It took me hours to recover, and I decided right there and then that cannabis was not for me.

Wanted to be accepted, in the company of Norma and Yolanda, I purposely tapered down my vocabulary and refused from that point on to allude to philosophy and theology which also alienated the common people of the *multis*. I decided to learn and practice the vocabulary used in *el mercado,* full of obscenities, incorrect grammar and bad words. Being a total snob had become repugnant. I learned them so well that up to now I can't get rid of some words and expressions that presently I use with my brother Teto when he makes an outrageous request: *"¡coma mierda hijueputa! ¡Vaya ver quien lo pisa cabrón!"* The word *puta* is always present in my speech. I let my hair grow down to my shoulders, the quintessential trait of a true hippy. I became unrecognizable to my pious aunts. *"Pobrecito Chepito, se hizo un mariguanero, ¡oh, qué horror Dios mío!"*

Had the Bishop decided to finally fetch me at that moment in my life, he would have taken me to be the devil incarnate possessed by demons and would have ordered an exorcist right then and there. I had become the perfect subject for an exorcism session, but little did he know that my behavior in truth was a desperate cry for somebody to come help me to make sense of it all. As much as I wanted him not to, the Bishop abandoned me, never sent for me, and never tried to reach me. Gustavo had left the Seminary, not me, but the Bishop had bundled me with Gustavo and understood me to also have deserted the Seminary. The Bishop saw me as Gustavo's sidekick and did not see the value of attempting to rescue me. I was unloved, undesired. So, I rebelled, maybe out of sheer spite of what he represented.

The girls did not welcome the new me at first. I had lost my allure as a saint and had become like any other barrio boy, common and ordinary. *"Me gusta mejor, así como era antes, no cambie,"* Norma would tenderly tell me. Later, the girls accepted my new me because they saw it as it was: my attempts to fit in with the group, although, no matter what, it didn't come out right. I felt fake. The girls took note of it. I was trying too hard.

For me, there was nothing more pleasurable at this time than to engage in forbidden activities that violated social decorum and family expectations, especially if I acted against the Church's dogmas, commandments and restricted code of conduct. I became a Don Juan in Norma's presence, almost a libertine. God will have to forgive me, echoing Stendhal, the French 19 century writer, who wrote in his Italian Chronicles' short story *"Les Cenci,"* quoting a Napolitano, the following,

> «*N'est-ce rien que de braver le ciel, et de croire qu'au moment même le ciel peut vous réduire en cendre ? De là l'extrême volupté, dit-on, d'avoir une maîtresse religieuse remplie de piété, sachant fort bien qu'elle fait le mal, et demandant pardon à Dieu avec passion, comme elle pêche avec passion».*

> (Is it not only to defy heaven, to believe that at that precise moment heaven can reduce you to ashes? Hence the extreme voluptuousness, it is said, of having a religious mistress full of piety, knowing very well that she is doing evil, and asking pardon to God with passion, like she sins with passion.)

Only in my case I was playing the role of the religious mistress. I knew very well that I was doing evil. I could also have asked, "Is this a sin? I do it intensely if it is one." This post-religious new life also reminded me of a Jewish aphorism: "If you are going to eat pork," as the Yiddish proverb goes, "let the juices run down your beard." I was ready for a total *destape* as the Salvadoran slang goes, an attitude of "everything goes" product of an escape valve after periods of extreme control, depicted well in one of the scenes in Verdi's La Traviata where Alfredo sings: *"...and may the fleeting moment be elated with voluptuousness..."* and

Violetta answers: *"...Everything is foolish in the world which is not pleasure. Let's enjoy ourselves, for fleeting and quick the delight of love is..."*

I was initiating a path of spiritual destruction and felt invigorated by my present circumstances. If only my mother knew at that time how far she was from redirecting me away from Norma and her associates, she would have desisted or fainted under the realization that my path had no return. I had been converted to the religion of sin. Her friend's daughter Marta didn't have a chance with me. For me, virtue did not lie in the middle anymore, as Aristotle defined it. For me, going to the extremes was where true virtue lay, and the only way I could fully experience life.

In my intense search to uncover all mysteries the Seminary had kept in secrecy from me, a deprivation at one time I wholeheartedly accepted, I passionately and relentlessly started to produce concrete instances where I could uncover them. I started to place my kisses and hands on Norma's body, wherever her fashion of the day and newly learned modesty allowed me. I initiated an exploration and conquest unstoppable to the end. The wise Yolanda sensed quickly my destructive pent-up inner energy, a hint of which she had seen since the moment we started descending the *Santa Lucía's* mount.

Yolanda one day decided to start leaving us alone in the house during my nightly visits. She stopped opening her legs and I did not see the red underwear anymore. She knew I was transforming in front of her eyes and became afraid of what I might do to her. She soon realized, however, that I would never try anything with her because of my love for Norma. Besides, she had her own amours to attend to and politely stayed away from the house until just before midnight and before Don Chico's return from work at the Casino. Little by little, I became unrecognizable to *mis tías* and *primos.* I marched steadily towards the deepest layers of hell and away from my pious and innocent seminarian past.

✳✳✳

Last year when visiting El Salvador, I inquired about Yolanda while walking around the old *multis* barrio, no longer on the outskirts of the city which has expanded erratically. I quickly learned her address and paid her a visit. She had become a dignified, very religious lady and respected in her community. She introduced me to her second husband and grown up children. Her first husband, one of the barrio boys, *el Chofo,* as we called him at that time, who had been the boyfriend she would run to see while I was on the sofa with Norma, was killed by the military squads during the civil war, leaving her with a baby girl. She cried in my arms as she filled me in on all that I had missed, letting me know how much she would have wanted me to be there as the person she had always trusted. She continued telling me that her daughter had died in her sleep 23 years later, all tragedies from which Yolanda has never recovered.

There were times during Holy Week and *las fiestas de Julio* when *El* Casino *Santaneco* was packed with landowners, day and night, forcing Don Chico to work 18-hour shifts, opting not to return home, sleeping instead in the casino's maid quarters. This sort of treatment of employees was and still is customary for Salvadorian Landowners, who expected them to be their butlers at all hours.

Norma would worry about her father and make trips to the casino just to ensure Don Chico was safe. (Later I learned he had a mistress, one of the housekeepers at the Casino, which explained his long absences from home.) Sensing that Norma was spending too many dangerous night-hours with me during his long absences, Don Chico decided to use one of his distant cousins to check regularly on Norma. He wanted at all costs to prevent Norma from becoming like her mother, Berta. From her first visit, this cousin immediately read the situation and knew that eventually Norma and I would end up in bed together. She told Don Chico, however, that there was nothing to worry about and assured him that all was well with Norma given my reputation as a son of God and Norma's sagacity. There was no chance of an unplanned pregnancy. She stopped coming to check on Norma and continued reporting to Don Chico that all was well.

There couldn't have been more favorable conditions for my desires to be satisfied and for my obsession to bite Eve's apple to reach a resolution. The time was ripe to lift the lid on the forbidden unknowns once kept so tightly inside Pandora's Box in the Seminary. Nevertheless, I still had lingering moral reservations and fears that restrained my impetus, strongly believing like a good seminarian that love shouldn't depend on physical carnal knowledge. But that just made Norma desire it with much more intensity, forcing me to gradually loosen my planned restraints.

The inexorable night came. It was impossible to resist. Yolanda knew it and stayed away. It took two years of such wild physical mesmerization and spiritual trance for the act to be consummated. It had been dry and pleasant for weeks, a surprising pause in that year's extremely copious rainy season, what we called winter in El Salvador. My 4th semester at the university, after the Christmas break, had already been interrupted by the military invasion of 1972, my prospects of becoming a lawyer forever thwarted, and I was spending the days idling at home. The *Santa Lucía* hill, visible from my balcony, showed newly sprung wild red and yellow lilies and carnations during the day. That night, Don Chico stayed away overnight with his mistress again. His cousin had long given up the task of checking on Norma and Yolanda, telling Don Chico that there was nothing to report. Norma still was fearful of her aunt and expected her to burst unannounced into the house at any moment during the day or night. Today, we started the same routine as soon as we sat on the green sofa. Soon, we turned the TV off and stopped watching the *Simple-mente María* soap opera. We had lost the thread of its plot long ago. Our long embraces and kisses did not permit a continuous watching. We both trembled with heightened sublime expectation.

We had not spoken about the appropriateness of our act before hand, but instinctively both knew that this night was the night. I might have uttered repeatedly the same typical shameless phrase many boys around the world use when enticing a girl into bed, "*Pruébame que tú de verdad me quieres para siempre. Dame una muestra clara de tu amor.*" We gradually stood up, making long pauses, without disengaging our interminable kiss, slowly walked across the living room, made another long pause in the middle of the kitchen, and another slow walk before I turned the doorknob of Norma's room that she shared with Yolanda. Norma kept the light off and refused to untie her belt to remove her already extremely tight blue jeans. Despite my insistent efforts the pants got stuck way above her knees and couldn't lower them. Pitch dark and in a total convoluted confusion, I didn't know what direction my act should have taken, and, at that precise moment, the thought of Norma not a virgin, only pretending to be one, invaded my heart. *She must be an experienced girl in lovemaking.* My mother's suspicions might have been right. Norma was pretending to be modest and inexperienced. I should have expected a free-flowing innocent skirt. Her mind long made, Norma should have known how to make it easy for me, but instead made it difficult to mask her past as an easy girl. Things moved fast, the act was strenuous and ended quickly, and when finished, I ran back to my house muddle-headed, tormented, frustrated and remorseful, not liking the new me. I cannot find words to convey my state of mind at that moment; the entire experience has remained obscure in my mind up to now. I very well might have imagined it all. Moments of extreme emotional intensity make your memories of the event either foggy or lucid, mine are foggy

The process of bringing down the seminarian person to transform it into the new person that I was going to become, as it happens to all adolescents in the search for their own identity, it was necessary, but heartbreaking

.

Chapter 23: The Separation.

For month later, Norma's mother, Berta, unexpectedly flew to El Salvador to fetch Norma with her Green Card in hand. Finally, the hard work at the cantina had produced results. Now the same cantina would welcome Norma, who knew that this day was going to come eventually, but not now, when she was intensely in love. She had come to disrupt her life.

Berta was overbearing, demanding, and never accepted dissent. Norma grew up deeply submissive to her and did as commanded. Don Chico was easy and handled Norma with love and understanding. Noma adored her father, but Berta knew only obedience from her daughter. Of course, it would have been unthinkable for Norma to mention me in the presence of Berta. The plane ticket was already bought and the flight to Los Angeles would leave in a few days. Norma was terrified.

My family had just returned to the ancestral home, after more than 15 years of a wandering family life. This was the house where my brothers and I had been born, on *Novena calle oriente* # 20. It was all thanks to Mama Chagua, who, before she died, asked that the property be transferred back to my mother. The big house had a lot of space and a huge backyard with the mango, lemon, custard apple and avocado trees, that my mother had planted to commemorate each of our births. The front yard was filled with roses and wildflowers, just as my mother loved them. Each of us could have our own room. The family was ecstatic with the return to the old part of the city, where our lives had begun. Norma and I couldn't see each other often, given the distance.

For two weeks, a persistent rain of small, cold, light drops had darkened the city: rain that Salvadorans call a *temporal*. This drowned out some of the festivities and traditions of the *Fiestas Julias*, and those to come, the *Fiestas Agostinas*, but Berta did not mind. She continued the party with her old friends from El Mercado that she hadn't seen in many years. Her visit took even more brilliance due to all the great noise of the festivals that venerate the mother of the Virgin Mary, Saint Anne, in July, and later, in August, the patron saint of San Salvador, the capital, that commemorate the appearance of Jesus "in radiant glory "to three of his disciples, that the Church calls the transfiguration. These parties were and are, not as religious as they should be, but a traditional excuse to get drunk and fornicate like the best atheists and pagans.

During the day, the pious joined the processions of the statue of Jesus out of the Cathedral. The priests and we the seminarians, with our special festival attire, would spray incense and holy water on to the parishioners. Presidents and politicians would attend the high mass in the morning and listen attentively to the Archbishop's sermon. An abundance of flowers added to the already colorful atmosphere. The orchestra and the seminarian combined chorus of the Minor and Major Seminary performed a sublime classical mass. All of these aspects were meant to create a truly spiritual, grand celebration. At night, however, those same people who went so piously to church celebrated by sinning as often as possible during the night time festivities, as was Berta's case. Such hypocritical behavior is the real contradiction of the church in Latin America.

Don Chico celebrated and remained with his mistress at the Casino during Berta's stay, expecting Norma to pass by and say goodbye before leaving.

A day before Norma left for Los Angeles, which was to be forever, Yolanda momentarily escaped her daily routine at El Mercado and walked to my house to share news of Berta's outings and to assure me that Norma would find a valid excuse to escape from her clutches that same night.

That night, Norma walked the 20 blocks alone from her humble apartment in the Multis to our new residence. Yolanda followed her much later.

As the drizzling rain continued, a solitary car drove by my house, crossing over the deep puddles of water that would always form by the gutter, splashing the muddy water against the front door, breaking the usual after-dinner silence. Because there was nothing to study or to do, I had decided to go to bed early. The university had already been closed for a month.

Norma's knock startled me. My musty room had its own entrance facing the street, which was not unusual for colonial houses. There were two such rooms in my house at the time, creating no need to go thru the *zaguán,* the big door in the middle of the house, to enter them. My parents were not aware in the slightest of Norma's visit. Half sleep, I opened my room's front door and smiled.

We had only a few precious moments left, and it was getting dangerously late for her return home. The National Guard had started its night watch in the city. We immediately buried ourselves under my linens and spent half an hour lying in my room, trembling in a close embrace, talking about our sudden, forced separation and promising each other to someday reunite. Before we knew it, she had to leave. Berta had already spent a small fortune on the lawyers and travel expenses so that Norma could have a better future in America. *Berta may be right* we were probably thinking to ourselves. *The decision, out of our control, may turn out to be for the better for both of us.*

That night, following the tradition of lovers throughout history, in those precious moments before their impending separation, we swore eternal love to each other. We kissed, embraced, and did not let go, after consummating our love for a second time. This time Norma felt at complete ease, without holding back or restrictions. Her customary thick-fabric and tight blue jeans had been substituted by a bright colored dress with a free-flowing skirt. *No need to pull any garment down, open buttons, or zippers.* One of my weakest and warmest blows could have moved the thin-fabric of the skirt all the way up above her waist. I don't remember if , while in bed, Norma confessed her pregnancy.

We soon said our goodbyes, coming back towards each other repeatedly for another quick kiss and embrace. I finally opened the front door of my room because the goodbyes were too painful. Just outside it, Yolanda stood holding a black umbrella and radiating with a picaresque smile of amusement. She had decided to come fetch Norma before Bertha could get suspicious. Yolanda had been waiting for what it seemed a long time, most likely she had heard what we had been doing together. Her smile gave it away. Norma stepped down onto the sidewalk. "*Adiós bicho feo.* One day I will send for you, after I find a good job in Riverside and save enough money." At that moment, there was nothing that I wanted more than to go north during one of the inter-semester-breaks at the university, if it ever reopened, with or without money. *No matter what*, I thought *we would love each other forever.*

✳✳✳

At that time in my life, the University had been invaded and occupied by the Salvadorian National Guard on July 17, 1972, almost a month before Norma left for California. Despite my love for Norma, soon after her departure I decided to stay put, betting that the government would be forced to open my school again soon after buckling under the pressure of the international protests in support of the students. I could not have been more wrong. A month after Norma left, I was still waiting for classes to resume.

It was just a matter of time before they put me in prison, just to make an example of this seminarian turned revolutionary. At the same time, the thought of a new northbound, exhilarating adventure and quest, with the lingering taste of Norma's kisses and the smell of her perfume, pulled me towards California. On my walk out of the city I stopped by Tío Michel's *"yuquería,"* to say goodbye.

"¡Chepito! ¿A dónde va tan temprano?" He said with consternation.

"Yo me voy para México de regreso. Ya no puedo seguir viviendo aquí," I said.

"Perdone Chepito, todavía no he hecho ninguna venta, acabo de abrir," he said, as he opened the cash register. *"Solamente tengo en la caja 10 colones. Aquí están. Buena suerte en su viaje."*

And with that, I started my long trek north; unaware, ignorant, and painfully oblivious to what lay before me.

Chapter 24: The Reunion

Now, looking back, I realize that my journey north, as daring and strenuous as it was, contained timely oases of tranquility and gestures of kindness, courtesy of a network of extended family members, close friends, and sometimes kind strangers, without whom I would never have made it to where I was going. The first rest I made was at tío Chepe's house where I received a generous loan of $100.00 that my cousin Sandra gave me to show the Mexican border officers, a requisite to let me cross. Next, I made a long stop in Puebla at the house of Gustavo and his pregnant wife, Elsita. He fed and sheltered me and issued me crucial U.S visa documentation I later used at the embassy in Mexico City.

After that, I stopped for a long time in Tijuana, at tío Juan's, my father's half-brother, who also provided me with food and a safe place to stay. After two weeks, he drove me to Los Angeles. We crossed the border without a hitch thanks to the tourist visa the US Embassy in Mexico City had issued me for 11 days. This visa was only made possible after the Embassy received a "telex" from the US Embassy in El Salvador stating that I was not a revolutionary trying to escape and that I had not petitioned for a visa before I left.

When we made it across the border, Tío Juan deposited me at my Tía Juanita's apartment in East LA, my fourth rest stop. There I enjoyed the company of my Ordoñez cousins who I had not seen since my childhood. Next hazy morning, her husband drove me to Temple City and dropped me at the house of my loving cousin and childhood babysitter, Alicita: my destination.

Just like the Greek gods intervened to help their adopted heroes when they needed to succeed in their quests and battles, my god or guardian angel influenced my journey repeatedly on my behalf, clearing away obstacles for me to reach my destination and fulfill my destiny. Obtaining a US visa, for example, was unimaginable to anybody in my circle of friends. The divine hand was palpable in that turn of events.

When I arrived at her house, Alicita, very graciously, put me in one of the spacious, newly furnished rooms facing a large green back yard with two lush, tall trees. The first night in that place, a place I envisioned would be my home for a while, I slept profoundly. I had finally arrived in America. I felt comfortable and accomplished. I slept the deep sleep of a victorious hero.

Alicita and her partner left for work ridiculously early next morning, so when I woke up, I walked to the Temple City's Saint Luke's church on the corner, spoke to the priest in Latin, and in an instant landed my first job ever, as a helper to the parochial school custodian. My first day in America and I already had a job. Things were too easy in this country, I thought. I felt on top of the world.

I came back home from my first day at my new job and, breathing rapidly, my heart beating like a drum, eagerly picked up the beige house phone from the table in the hall. Norma was on my mind and had been ever since the first day of my trek. I desperately dialed the phone number Norma had left with me the night before her departure. I repeated this action every afternoon before Alicita came home from work with no luck for three weeks. The female operator repeated over and over an incomprehensible message that ended with a repeating, high pitched tone followed by an operator's prerecorded message. Norma must have given me the wrong number or maybe her family had moved after her arrival. Next day, I paid extra attention to each digit so as not to skip any. I carefully completed the circle of each dialed number on the rotary phone. The connection was never completed no matter what I did. I feared Norma had purposely given me a wrong number. Asking Alicita for help was out of the question. Norma needed to be a secret for the moment.

At the beginning of November, exhausted from dialing the same phone number multiple times without success, I finally asked Alicita for help. It turned out that Riverside was in another area code and I needed to dial zero for assistance by an operator to complete the call. Alicita did it for me. Norma answered and did not believe I was in Los Angeles, thinking that I was playing games with her and only pretending to be in LA when I was really in Santa Ana.

"*Si tú no me crees, juguemos un juego. Dime donde nos podemos encontrar. ¿Hay un cafetín o restaurante cerca de tu casa? Dime el nombre, la fecha y hora cuando nos podemos ver. Hagamos la cita en este momento y te prometo que yo voy a estar ahí esperándote,*" I said.

"*Oh, bicho feo. No es posible que Usted esté aquí. No es posible. Mi Mamá y su esposo trabajan todos los fines de semana. Encontrémonos este sábado a las 11:00 de la mañana para ver si es cierto. Hay una cafetería en la esquina entre University Ave. y Douglas Ave. Espéreme adentro hasta que yo llegue, porque me tengo que escapar sin que nadie se dé cuenta. Mi Mamá me mata si sabe que fui a encontrarme con Usted,*" Norma answered in a whisper.

Alicita called a Yellow Cab to take me to the Greyhound depot near Temple City at 6:00 am on Saturday morning. The autumn gray sky sent a chill through my body and numbed my bare hands. There were no rain clouds. During the night, in mid-November, LA's temperatures could fall to the low 40s. The air was dry, soft, with the occasional, slight breeze coming from the Saint Bernardino Mountains caressing my cheeks. The sky was probably gray due to the high levels of LA pollution. Once at the depot, I didn't have to wait long for the bus to depart.

Three hours later, I found myself walking 10 blocks on University Ave., from downtown Riverside to the designated coffee shop. There was a feeling I had, walking on the street, that this was all an illusion, that it wasn't me walking, but another guy, lost in an unfamiliar city. The streets were empty this Saturday morning. I didn't see any open shops or people walking. The LA smog had given way to sunnier and warmer temperatures. Now a warmer, less refreshing air pressed against my neck and spread heat down my arms, drenching my long sleeve shirt in sweat within minutes.

The map Alicita had giving me came in handy. I sat at a table facing the street, my eyes fixed on the intersection with Douglas Ave where I knew Norma would be walking from. I did not wait long. Norma walked slowly down the street carrying a large belly. I had suspected such a thing would happen to her, but I was never sure. I doubted I was the father. I could hear my mother mumbling in my ear, *la puta de la Norma.* I did not care if I was not the father, most likely I was. A deep need to protect, and a sense of fatherly love and obligation, overcame me as I watched Norma making her way towards the coffee shop, and I knew then that the only action I could take was to marry her before the baby was born, no matter the costs. Norma has been faithful to me. I was the father.

After this first encounter, I traveled to Riverside several times to meet Norma at the coffee shop. On the third Saturday of November, at the time when most Americans were running out of inventive recipes for finishing their turkey leftovers, we hesitantly decided to leave the coffee shop and walk to her house. That same day I asked her to come to live with me in Temple City, and told her that I didn't know how, but I knew I could work hard and long to take care of her and the baby. My cousin Alicita had already accepted the prospect of having a newborn in her house with great excitement. It was left to Berta and her Chicano husband to accept the proposition.

I can only imagine now how I sounded to them. I am sure that I conveyed a super innocent desire to support Norma and the baby mixed with a macho attitude. After all, I had secured a job at the church on the corner the first day after I had arrived. This showed that I was an industrious boy with a great future, with better jobs to come once I learned English. I told them that my goal was to somehow, here in California, continue my university studies that had been interrupted by the civil unrest in El Salvador. My future was bright. Berta's daughter couldn't have been in better hands, I thought. I was a highly prepared person and success was my only destiny in this country.

After listening to my over inflated prospects for life, Norma's stepfather gave me a long cynical stare, did not make any comments, and instead offered me a ride back to Temple City. I had probably sounded like an extraterrestrial to him, totally outside of his sphere of understanding. Because of the lack of a definite response following my speech, I was sure he hated the idea of me and Norma together.

What happened next was not what I expected. Without saying a word, the Chicano disappeared into some rooms for a moment and came back with a new look. He had changed from blue jeans into dark colored pants, a loud shirt, and a black leather jacket. This was his idea of dressing up to impress my cousin Alicita. It was already night when we all left the house to get into the car. He drove a new 1972 Buick Electra. Berta sat in front; Norma and I sat in the back, afraid of holding hands, all of us in silence during the whole, long ride back to Temple City. I was expecting him to drive the new corvette I had seen parked in the side driveway of their house. Later, Norma told me that it was a stolen car and couldn't be driven yet.

Once in Temple City, Alicita very generously showed them my room where Norma and I could live with the baby. Berta and the Chicano, indifferent and uncommitted, promised to call to make arrangements for Norma's move. They never did. Norma never did. I never called and took Norma's lack of communication as a put down and understood that the Chicano and Berta saw our union as detrimental for them and for Norma. In their eyes, I was a charlatan who wanted only to obtain the green card through marriage with Norma.

Gradually, after a few weeks, it dawned on me that much more resources would be required to support Norma and her baby, which brought me into the realization that I was utterly unequipped for the task. I needed more time to settle down before taking on such a big responsibility. I knew Norma would follow orders from the intimidating Berta, who, after all, had brought Norma to LA to give her a better future. Norma wouldn't ever have dared to rebel against her mother. She was terrified and probably found it too risky to move in with me. She may not have had much of a loving relationship with her mother, but at least with Berta, Norma had financial security. If she were to move in with me and accept a life with a poor student, she would be giving up that security. My eagerness to continue my college education and eventually find a career drained all my energy and attention away from applying it to thinking about how to fight for Norma, diminishing my desire for her. My original personal commitment to her started to gradually wane and soon a profound, instinctual desire to escape took over my every thought. I was a coward. I skirted my responsibility.

Johnny, Norma's son, my first son, was born in December 1972. He would grow up thinking that Berta was his mother and Norma his sister. He found out the truth at age 16 while applying for his first driver's license after reading his birth certificate carefully, which listed Norma as his mother and Francisco Ruiz as his father. He soon started a frantic search for his father and a year later found me in Boston. Carolina invited him to live with us to continue his high school education at English High. He hated school, had dropped out during Middle School. He lasted a week with us in Boston. He went back to Riverside, California, feeling at peace, but our relationship would never mature into a father-son relationship, rather, he would finally accept Norma's husband as his real father in his life.

Carolina and I often think of Johnny with pity and a feeling of guilt for leaving him. It is not easy to accept the consequences of some of our decisions that at one time seemed to be the most appropriate and that later, it turns out, caused pain in some innocent people.

Chapter 25: Alicita, Ana, and Sharon

After deciding to forget about trying to marry Norma, I continued with my struggle to reinvent myself by creating a new independent life in America without the ever-present in-my-head commands of my seminarian life or economic dependency on others. The first thing I needed to do was to find a way to extend my US visitor visa. The only possible solution was to apply for a student visa at the Los Angeles immigration offices and list my cousin Alicita as the petitioner, stating that she would provide an affidavit of support. For sure, this would be a done deal, or so I thought.

So, one early rainy November morning with a 45-degree chill in the air, I, in my one long sleeve shirt, walked to Las Tunas Drive and took the bus to the Los Angeles immigration offices to file for a student visa, without even consulting Alicita. I understood her support to be logical and expected. She had served as my babysitter in the Hacienda back in El Salvador when my mother was too busy or needed a respite from my constant hyperactivity, so I was sure she could be trusted to vouch for me. When today I read the student-visa form I completed that day, I found it comical the many English spelling mistakes I had made on the page, even though I used a Spanish-English dictionary. By the looks of it, I did not doubt for a moment at that time that the visa would be granted upon examining my seminarian background. For sure, the immigration agents would call me soon for an interview to issue me the visa. This proved to be a big mistake.

Meanwhile, I looked for a blue pen and added a matching zero to the number of days on my current visa. The visa issuing counsel in the U.S. embassy in Mexico City had written "11 days" by hand using a blue pen and had conveniently left sufficient space between the number 11 and the word "days." Nobody would be able to notice the extra zero. Besides, it was perfectly normal to grant a 110-

day visa. If an immigration officer were to stop me to ask for my papers, the 110 would prove my legality. I would have the student visa soon anyway. This gave me peace of mine, but, thank God, I ended up never having to show it to any official.

Around a week later, when I entered the house from work, I found Ana Funes, Alicita's roommate, waiting for me at the door, fuming, green with anger, yelling at me, saying that I had jeopardized their livelihood in this country by going to immigration and filing for a student visa without their permission.

"No sabía que tú eras tan estúpido. Fuiste a dar el nombre de tu prima a las oficinas de inmigración. ¿No te das cuenta de que Alicita está ilegalmente en este país y que ahora la van a deportar porque tú les diste su dirección? Acabamos de recibir una llamada de inmigración preguntando por Alicita y su petición para mantenerte. Quiero que te vayas de esta casa inmediatamente," she yelled hysterically, seemingly on the verge of fainting.

Ana kicked me of the house. I remember Alicita coming out of the bedroom to look at me as I left with her big, black, sad eyes. Alicita lowered her head in shame. She had already submissively accepted Ana's decision knowing also that I had put her life in U.S. in jeopardy. Much later in my life, I learned that Alicita was Ana's partner. Ana was a legal resident, spoke English fluently, and was the social worker at one of the L.A. women's drug rehabilitation clinics, a well-paid job. Ana had a strong hold on Alicita's life and used her legal status as a power tool. Alicita lived in constant fear of upsetting Ana. Her punishment, were she to contradict Ana on her decision to kick me out of the house, would most likely have been a heartless denunciation to immigration officers and a definite deportation. There was nothing for Alicita back in El Salvador. Alicita looked at me with intensity and guilt, powerless to say or to do anything in my favor, as Ana continued her tyrannical rule over her by ordering me to leave.

Now, 45 years later, I understand Ana's reason. Unexpectedly, I had come to disrupt her idyllic and controlling relationship with Alicita. Ana's favorite 33 long-play record at that time was a newly released album by Barbara McNair. Her favorite song, "For Once in My Life," she played every night after dinner. This song became the first song in America whose lyrics I tried to understand. I did not see it then, but now I know her sick love message to Alicita was very clear: *"I love you because you need me, and I can control you."* On my part, Ana's decision to kick me out of the house made me confront my intense fear of being totally abandoned and the necessity to usher all my strength and wits to survive, not unlike the common issues faced by all new immigrants: where to escape, where to sleep at night, how to get food, where to live. I had not yet lived two months at Alicita's when I had to leave, a very short time, and not enough for me to have any other options lined up. I had no place to go. Where could I have gone?

Families often carry secrets, but never forever. The truth often reveals itself during family crises, emergencies, and deaths, but not always with positive effects. I had assumed that Alicita was a settled, permanent resident after having lived in this country for several years, traveling back and forth from El Salvador to LA without a hitch. My assumption could not have been further from the truth. Immigration officials did not have any records on Alicita; to the US government, she did not exist. When the immigration office called to talk to Alicita, Ana said that there was no Alicita living at that address and that most likely my application was a fraud. Officials never called again and never came to the house to investigate. Ana's anger and fears proved to be unfounded in the end. Teto now tells me that maybe Alicita used her look-alike sister,

Martita's, green card to cross the border for the longest
time, the guard in Tijuana too busy to notice the difference.

The week before being kicked out of the house, the
priest at Saint Luke's had told me that he could no longer
afford me as the parochial school custodian's helper and
let me go. The next day, I walked the streets of Temple City
and Rosemead, and visited the schools around the area
hoping for another arrangement like the one at the
church. I couldn't have known the hiring difference between parochial and public schools. All my senses were on
high alert again, constantly in an acutely vigilant state of
mind to find every job option possible. I stopped first at a
public school. It was very early, and the fresh, late-Novem-
ber breeze was invigorating. The teachers waiting outside
for the front doors to open happened to speak Spanish and
told me that I could apply for a job as a cleaner at the
central offices. I saw that as much too complicated and
would take too long. I needed a job immediately.

One of the other teachers came up to me and gave me
walking directions to the Lincoln Elementary school. I continued on East Broadway, took a left on S. San Gabriel
Blvd, and then a right on E. Grand Ave. Half an hour later
I was entering the school and standing in front of the re-
ceptionist's desk. She, immediately sensing my hesitation,
spoke to me in Spanish. I stared at her yellow-hair, probably for too long, and then lowered my eyes to her
accentuated, thick lower lip. Her Spanish was flawless and
her accent Central-American, addressing me with the col-
loquial *vos*, instead of the formal *usted*. She had just
warmed my soul.

Sharon, recently back from Costa Rica with her husband Jorge and young daughter Natalie, had decided to
volunteer at Natalie's school answering the phones in the
mornings. Volunteering brought Sharon out of the house
and gave her a renewed purpose in the otherwise boring
and isolated life carried out by most white American

housewives in the early 1970's in Rosemead. I, with my usual speaking style, always enunciating words with great feeling, did not waste time in relating my situation to her. Sharon's face brightened up, excited by an encounter with a Central American in a heavily Mexican immigrant population.

She left the desk, invited me to sit outside in the school's playground, and recounted her happy adventure while on her two-year stay in Costa Rica. There, she was the center of attention and admiration, practically a sensation, within her husband Jorge's family. Costa Rican men would stop to whisper *piropos* at her while walking on San Jose's Avenida Central. This idealization and constant attention from the local men that only Latin women usually had to endure made her feel beautiful and powerful, but Jorge found it unsettling. The day after he found out that one of his uncles disrespectfully had been trying to seduce Sharon for a while, and doubting Sharon's commitment to their marriage, Jorge decided to bring his family back to the States.

At the end of our intimate exchanging of stories, Sharon offered me help finding a job and insisted on driving me home. I had only walked around three miles to get there and found it unnecessary to be driven back home. It was too soon in this city for me to realize that nobody walked in LA. Her new light blue 1972 Toyota 1600 station wagon took me back home in no time. I, innocently, asked her to come in for a drink of water. Once inside the house, she followed me to the kitchen and I promptly handed her a glass of iced water. As she grabbed the glass with her right hand, she held my hand with her left one. I did not respond as I tried to read her intentions. She laid the glass of water softly on the white linoleum kitchen counter without looking at it. I waited for the water to spill and the glass to shatter all over the ceramic tiles. It didn't. Sharon silently kept her eyes on me without flinching. With an abrupt and sudden jerk, she pulled me towards her, now using her two hands, and started kissing my mouth desperately. She then pushed me slowly taking short steps, pressing her breasts against my chest, forcing me to respond with similar steps backwards, not unlike two intimate tango dancers moving in time with the music.

Next, she steered me out of the kitchen, looking for a comfortable place to land, all the while with her mouth sucking mine without letting go. We finally reached my cousin's bedroom door. Sharon hesitated in the hall, concerned about mistaking this bedroom for mine. She then opted to angle me backwards against the wall, short of breath. Her kisses moved to my neck as she undid the buttons of my long-sleeve shirt. One snapped and I heard it land on top of the table in the hall. I made a mental note to retrieve it later. I was very fond of the light-pink new long-sleeve shirt I wore that day. Alicita had just driven me to buy it at Sears. Its fabric was thin and let the Californian breeze refresh my skin.

Confused, I allowed her to do with me whatever she wanted. A forceful rejection would have put her to shame and I thought it improper and disrespectful. I had just met her. How she was treating me was obviously, or so I assumed, the norm in America and I had to adjust to this new culture. I, however, now suppose that I was easily seduced and made vulnerable by my own overwhelming desire to explore the world.

Suddenly, releasing what seemed to be a previously repressed, strong, pent up desire, Sharon pushed me towards the living room sofa and wasted no time in lowering her blue bell-bottom dress pants. Next, she threw her white blouse to the floor and did not wait for me to snap her bra open, as I had learned to do with Norma. She undid it herself and threw it next to where the blouse had landed. Her breasts were pinkish white with straight and thin nipples, her arms and legs long and thin. She reminded me of an egret bird just before it snapped a small fish out of the water.

I panicked at the thought of Alicita or Ana coming home early and finding me with a stranger in the living room sofa. I may have been biologically ready, but my mind was filled with Norma's face. Sharon mounted me frantically, but then slowly moved her hips up and down, moaning softly with her eyes closed. I watched her intently, waiting for her next move, not knowing when it all would end. After what seemed to be a long time, Sharon burst into yells and shrieks before collapsing her body on top of me, exhausted.

I had kept in absolute silence the whole time. I had felt no need to show her that I was a macho man bursting with virility by taking control of the situation. I just let it happen. This was my second time in bed with a woman, but this time turned out to be a solely physical act void of emotional attachments. If I were to go to confession with one of the Seminary priests, I would have received angry admonitions, a long mortification, and a steep punishment. During the act, Norma's face never left my mind. For whatever reason, my nose bled towards the end and Sharon tried gingerly to stop the bleeding. Later, she took one of the sofa beige cushions that my blood had spilled on to the kitchen to treat it with a liquid other than dish soap to wash it out.

The experience was horrible. I didn't know what had just happened, but I did know that after her carnal desires had been satiated, Sharon would be predisposed to provide me with any type of assistance. At this time in my life, I just went with the flow of social interactions with the passive aim of exploring and experiencing life as it came to me, and for that to happen, I had to yield control to others. I was reluctant to participate in what appeared to me to be sinful acts: the teachings of the Seminary, those from Padre Chus especially, were ever-present at the back of my mind. In a sense, others probably took advantage of what they saw as a willingness to accept their approaches. They saw my new and uninitiated immigrant state of mind as weakness to exploit for their own personal gain, which at this time I was too inexperienced to understand. In a sense, with Sharon, though I didn't know it then, I had just become a sort of male prostitute.

After a short while, Sharon abruptly jumped up from the sofa and left me naked, saying that it was already time to pick up Natalie from school. After getting dressed and before she left, Sharon turned to give me a long, wet kiss. "Your mouth is so delicious," she said as she closed the front door behind her.

Recently, when I visited Ernesto, I asked him if he had any idea why Sharon would have said that. He said that at that moment in my life I looked like a pious virgin ready to be deflowered. Sharon felt she had made some kind of conquest. Her behavior, however, corroborated the misconceptions about American women Salvadorian men had grown up with in the 60's: white Californian women were independent, daring and easy, as shown in the American movies. By stark contrast, afraid of social recrimination in the small towns and social circles, and ashamed of religious admonitions, Salvadorian girls took very long before sleeping with their boyfriends, if ever.

Soon after Sharon had left, Ana stopped at home accompanied by one of her addict clients. My nostrils were quickly saturated with a smoky herbal smell: a mix of tobacco, marijuana, and cheap perfume combined with an unwashed body odor. I quickly left the house for a walk around the neighborhood to think about what just had happened, breathing deeply to make sure my nose did not bleed again. I noticed that my shirt was stained with a couple of drops of blood, now dried brown from oxidation.

I found it very strange that Ana would bring a client to the house. Maybe that was her routine, or maybe Ana was also an addict and came home to do drugs and have sex with her clients. She did not expect me to be home so early. When I came back from my walk, I found Ana's client sitting on the sofa where Sharon had just pleasured herself with my body. I went straight to my room without uttering a word as I passed by her. I opened the top drawer of my bureau to check on my savings. My entire cash bundle was gone.

I burst into Ana's room. I remember I found her in bed, maybe taking a nap or something else. I told her that her client had just stolen my money. She shook her head violently to fully wake up, stepped into the living room to search her client in front of me, but she did not search, only asked. Her client denied the accusation. I knew she had probably stuck the several hundred-dollar bills deep inside her underwear. There was nothing I could do to retrieve the money. I thought about jumping on her to forcibly undress her, but the social norms of respect and decorum prevented me from doing such a thing. Ana was the authority of the house, much older than I was. I had to respect my elders. Today, were a similar violation on my property happen to me, I would become incensed and disregard all social norms and respect for authority, resulting in a more aggressive act, probably at my own risk.

At that time, I was still under the influence of the Seminarian ethos and civility. It hurt me to see the money the priest had paid me for cleaning the school vanishing in an instant. Ana did not cooperate with me, did not show any concern, and took the incident as normal. She might have thought I had forgotten where I had kept my money in the first place, or, maybe she was an accomplice. Welcome to America! Her client had also taken the addressed envelope where I had just inserted a one-hundred-dollar bill for my Guatemalan cousin, Sandra. I had promised to pay her $100.00 loan back as soon as I crossed the border and found my first job.

The robbery had very negative repercussions in my life. I couldn't pay Sandra as planned. My good intentions were never recognized by Sandra. Soon after this incident, Sandra sent me heated letters reproaching my sleazy conduct for not doing what I had promised. I became a thief in her eyes. My robbery excuse was hard to believe and therefore only confirmed her suspicions. There is nothing that hurts more than being accused unjustly for an act that one did not commit; all caused by another injustice, in my case a robbery. It hurts. It changes you. The chances of dancing tango with her on our next reunion became null. After two horrible experiences in one day, my search for a new job became even more desperate.

Therefore, when Ana told me that I had to leave the house because I represented a danger to Alicita's immigration status, I immediately called Sharon and asked for help. I don't remember if I cried as I said goodbye to my cousin and childhood babysitter, Alicita. She didn't utter a word; such was her submissive attitude towards Ana. My childhood babysitter, my first cousin, was abandoning me to fend for myself in the face of unknown cruelties in an unfamiliar city, country, and world. I felt frighteningly unprotected and a strong desire for one of her long hugs and multiple motherly kisses, as was her habit every time I scraped my knee running in the hiking trails of the Hacienda, overcame me. She, instead, wiping her eyes with her fingers, lowered her head, turned around quickly, and with urgent steps disappeared into the shadows inside the house. Ana stood in the threshold of the front door in silence, but her body language gave the clear indication that the sooner I walked out through it, the better. I suspect now that Ana's desire was to get rid of me and had found the perfect excuse. She wanted to be left alone with Alicita. I think I was, probably, crying when I phoned Sharon. There is no way I could not have been crying.

It had long since gotten dark as I waited outside on the curb for Sharon. A smooth, cold, November rain covered the stone tiles of the walkway to the house and gave it a glassy sheen that reflected the shimmery street lights. The wavering images of the street lights in the water made me dizzy and I plunged into a deep pool of sorrow. Sharon came to pick me up within 20 minutes in her Toyota. I didn't have any possessions other than Teto's green army duffle bag packed with my clothes ready to go. Sharon drove slowly back to her house. The LA rain had become unusually intense, making the gutters overflow and form dark, nearly unperceivable pools around the street curbs. According to Sharon, the lightweight Toyota was prone to hydroplaning.

Her husband Jorge was waiting for us at home and quickly suggested the garage as my quarters. He would bring out an old mattress for me, but Sharon protested and installed me in the guest room while her daughter Natalie stared at me wide eyed, wondering why this new person was coming to live with them, maybe thinking I was a Costa Rican relative.

The next morning, Sharon, who had recently found a secretarial job at a local insurance company, and Jorge, who made bundles of money being a lineman in the desert for the California Bell company, left early for their jobs. I soon became the de facto babysitter for Natalie, walking her to and from school while I tried to find a new job. At this moment, however, learning English became more important to me than a job. Sharon was able to convince Jorge that they needed to support me while I found my way in America.

Sharon was in love with me, I did not feel the same for her. At this time, I did not have any other choice but to follow her desires. I was fighting for survival, and had to take advantage of any opportunity, regardless of the consequences. That I could be the cause of the destruction of their marriage was not one of my considerations. I imagined that infidelity was expected from white America women. Jorge would have known this, but he never suspected Sharon's midnight barefooted walks to my bedroom. I became blind to everything else, but to my survival. I let her come to my bedroom in the middle of the night as often as she wanted. Some nights she visited me twice, just after midnight and before sunrise. I did not derive any pleasure from those encounters, while she repeatedly achieved ecstasies. When asked about Jorge, she insisted that there was nothing to worry about. He was a heavy sleeper.

For some people, the personal quest of pleasure and quick satisfaction of instinctual urges overrides all other needs in their lives. They risk it all for some fleeting moments. This is what some people call lack of self-control or addiction. Sharon risked the wellbeing of her family every time she ventured into my room at 2:00 am. Half asleep, I performed passively and let her do most of the work. Every morning, upon waking up, I had a hard time recollecting the specifics of what had happened the night before. Sharon did something else by her licentious conduct. She shifted my conception of women in general, from an idealized, almost spiritual version kept on a pedestal, and fostered while in the Seminary, to a more concrete human figure whose corporal satisfactions were uncontrollable and thus inevitable, despite the negative outcomes for others. This new understanding of the kind of satisfaction that had to be fulfilled at all cost was the total opposite of what I had internalized in the Seminary, where I was taught that pleasure was a side effect of life, never its purpose, and when it came, it needed to be controlled and soon extinguished.

Furthermore, Sharon corroborated the common stereotypes Latin men had of American white women as sex maniacs and easy to take to bed. She used me as her new sex toy to obtain inordinate physical pleasure, knowing that I was inexperienced and almost a virgin since I had been only with one woman, Norma, in my entire life and for only a few fleeting moments. It did not take a long time for me to accept her role as a mentor of pleasure at night, not wanting to jeopardize the sense of security I felt and the economical help she provided outside of these encounters. I also became aware that her sex-mentor role increased her dependency on me as it intensified her own sexual pleasure to the maximum. I don't remember Jorge and Natalie waking up ever at night from Sharon's loud screams and moans of pleasure that would quickly become muffled under my pillow. On my part, I just wanted a short respite in my struggle to survive. My mind was always somewhere else, with Norma.

Chapter 26: Jorge

Sharon sent me to the South El Monte day school for adults to learn English in an open enrollment ESL-1 program for beginners. Jorge gave me his standard black 1970 VW with a new 1972 engine that I helped him install one weekend. I drove this car back and forth from school, all the while never having a driver's license.

I had driven a car only once before and that was under extraneous circumstances at the end of my propaedeutic year in the Juan XXIII minor Seminary in Santa Ana. One November Sunday, early morning, a chauffeur drove us, five seminarians and Padre Camilo, in an old, green, Willy's station wagon that had been donated by one of the rich benefactors, to the outskirts of the coffee plantations of the Tacuba Mountains. Our job was to hike up and down the trails while singing religious chants and stopping periodically to announce ourselves at the village chapel to all inhabitants and coffee pickers. "*Vengan todos ustedes esta mañana a oír la palabra de Dios. Habrá bautismos, confesiones, confirmaciones, y matrimonios. El Padre Camilo Girón va a dar misa.*" Late afternoon we waited for the chauffeur to take us back to the Seminary. He never came back. We found the jeep with the keys inserted parked in front of the chapel.

Padre Camilo was nowhere to be found. Being the *celador,* the prefect, I was supposed to assume leadership. The way I did it was to tell the other seminarians that I was going to drive us back to the city, which I did. I drove the jeep as if I had driven daily my entire life. Down the switchbacks, the jeep swung to the left and swung to the right sharply as I negotiated the tight curves of the dirt road, trying not to look down the precipice. I regard this as another case of divine intervention in my life. There is no other logical explanation for having survived the long trek down a very dangerous road. The seminarians had a blast. Their bodies accompanied the swings of the vehicle and uttered a long "aaaahhhhhh" as they slid from side to side in the back seat. We found Padre Camilo at the seminary. With an astonished face he asked, "Who drove el jeep?" "Chico drove it," the seminarian responded in unison. "I didn't know Chico knew how to drive!" he said. "I didn't know either," I said, laughing.

So, evident by my experience driving down the mountain, driving came naturally to me. I just drove out of Jorge's driveway, fitting the reverse gear into place with a smooth motion without producing any creaking noises out of the transmission box. Maybe the reason for my instinctive driving was that when I was four, my father often asked me to change the gears of our green and blue 1952 Chevy pick-up truck as he drove. Its metal stick gear shift came out of the floor and had a hard metal knob screwed on top that showed the gear numbers and a shifting diagram imprinted on it. I would stand behind this stick. The black knob, which was almost as tall as me, often knocked into my forehead from the vibration of the car forcing me to grab the stick shift with my two hands and wait for my father's instructions.

"*Cuando yo le diga, usted mueve la palanca para atrás. De la velocidad 'primera' a la velocidad 'segunda'. Y cuando yo le indique de nuevo, la mueve un poquito rápido hacia la derecha sin soltarla e inmediatamente la empuja bien fuerte hacia adelante para que entre la velocidad tercera.*"

Another reason I fearlessly jumped into the black VW beetle without ever having really driven a car before, had to do with the perfect design of the Los Angeles streets. With high concentration, I would drive Jorge's car and shift gears with the proper use of the clutch, without producing the expected transmission grinding sound of an unexperienced driver. The roads appeared to usher me easily to my destination. Often, I had an El Monte police patrol car behind me, trailing me for several blocks, something that would have made any other Latino immigrant anxious, but I never made anything of it. I felt invincible and immortal.

I soon became Jorge's compadre. During weekends, he was very proud to show me the amenities of LA and its surroundings. We became a trio with Sharon. Living with them, I was exposed to the vibrant LA nightlife. Jorge took us to flamenco performances around La Ciénega Blvd, to dance clubs on Sunset Blvd, and to popular restaurants in West Hollywood. One weekend in early January, he drove us to the snowy Saint Bernardino Mountains. This same weekend he taught me how to install chains around the tires to improve the low powered Toyota station wagon's traction. During another weekend, Jorge drove us to Magic Mountain to the delight of Natalie. After dinner on weekdays, Jorge often took me to the Rosemead public library to read and study. At times, I felt Jorge was treating me like a much younger brother or a son that needed to be instructed in the realities of life. I easily played along and soon assumed the role of a student. This is what I was trained to do in the Seminary: to be a sounding board for the community's sentiments and to constantly enrich my soul with new knowledge. This induced him to take the role of a mentor to perfection, and I took the one of a motivated pupil, which was precisely the role that a seminarian was indoctrinated to play.

This was not the first nor would it be the last relationship where I would assume the motivated pupil role. Under this role, I attentively and humbly followed the mentor's recommendations without dampening my inquisitive attitude as the disciples may have done with Jesus. My behavior, in turn, motivated the mentor to continue assuming and perfecting his role. Taken together, this dialectic provided continuous inspiration and encouragement to the relationship.

Jorge never asked me to contribute economically to the household. He felt lonely, found our conversations intellectually enriching, and was soothed by my Central American Spanish. I reminded him of what he was 15 years prior when he emigrated to LA from Costa Rica. In a sense, I brought the ambiance of his homeland back to him and this made him happy. I often think about him every now and then. I have been looking for him for a long time on social media without success. He may not be computer savvy or may guard his privacy. I would like to see him to ask for forgiveness and thank him for his unconditional generosity and support. I often also wonder what became of his daughter, Natalie.

The 1972 winter I spent with this family proved to be a very wet winter in Los Angeles, especially during the month of November. This time in my life is etched in my memory as a long, grey, wet, and very cold period, not like the dry ones experienced recently in perennially sunny Southern California.

Chapter 27: Ernesto.

One early, sparkling January morning of 1973, holding a twin-wire blue notebook with 100 sheets that I bought for 89 cents, and a black pen I took from Sharon's kitchen counter in my shirt pocket, I showed up at El Monte Union High School District School for Adults. Its one-floor-low-ceilinged building looked as if it had been assembled using prefabricated classrooms put together like Lego blocks. The adult education center was located across the street from the El Monte Police Station. One block down the street, a large, metallic art deco sign with thick and wide 50's style letters announced the El Monte shopping center, a sort of arcade. The rear of the school connected to an open green field with a picnic area away from the traffic noise. Three isolated wooden benches with a round table to their side stood at the right, their varnish faded to an ugly, pale brown, and I wondered if anybody ever ventured to the back of the school for lunch.

After an initial diagnostic test, I was placed in the ESL-1 class with Ms. Phillips. I had done very poorly in the English for beginner's class at *El Colegio San José* in Santa Ana. I couldn't ever decipher sets or strings of unpronounceable consonants so common in English, which invariably interfered with my attempts to glean any meaning out of the words. How are, for example, the *shr, nts, ght, thr* sounds in words like shroud, counts, thought, and threw pronounced? I could never understand how there was no vowel between those clusters of consonants. Luckily, there were no oral or reading tests at *el Colegio*. The priest who was teaching us did not know how to speak English. Our task was to write Spanish translations from short English paragraphs. I resorted to learn English vocabulary using Spanish pronunciation, which does not ignore any vowels, but ignores strings of consonants. This did not work. I became highly frustrated and developed a deep aversion, close to hate, towards the English language. Now in El Monte, my survival instinct had kicked in and I had to put my negative attitude aside. I had not had women as teachers since elementary school. I felt as if my mother was teaching me. Ms. Phillips' sincere smile and caring eyes made me feel immediately welcomed. There were 10 students in the class, a mixture of Mexicans, Central Americans, and Cubans. I could see that Ms. Phillips was made to teach immigrants and understood the best and gentlest methods. We respected and loved her.

On the first day of classes during the morning break, as I walked out to the back field for some fresh air, I heard a voice coming from behind calling for my attention.

"¿Cómo te llamas?" a short and stocky, young guy asked me, smiling happily.

"Francisco," I said.

"Oye, ¿Quieres comerte un taco? Te invito," he stated with confidence, almost like he wanted to show off, without letting go of his smile.

"¿En cuál restaurante?" I asked.

"No seas buey. ¿Acaso no sabes que aquí uno compra comida de las trocas enfrente de la escuela?" He said, surprised to encounter someone incredibly ignorant of LA culture.

"No. Yo nunca he hecho eso en mi vida." I said, taking on an air of importance. I thought buying food from a truck was too strange for me.

"Vamos. Antes que se nos acabe el tiempo. No me gusta regresar tarde a la clase." He concluded.

We sat on one of the pale wooden benches to eat our tacos directly outside the rear door of the school. Soon, other students gathered in small groups around us, introducing themselves with short narratives of their lives. They talked about how they ended up in Los Angeles, their living arrangements with family or distant relatives, what they were trying to achieve, and how important it was to learn English to succeed in this country. Their other option was to return home knowing English and pray that they would find a better job with their new skill. The Costa Rican was sent to the US by his parents after finishing high school with the purpose of studying English before starting his first year at the university back home in September. The Cuban said the US government was paying him to learn English, and that he lived in a subsidized apartment. I felt extremely jealous to hear his story. Why would the Cubans get such better, more humane treatment? Of course, all in the name of anti-communism.

Most of the students, however, were poor, but highly motivated and aware that there was no real success possible without English. Their families were supporting them while they studied for at least six months. Upon hearing that I was looking for a job, my new friend offered to drive me to the factory where he worked nights after school. He would talk to the manager. I would most likely be hired in light of my new friend's reputation as a hard worker. I had just met Ernesto, a Mexican from Guadalajara, and someone who soon would become my best friend.

I had never seen a factory, but I knew that factories paid well for repetitive, physical work. The idea of a factory also made me think of a moral told in the Seminary. The Bishop Barrera used to tell us the story of a seminarian in Belgium that asked for permission to take a leave of absence for a semester to work undercover in a factory. He wanted to acquire a real-world experience by identifying with the lives and struggles of underpaid factory workers who most likely would be part of his future congregation. Soon after his arrival at the factory, the workers were surprised by the seminarian's humility, commenting positively on his demeanor, speech, love, and respect. He also showed a highly developed optimism and work ethic, combined with a sense of calm, patience, and leadership, especially when the workers confronted problems with the tasks assigned by management. The factory workers con-cluded that the new hire's behavior could only be explained if he were a son of God, a priest, or a true Chris-tian. There couldn't be any other explanation for his comportment.

Bishop Barrera would conclude the story by saying that as priests, our congregations would pay close atten-tion to our behavior and would want to emulate it. It behooved us to comport ourselves just like Jesus Christ would have in all aspects of our lives, without bragging about it, or using the habit for our personal gain. A true Christian needed to show, not tell, by example. I was will-ing to follow his instructions in this gringa factory. Perhaps not showing holiness, but much courage, respon-sibility, initiative and observation.

We stopped at Ernesto's house on our way to the fac-tory. He wanted a change of clothes. A small shed containing garden tools at the end of the backyard of a small, ranch style house was where he lived, which was hardly visible from the street obscured by overgrown bushes of maidenhair fern and hoary manzanita. The owner of the main house was a UCLA University professor who Ernesto had befriended and who gave him shelter in the shed in exchange for yard work and errands. Ernesto slept on a stained futon mattress placed on the floor and had access to the bathroom and kitchen while the profes-sor was away teaching at one of the California University system campus.

Ernesto came out of the shed a few minutes later wear-ing an old, plaid flannel shirt, like you would see the East LA Chicano's wear in the streets, and a pair of blue jean overalls, like the ones factory workers wear in black and white 1940's Hollywood movies. He reminded me of one of Luis Buñuel films, *Los Olvidados*.

The shift at the factory started at 4:00 pm and ended at 12:00 am. I then remembered how the expatriate Sal-vadorians, like my cousin Alicita, would come back home to El Salvador for Christmas vacation, driving a new car, a Falcon or a Mustang, with Californian plates, their wallets full of dollars. They often spoke about how their dollars had been acquired by working hard, including overtime, in a factory.

Alicita came back home to Santa Ana with Irma, not Ana, for Christmas vacation in 1967 driving a 1966 Falcon. She organized an extravagant party that year, with endless liquor, music, and food. It appeared that the whole town of Santa Ana showed up, some just to look at the new Falcon coup. Alicita's house, *La gran casona de Los Menéndez Castro,* was one of the largest in town, and could easily accommodate hundreds of people in its corridors and multiple patios.

I, on leave from the Seminary, attended the party with Teto and my parents. Irma, well endowed, made a point of tempting me all night by inviting me to dance cumbias under the disapproving eye of my mother who protected me like a Venetian vase. Irma kept me in a tight squeeze all night, pressing her large firm breasts against my chest, and feeling and rubbing my permanent erection with her thighs expecting a full inevitable ecstasy, which I made sure, with extraordinary mental power and control, to avoid. I suspended my desire at the point of almost, which was highly pleasurable in itself. I resisted it up to the end of the night, when finally, my mother decided to pull me away from Irma. Teto now tells me that Irma wanted to take me to her room to make love to me exclusively to prove that all priests were hypocrites and celibacy was a myth. Irma, half-drunk, ended up driving us home to the *multis,* Apt. #34.

The next day Bishop Barrera announced that Gustavo and I would be going to Puebla, Mexico, on a 7-year scholarship towards master's in philosophy and a doctorate in theology. I felt worthy of it. I had been tempted like never before with Irma, and I had not succumbed. It also helped me that the Bishop had been extremely impressed by my ability to organize in short notice a community boys' choir for the Christmas festivities. But even now, years later, I have my doubts about whether the Bishop sent me to Mexico because of my own merits or because I would be a companion to Gustavo, his favorite. We left with the Bishop for Mexico that January of 1968.

Four months later, around the Spring, I received a letter from my mother, stained with tears, telling me that she had decided to accompany Alicita and Irma on their way back to Los Angeles to find work. As I read the letter, I could imagine the tears in her eyes when she continued to tell me that on her way up, she had stopped in Puebla to see me. Sadly, the old ignorant concierge at the Seminary did not bother to announce her visit to the administration. Rector Huesca had ordered complete silence during our retreat of fasting in spiritual preparation for Holy Week. It was April 5, 1968. Despondent, my mother walked back to the Falcon, crying, not wanting to upset the unknown norms of my new cloister, God forbid, inadvertently aiding in my sinning. Impatient, Irma hurried to get to Los Angeles. They just drove away. I wouldn't see my mother again until the summer of 1969.

Fast forward back to meeting Ernesto and the possibility of a new job, I couldn't contain my excitement. I was about to become one more Salvadorian making a lot of money by working hard in a factory. I saw myself going back to Santa Ana inviting my entire family and friends to a big Christmas and New Year's fiesta, courtesy of my pockets full of green crispy dollars, with my Mustang parked in front of the house. I would ask la *Niña María* de Chalchuapa to make one hundred *panes con chumpe and* hire *la marimba del pueblo* to play my mother's favorite songs all night.

This time I would forgive my father for being an alcoholic and would order the best-imported rum for his delight. I would want him to be proud of me and say, "Chepito left us. We thought he was dead, but he came back after succeeding in LA. I never thought he had it in him." Images of the ancient rites of passage flooded my imagination. Yes, I represented the Greek hero who had left Athens on a quest, survived the wilderness and savage beasts, and had come back home after transforming into quite a man; marching into the dusty town triumphant, with the skinned hide of a lion on his shoulders. Those thoughts filled my heart with extreme happiness. I would also make enough money to give back the $100.00 Sandra, my Guatemalan cousin, had lent me, finally repaying that debt and releasing a weight from my shoulders.

On our way to the factory, Ernesto's old green Plymouth sedan sputtered and stalled suddenly at one of the intersections, jolting me back to the present, and casting a cloud of doubt over my possible first day of work. Ernesto had paid $400.00 for the car, knew its quirks, and therefore knew how to fix it. He got out of the car, opened the hood, loosened and re-tightened some gaskets, wiggled some hoses, then got back in and asked me to get out and push the car from behind. I tried my hardest to push it down the street without success. Noticing my failure, a group of idle Chicano boys with oversized pants ran from the sidewalk to help me; a broken-down car in the middle of the street driven by Mexicans a familiar site in LA. The Plymouth sedan started again, and we continued our trip to the factory. *To survive in LA, I'm going to have to learn about car mechanics,* I thought. *Yet another addition to a long list.*

Ernesto eagerly walked me to the main office to present me to the manager. The blonde-haired, blue eyed manager looked at me, gave me a blueprint to read, and asked Ernesto to translate. He pointed to the paper and uttered a sequence of questions to see if I at least understood what the blueprint instructed me to build. The black and white blueprint showed different diagrams, arrows, circles, squares, rectangles, bars, and angles with a list of materials, mostly metal bars of different dimensions, weights and sizes. It also listed steps to be followed to construct an ornamental fence. The diagrams were easier to understand than the first geometry lesson I had had at the Seminary, but I knew that the directions written in English would present a challenge. I kept my doubts to myself, however, and I was hired on the spot. "He'll have table number 3, next to yours, Ernesto. Show him how it's done," the manager said.

The factory building with fluorescent industrial lamps hanging close to the high ceilings looked rather small. The fumes and gases containing aluminum, arsenic, and beryllium obscured further the masked faces of the employees working on the dimly lit floor. I had no idea how the workers could read their opaque blueprints. Upon entering, I coughed instantly.

The raw metallic smells of the factory brought me back to the time in Chalchuapa when my mother, prompted by her rich sibling, insisted that I learn a trade. *"Rosita, tú tienes cuatro varones. Tu única salvación de tu pobreza es el poner a trabajar a tus hijos lo más pronto posible. Olvídate de darles estudios.,"* my mother's siblings often repeated. I had just turned 12, was doing well in the sixth grade, but faced a very uncertain educational future. My father's alcoholism had finally devastated the entire family and there was no money to pay for my secondary education. She decided that learning car mechanics would help me create a source of income without a high school diploma. Her brother, Tío Chendo, who had an engineering degree from the University of Chicago and was the owner of a coffee mill and car shop, would train me. I spent two months of vacation at his shop before starting the seventh grade in Santa Ana. He was not a good teacher and I didn't learn anything. He only made me clean dirty scrap metal all day. I soon stopped going to his shop, but the toxic smells of his mill and car shop, the same ones in the LA factory, remained inside the deepest nooks of my nostrils.

In the Los Angeles factory, there were twelve heavy, metal, rectangular tables with aluminum edges and tops, 15 feet long and six feet wide, in two groups of six tables placed side by side. When I entered, a shower of shooting sparks sprang out of each table illuminating the plant and large amorphous shadows formed on the high metal walls. On the longest side, the plant opened wide to a large patio. This was considered the welders' common area, where supplies and specific cutting machines and furnaces were kept. Welders waited in line at the start of the night to have access to them. The sooner you cut your materials the sooner you could start and finish the allotted blueprints.

The job consisted of finishing 12 feet of ornamental wrought iron fencing every night by using electric welding guns. Each welder started with a blueprint handed to them by the engineer at the factory office and then proceeded to cut all the parts needed: posts, end posts, stays, rails, and bars and rods of different dimensions from pre-manufactured materials. Each of us was given an industrial welding helmet. There were no gloves or filtering masks, only the thick opaque glass of the helmet to protect my eyes. My "sissy" hands, as they were described by the custodian at the Saint Luke's parish in Temple City, were still as such.

Ernesto sensed that I was an intellectual, not a laborer by nature, and with great patience spent the first night next to me at my heavy aluminum table teaching me the art of electric welding. I found that one needed to treat the metal with great care to avoid unnecessary perforations that might widen the planned seams, where the bars and the rails, for example, met, rendering the welding and metal pieces useless. In such a case, one had to throw the damaged pieces onto a pile kept in the outdoor common area, hoping that those pieces could be salvaged by another welder. Having to go back to the cutting machine was intensely avoided by the workers. This further delayed the completion of the job and put the worker in jeopardy of being let go by management. The discarded pieces created waste and increased the cost of production. The foreman kept an eye on the size of the pile. It took me the entire night practicing on other welders' damaged pieces to finally produce perfect seams. Ernesto ran back and forth between his table and mine supervising the quality of my work.

The white foreman came by several times to assess my progress. At the end of the night, he announced that I was ready to have my own load the next day and be paid $2.00 per hour, which was for me a fortune. But I was not ready. During the first week at the factory, Ernesto continued to run back and forth every night between his table and my table to help me finish my 12 feet of ornamental ironwork.

"*¡Pinche buey! Vengo a ayudarte a terminar tu trabajo, nada más vigila al forman. Cuando se de vuelta al final de la planta me dices, para yo irme de regreso a mi mesa. Cuando él regrese de su caminata de inspección y pase por tu mesa, tú nada más tienes que hacer el mate que estás pensando, y examinando con tus ojos bien pelados tu soldadura, o ponte a leer el plano, como si estás leyendo lo que te hace falta por hacer,*" Ernesto whispered in my ear after suddenly appearing at my table.

He had been observing me for a while and noticed that I was struggling with my welding seams.

"*Yo no sé por qué me está tardando tanto. Es que estoy haciendo hoyitos innecesarios, se me pasa la mano, no sé cómo controlar la pistola, y tengo que descartar los pedazos,*" I answered anxiously, in constant fear of being fired on the spot.

The first week I did great work with Ernesto's help. The foreman was pleased to see the finished iron fences with all their ornaments perfectly curled and the welding seams smooth on the bars and asked me to continue coming every night to work. Around 1:00 am, Ernesto would drop me back home at Jorge and Sharon's house.

Having a new job at night created a new routine around the house. When I got home around 1:00 am, I found the house dark and silent, but knew that Sharon was not sleeping, just waiting. I knew Jorge and Natalie were sound sleep like always. They were heavy sleepers. Sharon would hear me in the shower and estimate the time it took me to walk to my room and get under my covers to go to sleep. She would then cross the living room to enter my room to get her pleasure. The only need I had at that moment was to sleep, making me generally unresponsive. She did not care. Somehow, she always got what she wanted regardless.

After a few weeks, the inevitable happened. One night, Sharon did not come to my room. Next morning, Jorge surprised me by asking me if I loved Sharon. I did not respond.

"*¿Dónde está Sharon?*" I asked, with my heart in my throat.

"*Ayer se fue a vivir con una amiga que tiene un apartamento en West Hollywood. Me dejó solo. Se llevó a Natalie. Si tú la amas, tú te puedes quedar con ella. Yo me voy a vivir temporariamente cerca del desierto donde estamos poniendo torres con cables eléctricos para llevar electricidad hacia algunos pueblos lejanos. La compañía de California Bell me da donde vivir,*" answered Jorge with a somber tone. I did not say anything. I barely had time to figure out why Jorge wasn't beating me to death on the spot before I immediately had to think about my next move: Where was I going to live now?

Jorge, reading my mind, continued, "*tú te puedes quedar en esta casa. El alquiler está pagado por dos meses más. Un día de estos, Sharon va a venir a buscar sus cosas y a llevarse los muebles. Si tú todavía estás aquí le puedes ayudar a mudarse a su nueva casa.*"

"*Por supuesto,*" I said, showing an eagerness to serve and please, "*cualquier cosa estoy dispuesto a hacer,*" finishing my glass of orange juice, and getting ready to leave for school. I hadn't driven the black VW for a while after I met Ernesto.

Ernesto came to pick me up right on time and we left for school. That was the last time I saw Jorge. One year after this incident, I called him one day from one of the public phones at the entrance of the Mugar library, at the Boston University Sherman Student Union, during my first semester as a freshman in 1974. I wanted him to be proud of me. By then, he had divorced Sharon, married a Latina woman, become a Jehovah Witness, and found complete bliss. When I asked about Sharon, he told me that she had also remarried and had become a Jehovah Witness. He gave me his new address in West Hollywood. Through the phone, I heard a young female voice with a Colombian accent calling him *corazón* from someplace in the house, to which he replied, *"ya llego."* He refused to give me Sharon's phone number. I wanted her to be proud of me too, now that I could speak more English with an extensive, academic vocabulary.

That day, when I came back from work at 1:00 am, I walked around the silent house and an indescribable loneliness mixed with fear made me tremble. The brotherhood and camaraderie deep-felt in the Seminary were long gone but its absence never ceased to affect me. Jorge had reproduced that feeling, but now that I was alone yet again, a deep depression spread through me. When I got up the next day to an empty house, I burst into tears, confused about the purpose of my life, lost in the present, and facing an imagined but uncertain future. My mind quickly veered towards my past life. Did Teto go back to the army under my father's insistence? Was Gustavo and Elsita's first baby born without any problems? Were my parents, especially my mother, wondering about my whereabouts? I started to believe how foolish I had been all these years thinking that the Seminary motto *"Ad Maiora Natus"* was a prophecy that would be fulfilled within me, regardless of the strength provided by life's obstacles. Instead, I might have been doomed for failure.

I had resisted writing a letter to my parents about my struggles. I wanted them to hear only successes, not failures, and felt it was not yet the moment to get in touch with them. Teto told me recently that I had made a mistake not writing sooner. My mother cried everyday thinking I was already dead, killed some place on my way north.

Norma also popped into my head as I sat on the brown sofa in the living room. Norma had a baby and it was most likely mine, but there was nothing I could do about it at that moment. I had no money. I did not have a permanent job. I was nobody. Her mother, Berta, had already forbidden her any contact with me. I did not combat Berta's orders. I did not fight for my first love. At the present, I used my strengths towards surviving and conquering this new country. Norma would have to wait. Soon I started to doubt my love and responsibility towards her again and felt a sense of freedom when I thought about just giving in to Berta's wishes and never reaching out to Norma.

Later, I learned that Berta had a suitor for Norma way before she came to El Salvador to scoop her up. She had already promised Norma as a spouse to some Californian man that frequented the cantina and the bordello. Norma did not fight her mother's intentions for her. After my lengthy silence, Norma welcomed that man, and was later forced to marry him. Berta convinced her not to ever tell her new husband that she had a child. The child, I later learned, grew up thinking that Berta was his mother. Norma's new husband was easily duped. Norma never told him the truth. Norma knew, as did I, that she had to survive in her new country and made decisions that would assure her stability.

Today, before leaving, Jorge had left the refrigerator filled with food. The black VW was no longer parked in the driveway, neither was the Toyota. For a moment, I had expected him to leave the VW behind.

"*Ernesto, yo tengo una casa libre por dos meses si tú quieres vivir conmigo, te puedes mudar,*" I asked him at school that morning.

The same day, Ernesto moved to my temporary house after work. Not having possessions or stable relationships is liberating, one can take off at any moment to any place in the world, with or without money, by foot, by car, by plane, by boat, without the tears that come with saying goodbye and with the reassurance that nobody will be hurt when you leave. The bags must be packed on the way: there is never time to be organized. Ernesto brought a small suitcase with some clothing, walked across the living room and nonchalantly moved into the small bedroom. He had practice in these matters. As is expected by many new immigrants, the initial phase of a new life in America emulates that of any experienced nomad. One must be ready to move, dictated either by the region where work can be found or by the fear of being deported. A new immigrant's housing situation is rarely permanent.

Ernesto's presence in the house created in me a new sense of security and stability. He was the one who knew how to survive on the streets, having acquired that experience early in life on the streets of Guadalajara It was also reassuring to me that Ernesto's presence would recreate the living conditions, camaraderie, brotherhood, and the sense of belonging to a team that had each other's backs that I had had back home with my three brothers, and at the Seminary with my fellow seminarians. I had always excelled under those conditions. I admired Ernesto's practical solutions to daily living. I never understood how one became so apt for survival in a big city. For Ernesto, it was second nature to know what to do in any situation life threw at him. He was a man of action. My hesitant and over reflective approach to making decisions made him more assertive, which compelled me to follow his lead. I had not lived as much as he had, and he knew it.

He recently told me that my speech, the way I formed my complicated sentences in Spanish, and worst of all, the content of my conversation, was out of this world. I was quick to philosophize about every minute moment of my life, sprinkling my thought processes with quotes from Kierkegaard, Schopenhauer, Kant, Sartre and Teilhard de Chardin. I expressed absolute thoughts and conservative ethical codes and dogmas. He told me that he has never forgotten a conversation we had where I talked at length about Freud and his psychoanalysis, and how my indoctrination during the seminarian years were controlling my instinctual desires.

He saw me as a special case, as the friend whose way of being needed only to be tolerated, not necessarily understood. I lived in the clouds, but LA required concrete actions towards survival. I was without doubt an outsider, an immigrant, but also a misfit in relation to the predominant LA narcissistic, pleasure seeking, culture. Ernesto knew immediately that I was doomed for disaster in LA and his protective nature, triggered by my condition, compelled him to teach me street survival skills. At the same time, he was attracted to my ways. I opened a new and unknown world of ideas to him.

We soon entered into a hectic daily routine, twisting our tongues practicing English pronunciation at the El Monte Adult education during the day and bending our backs and necks welding ornamental fencing at the factory at nights. We knew only the taste of fast food sold by Mexican Food Trucks: tacos for lunch at school and tacos for dinner at the factory.

Our routine was interrupted one early morning weeks later by Sharon who came to pick up some forgotten items, totally disregarding the furniture. Her desire of starting a new life negated her previous existence with Jorge. She had never loved him. Jorge had one day told me that he had met Sharon, only 17 at that time, one weekend night walking on Sunset Boulevard. She had run away from home, was living on the streets, using drugs, and sleeping with rich men, not unlike a seasoned prostitute. Sharon had come up to him to ask for money. He saw only innocence and beauty in her and decided to rescue her, brought her home, and soon married her; taking her away from what he considered to be a sad and desperate life. Sharon became pregnant and had a girl. Soon after, Jorge moved the family back to Costa Rica for a new start, to fully rehabilitate Sharon. I had my suspicion that this did not work because Jorge hinted one night, while at the library, that Sharon had slept with one of his Costa Rican uncles during that year.

The day Sharon came back to the house was a Saturday in the spring of 1973. She had come with a female friend and after collecting her things asked us to go dancing that night with them at one of the new discotheques on Sunset Boulevard. It might have been The Roxy or maybe the Rainbow Bar and Grill. The idea of having fun by spending hard earned money on frivolous pleasures like going out dancing on Saturday nights was incomprehensible to us. Why would Americans do that? The hard dollars made at the factory had to be used for subsistence an, if possible, put towards savings. We kept our cash in our suitcases, mine in the bottom of Teto's duffle bag. The future was forever uncertain. The girls insisted. They would pay for everything. The thrill of the unknown made Ernesto and I acquiesce. Sharon probably wanted a last taste of my company.

We danced all night. At one point during the night inside the discotheque, Sharon came close to me and instinctively placed her lips against mine. Unapologetically, she planted the longest, juicy kiss on my lips, as if she was afraid of never again being able to recreate the same sensation for the rest of her life. I responded in kind and for a moment, I got the sensation that maybe this was a normal American behavior.

It seemed that an invisible magic glue had been poured between our bodies that made it impossible for us to separate. Sharon was overtaken by her emotions and lost herself in her lust to only finally unglue her body from mine when her friend, leaving Ernesto alone in the middle of dance floor, came to check on her. "I know we have to leave, but, please, before we do, I want you to kiss Francisco. I want you to feel what I feel. I want you to taste the deliciousness of his mouth. I want to share him with you," Sharon said in desperation. Her friend pushed her away to quickly kiss my lips, staying there as long as Sharon had, afraid that the strong sensation Sharon referred to was going to elude her.

Finally, Sharon interrupted her friend's kiss to say good-bye. *Adiós Francisco. Tenemos que irnos.* That was the last time I saw Sharon. Until today, I don't know if it was my lips or my abundant expressions of inexperience and innocence that caused Sharon so much excitement. *"Estas mujeres gringas están locas!"* Ernesto said. *"Sí, están locas,"* I responded. We drove home at 4:00 am. For once, Ernesto's car did not breakdown at any red lights.

Chapter 28: The Alleged Stolen Car and the two *Gringas*.

"Ernesto! Wake up! Come to the gate! Open the door! It's me, the professor!" The clanking at the metal gate was persistent and loud. My motivation to get up and walk up to the window was quickly smothered by my cozy bed and companion who had sapped all the energy out of me. It was one of those Sundays that compelled me to sleep in until noon. Today, Laurie added to that desire. I cursed the person who dared wake us up so early. I didn't open my eyes and stayed in bed, unlike Ernesto who, recognizing the voice of the visitor jumped from bed, leaving Debbie behind, and ran to his window to see the professor at the gate, "Ernesto? Are you there?" It was 6 o'clock on a gray Sunday morning, as many are in LA.

After the month's rent Sharon and Jorge had prepaid for us to stay at their house for free ended, Ernesto found another house to rent cheaply very quickly. His survival skills and successful moves from place to place never ceased to surprise me. I never knew how he managed to find a new house for us. Still in his pajamas, Ernesto ran to the gate to meet the professor. I found it odd that the old guy would rush to our new house. By this time, I was already looking through my window. Evidently, Ernesto had shared our new address with him after moving out of the shed in his backyard. Lucky for us because the day before, El Monte Police Department had come to the professor's house looking for Ernesto. The owner of a green Plymouth sedan had just reported his car stolen from one of the El Monte parking lots adjacent to the school. That past Friday, the taco truck owner had seen two students coming out of the Adult Education Center driving away in a car that matched the description of the stolen car. The detectives had interviewed the students and the teachers at the school and all had said that Ernesto was the student who drove such a car, but they attested to Ernesto's honesty, integrity, and excellent comportment and wouldn't ever suspect him of stealing a car.

Ernesto told me years later when we were reunited in LA that he had gone back to the school months later to find out what the people there had told the police. Apparently, they explained that Ernesto had been seen of late with his friend Francisco, me, very often and they had just moved with two American girls to share a rented old house at the edge of Hacienda Hills. Francisco was also in good standing at the school, they explained. Both were respectful, excellent students, and presumed to be of high moral character. Neither of them would ever attempt to steal an old car. There must be a big misunderstanding or a mistaken identity.

The other possibility was that there were two similar cars in the area. Ernesto was without any doubt innocent. Ms. Phillips was the one who met with the detectives, showed him our perfect attendance and high grades in English and very strongly defended us. Ernesto told me these details recently when we found each other through Facebook, after more than 40 years of this incident and his family and my family met in L.A. That day, we took a walk down Santa Monica pier and this incident, that had propelled us to leave LA to come to Boston, became our first subject of conversation.

That early morning at the gate of our new house, the professor begged Ernesto to get rid of the car and he added that those "blond girls" had duped us and absolutely were bad news and that we had to drive them as far as possible from LA to get rid of them. The professor suspected the girls were running away from justice. The rumor was that the detectives now were also looking for the girls. We could be suspected as their accomplices. Ernesto declared his innocence to the professor. He had bought the ugly old green car, a piece of junk, from a friend who had decided to go back to Mexico. As far as the girls, we would get rid of them, Ernesto reassured him.

The professor was insistent. The police wouldn't take any denial of wrongdoing as a valid answer from an immigrant with questionable papers, and Ernesto would be handed to "*la Migra*" for deportation to avoid further investigation and paperwork. I would have been also included in that plan of action as an associate of Ernesto. Dirty Mexicans, as we all Hispanics were in the eyes of the police, were all undoubtedly psychopathic liars.

The car was only one cause for our decision to leave LA. Two weeks earlier, we had met two girls on Wednesday when coming out of the school, Debbie and Laurie. They stood in front of the entrance under a white alder tree and came up to us as soon as we exited to ask us for a $20.00 bill. Their money had run out while visiting LA for the weekend and they were desperate to get back home to some small town in northern California, or so they said. We were lonely and welcomed the interaction and flirting with these girls. Finally, I had the opportunity to practice English in a real-life situation. Ernesto gravitated towards Debbie and I towards Laurie. We asked them to come back to the same spot after school that Friday when we would get paid, but first we had to drive them to our house, have them stay there until we came back from work around 1:00 am, wait for the banks to open on Saturday, to give them the $20 dollars.

We told them that we had to move quickly because we were moving into a new house during the weekend. Ernesto and I were always on the move, building, destroying, exploring options, discarding some, and impetuously embracing others. Our lives were taken as unfinished adventures pregnant with great possibilities. We didn't consider any of our actions to be leading us into danger. We had no fear. Whatever was doomed to happen, we would embrace it as did the Greek heroes who inexorably marched into their tragic fates. The girls represented another of those moments offered by destiny, we thought. We had to capture it, with the hopes of discerning what role this new piece in the bigger puzzle that was our future, could play.

Everything went as planned, with one big difference. We had taken the girls' intentions at face value, but on Saturday morning they had already fallen in love with us, or we fitted into their grand design, or they looked to lay low for a while, or for whatever reasons, they dreaded to go back home. We understood that they were looking for stability, independence, control over their own lives, and love: things, it seemed, we were all lacking and possibly willing to offer. They refused our $20 for the bus fare to get back home. We returned the favor by accepting their companionship. That morning, the girls happily helped us put all our meager possessions into the old Plymouth and move out of Sharon's house into our new house.

By this time, I had failed to notice that the girls didn't carry any luggage, just a medium size brown canvas pocketbook with wide straps ending on an oversized knot over their shoulders. That morning, our moving process was repeatedly interrupted by our long rests on the driveways for intense long kisses and hugs. We accepted it all. Full of nervousness about such future uncertainty, but with our sources of fear fully covered by their kisses. These preliminary moments of the positive potentials of a love relationship, at a life crossroads, do not come often in life. I embraced it with great intensity. I was exhilarated to make such a grown-up decision as to move in with a woman that I had just met. How had I become, under the eyes of my superiors at the Seminary, so promiscuous? Had I not learned anything about celibacy, permanent pure love, control over my own carnal desires and passions?

After what I felt was a blatant betrayal to my clerical vocation and religious commitment in the eyes of the Bishop, I had put into question all tenants the Seminary had taught me, including God's intentions for my life. At the present, with the unleashing of all my passions, somehow the future did not look uncertain anymore. Norma was relegated to a very distant memory. The weight of a new love relationship would firmly plant me in one house, one job, and one city. Maybe just for a moment I needed to take a long pause and suspend the search for a better future I had started 10 months before. That Saturday, I sensed the start of a great beginning that had all the ingredients of a settled life that would certainly put down deep roots in a new country. After several false starts, things were beginning to work out.

Once moved into the new house, the four of us drove to Ralph's to buy groceries. We let the girls loose in the supermarket. We wouldn't have known what to buy. I could see they were very hungry and they quickly assumed the role of housewives, eager to please their new pseudo-husbands, whispering to each other lists of groceries and ingredients needed for certain enticing recipes. We knew only hot dogs and tacos sold by food trucks. This was the first time I experienced the dynamics of power that money could exert. Ernesto and I would work six days per week including overtime, the girls would stay home, shopping for groceries, cleaning and cooking for us, and taking care of their toilette the rest of the day. Our Latin background and our own experiences at home did not let us see it any other way. We were strong men and needed to protect and work hard; the girls were beautiful and needed to reciprocate with tenderness and love. We paid the hefty grocery bill without hesitation.

On the drive back, I imagined our dinner table set up properly, with flowers and candles. The girls would place the plates, brought from Sharon's house, with great care over the new, just purchased, red tablecloth. The newly perfumed and made-up girls would cook, while we waited for dinner in the living room, watching TV on Sharon's TV, smoking our Marlboros, with the girls' laughs as a soundtrack. The car radio filled the cabin with Natural High, one of our favorite songs by the Bloodstone. Ernesto with his great tenor voice started to sing with a big smile on his face, *"Why do I keep my mind on you all the time? And I don't even know you. Why do I feel this way? Thinking about you every day."* The radio continued with So Very Hard to Go by Tower of Power. *"I knew the time would come. I have to pay for my mistakes."* The girls swung their bodies, lifted their arms and joined Ernesto; I hummed pretending to know the words. We might have sounded in the manner of loud happy couples at the start of a long drive with no destination in mind just for the pleasure of feeling unrestrained, unshackled, and the great expansive feeling that total freedom inspires. Some onlookers might have thought it suspect, the loud scene of two tanned presumed Mexicans having fun in the company of Scandinavian looking white girls. Luckily, there were no LAPD officers in sight.

"You don't say 'Give me your mouse', Laurie tenderly with a big smile told me that night after dinner during our foreplay. "You say, 'Give me your mouth'." "Mmmmmoo-ouuuthtthth," she repeated under my attentive look at her tongue, which stuck out between her perfect white front teeth. That night, I learned that some English sounds needed special attention and repetition if I were to replicate them. During the night, I repeated countless times "mouth," under Laurie's great amusement. I had just acquired a loving and patient teacher and, as everybody knows, there is no better way to learn a new language than by dating someone who speaks it.

However, there would be only one night of blissful love spent at our new spotless house, the girls had made sure of that: the refrigerator full, the uncluttered furniture in the right places, and our new lovely girlfriends looking angelic. Sunday morning, the professor would be shaking the iron fence with all his force to wake us up and demanding that we get rid of those girls.

"The professor said that the parents are looking for these girls. They haven't been home in a while," Ernesto loudly announced as he rushed back into the house. The girls, sensing danger, were already gathered in the kitchen and had started to cry uncontrollably, with their faces expressing deep fear and disappointment. I couldn't decide if their tears were caused by the doom of an upcoming, unavoidable, harsh punishment courtesy of their families, or by the inevitable dishonor associated with lying to us to obtain sympathy and love. One day they had escaped their familial nightmares to try their luck, like countless others, on the LA streets, just to find an unsuspecting pair of stupidly innocent, gentle, thoughtful, charitable, and hardworking "dirty Mexicans" who were willing to offer solace and provide for them as long as they wanted, only for it to end abruptly now.

They refused to answer any of our questions and continued crying uncontrollably.

"We need you to leave this house. We are willing to drive you home, wherever that may be. We don't care what you have done. We don't want to know why you are running away," Ernesto told them after a couple of hours, just before lunch.

Debbie, the slender one from Wisconsin with intense green eyes and a disarmingly tender smile, pulled Laurie, the chubby one from LA, aside. The decision was made.

"Yes. You have to drive us home. This is my address in Arcadia with my phone number. This is Laurie's address in Temple City with her phone number. Promise us that you will not forget about us," Debbie said.

"We want you to drive us both to Debbie's aunt's house," Laurie said.

I decided to give Alicita's phone number to Laurie.

"My phone," I said.

We skipped lunch. The girls picked up their canvas pocketbooks with tears still in their eyes, walked out of the house, and sat in the back seat of the green Plymouth.

This time we didn't stop in the driveway for hugs and kisses, as to insure the finality of their departure. Debbie directed our way to her aunt's house without hesitation, turn by turn, as if she had driven those same streets many times before. Ernesto turned the radio on. The most popular song in LA that week burst out of the speaker. It had become our song. The girls started to mumble it and soon began singing at full blast, accompanying Tony Orlando and Dawn, "*If I don't see a yellow ribbon tied on the old oak tree. Do you still want me?*" Crystal tears rolled down their pink cheeks, but they turned to look at us with a reassuring smile. "Stop! Stop right here"! Debbie suddenly yelled. "This is two blocks from the house. We are going to walk the rest of the way," she ordered. The girls quickly opened the car doors, jumped to our windows, gave us a big long kiss, crossed the street, and walked on the sidewalk keeping very close to the leafy trees as if looking for protection as they locked arms for comfort. What just moments ago had looked like a permanent future, had ended in white smoke. Our fate was not inexorable after all but pointed towards different directions.

Chapter 29: Back to Alicita's House

The temperature was climbing by the day and the dry heat of LA started to be intolerable. We had to vacate our short-lived new house and find temporary housing to give us time to plan our next move. Up to now, my life in LA had been subjected to unbridled improvisations, reacting to events and people, no grand master plan involved; surviving at all costs was the only tenet. I decided to call Alicita from the school's public phone to beg her to let me stay in her house for a while, until I knew what step to take next in my life. I hadn't spoken to her since I had been kicked out of the house by Ana at the end of November and I remained uncertain about the action the LA office of immigration had taken about my invalid student visa application and whether or not it had affected Alicita's status negatively. I hoped our family ties would prove stronger than fear. I told her that I would be coming with a male friend.

"*Le tengo que preguntar a Ana. Estoy seguro de que ella va a consentir puesto que nada pasó malo con ese asunto de la emigración. Nunca vinieron a investigar, ni nunca volvieron a mandar cartas, ni para ti, ni para mí. Yo creo que el enojo ya le pasó a Ana. Hablàme más tarde para decirte,*" she said with a happy tone as if wanting to make amends, hoping for my forgiveness.

Ana consented to our arrival, with the stipulation that we live in the back porch of the house. She took it as an act of charity as she would have normally offered it to any other homeless young men that she might have encountered in her practice as a social worker. We moved in on the same night, after which Alicita and Ana continued with their lives, ignoring our ins and outs, maybe as a means to protect theirs. Now that I remember, they dismissed us completely as it to send a message that our arrangement was temporary, no need for socializing or getting used to each other. Also, our working schedules were very disparate and did not allow for common time at the house.

A tall side-gate led us into the backyard. The large back porch had large screen windows all around it, and a screen door. It was used to store old furniture and many cardboard boxes stacked one on top of another. Two twin mattresses had been left on the floor, as if the women had had some guests living in the porch before, with no blankets, linen, or pillows for us. I had to use Teto's army green duffle bag as a headrest. The nights were breezy and cool and two tall sycamore trees gave the backyard permanent shade during the day. We slept with our clothes on, ready to jump out bed, just in case *La Migra* came calling.

Ernesto and I sensed that we were entering into a decisive period of transition in our lives that forced us into deep reflection. Up until now, our main concern had been our daily survival: work, food and shelter. Starting at this moment, however, we felt the need to take the next big step towards a brighter, more permanent, and stable future. The risky incident with the girls had shaken us to the core and compelled us to reevaluate our ways; tough decisions needed to be made. During this period of respite, we launched into dense conversations about all types of subjects while in the dark well into the night. We agreed that no matter what happened, we were committed to remain friends, brothers, and forge ahead in this country together. My idea of going back to El Salvador was put on the back burner, there to be revived only under extreme circumstances. Ernesto never thought about ever going back to Guadalajara.

Not long after, our bond deepened as we disclosed more lengthy details of our lives before coming to America from the safety of our respective pillows. I described my daily routine in *el Seminario Menor* in Santa Ana. didn't delve much into *el Seminario Mayor* in Puebla, except the description of some of my philosophy courses. I kept my complicated past with Norma a secret, I was ashamed, afraid of his disapproval, but I found great refuge in retelling to Ernesto my experiences at the Seminary, where I had felt secure and safe, leading a very predictable life. My accounts calmed me down; they infused me with renewed strength and optimism. Afterwards, happiness entered my heart, as if the present turmoil was assuaged by the comforting thoughts of a spiritual life long gone.

In my monologues at night, which Ernesto interrupted often to demand clarification of terms and people ¿Quién era ese Freud? Dime más acerca de ese filósofo o psicólogo, I described enthusiastically the content of my philosophy and psychology courses, my year of pre-law at the Salvadorian university, and my reasons for coming to America. I mentioned Norma only until recently when we reunited in LA, 40 years later. What I did tell him during those nights was that my aim in life was to obtain a doctorate in something and to one day return to El Salvador as a university professor to influence the country's politics, a goal that many expatriates have while living abroad.

I was working in a factory now, but unlike countless Latino immigrants, I told him I saw myself primarily as a university student with a very unusual academic background on a break from his studies, doing laborer work. After all, how many almost-to-be-priest-Latino-recent-immigrants were there in LA in 1972? My nightly talks about Scholastic Philosophy literally put Ernesto to sleep, but not before infecting him with the education bug. "Objects are made of two elements: Essence and Accidents. You define objects based on their immutable essence, not their ever-changing accidents. The trick in life is to find the essence of things. Happiness rests on it," I told him. Soon he started to see his future to include a college education. If I could dream it, so could he. During those nights, he reciprocated by telling me about his childhood in the streets of Guadalajara, the father that he never knew, and the struggles of his mother who had to abandon him for long periods of time to work nights. His mother didn't want little Ernesto to see what she had to do to survive.

Our nightly conversations continued. *"Esta era mi rutina diaria en el Seminario Menor en Santa Ana. Te la quiero contar para que te des cuenta como era mi vida enclaustrada,"* I told Ernesto on one of those nights. He ended up dozing off several times as I attempted to tell him everything I could remember, but I would just press on through the winding paths of memory in my mind, determined to keep them alive.   Here is a representation of the daily schedule I recounted to him.

AM	**Actividad**
4:30	*Oraciones matutinas dirigidas por el Celador (el seminarista líder), que las leía del breviario* (We got out of bed and kneeled on the floor, half-asleep, to repeat the prayers, a version of the "Laudes" in the mediaeval monasteries). The "Celador," read a stance of Psalm 94 alternating with our antiphon:

> *"Señor abre mis labios. Y mi boca proclamará tu alabanza". "Venid, aclamemos al Señor, demos vítores a la Roca que nos salva. Aleluya." "Venid, postrémonos por tierra, bendiciendo al Señor, creador nuestro. Porque él es nuestro Dios, y nosotros su pueblo, el rebaño que él guía."*

4:40	*Gimnasia Sueca, dirigida por el Padre Chus, su propia idea.*
5:00	*Baño, hacer cama, y ponerse el uniforme del colegio San José, camisa mangas cortas de color blanco y pantalones kakis. Los de quinto curso se vestían ya con sotana.*
5:30	*Meditación en la capilla del seminario* (This was the time for individual conversations with God)
6:00	*Misa*
7:00	*Desayuno - leche con pan, no café*

7:30   *Caminar 20 cuadras de dos en dos al Colegio San José a tomar nuestras clases seculares que empezaban a las 8:00 am con los sacerdotes y hermanos Salesianos*

PM   ***Actividad***

12:00   *Caminar de regreso al seminario a almorzar*

12:30   *Estudio en nuestros pupitres respectivos*

1:30   *Caminar otra vez al Colegio por las dos clases de la tarde*

4:00   *Regreso al seminario para deportes: fútbol y básquetbol*

5:00   *Coro*

6:00   *Cena*

6:30   *Rosario en la capilla del seminario*

7:00   *Estudio*

9:00   *Capilla, a rezar y cantar y meditar. Reflexión del día con el Rector y recibir su bendición después de un canto*

> *"Señor otro día pasó bajo tu protección. El sol sus fulgores nos dio y ya la noche llegó. A ti nuestro señor se eleva nuestra oración para pedirte señor nos des tu bendición". (we finished the day with the vespers)*

During moments of crisis, turmoil, and immense change in my life, I have often yearned to be magically whisked back to the protective, nurturing, and safe cocoon of the Seminary and let the sanctuary and spirit of its brotherhood bathe me in its light once more. The Minor Seminary functioned similarly to a summer camp in the Northeast of the United States, where hundreds of camp songs, triggered at different moments and occasions during the day, are sung, not unlike a Yeshiva in Jerusalem; where I witnessed my son, Eric, engage in such euphoric and constant musical interludes. One seminarian would start a song, sometimes for no reason at all, and soon the whole group would join. If one noticed somebody doing something great, the *Bravo, Bravo, Bravísimo* song would be sung to honor a peer's accomplishment. Many songs were sung for religious and spiritual purposes, and at different times of the day. When we got up, before eating, and before going to bed we would sing as we kneeled to ask the rector to give us his benediction.

The Seminary's strict adherence to a code of discipline also fostered an atmosphere akin to that of a military school. An inordinate emphasis was put on honor, integrity, physical strength, and punctuality in following the daily schedule. Slow and tardy seminarians were ridiculed by the group. The Bishop had a classmate named *Procopio* while studying as a seminarian at the *Pontificia Università Gregoriana* in Rome who got up late in the morning, came late to mass and classes, and accomplished his daily tasks with palpable laziness. *Procopio* became the moniker for seminarians found wanting in those areas, particularly for tardy ones. The tardy seminarian was shamed in front of the group by the rector and classmates, calling him loudly *Procopio*: "*¡Ahí viene Procopio!*"

Some of my most cherished memories from my seminary days are of my time in the seminarian Choir. It was the best in town and invited often to perform in public places and in special church ceremonies. Our repertoire was extensive. Padre Chus, the rector, was a composer, pianist, and great music director. He taught us contemporary and classical music.

During my first day at the Minor Seminary, the organist, a seminarian high school senior, brought me to the piano to test my voice by playing each note of the scale in *do mayor*. After playing the *mi* note he realized that I could barely carry a tune. He tried different scales on me to no avail. The *do-re-mi-fa-sol-la-si-do* notes were flat. The word quickly spread that the new seminarian couldn't sing and would be useless in the chorus. My classmate Gustavo had entered the seminary two years before me and had kept a privileged position as the soloist with his angelic *voz blanca*. The *voz blanca* is the voice young boys possess before they reach puberty. In the Minor Seminary, there were seven prepubescent 6th graders in the *voz blanca* section of the chorus and I was one of them. Padre Chus quickly ordered me to just open my mouth without uttering any sound. "Pretend to be a fish," he instructed one day during practice, "I want you to just open and shut your mouth without making a sound and stand behind Gustavo."

Nobody was excused from chorus practice. All seminarians were required to be a member, so because Padre Chus couldn't kick me out, he had to come up with a way to ensure my apparent lack of talent wouldn't be an issue. As was mandated by the rector, I stood behind Gustavo in the middle-front of the chorus where I got the privilege of listening to all our works in a multi-phonic manner, with the basses on my right, the baritones behind me, and the tenors on my left.

There was always a new piece to learn for such and such festivity, religious or otherwise, so we were in constant rehearsals of *motetes, oratorios and madrigales*. For the 60th priesthood anniversary of Monsignor Agapito, Padre Chus wrote a play to honor his life in which I had a short line as a member of a small *pipil* tribe. Gustavo played a young Agapito. Monsignor Agapito had come as a Spanish missionary in 1895. One scene of the play showed Monsignor Agapito when, before leaving Spain, he innocently had asked his superiors for advice on how to defend himself in case of a *pipil* uprising.

The overture of the play, unbeknownst to me at that time, had us singing "*Loor a ti gran sacerdote de Cristo...*" to the tune of Wagner's overture for the opera *Tannhäuser*. Padre Chus wrote lyrics to the melody of several classical pieces whose titles I would discover much later in Boston listening to WGBH classical radio. For the birthday of Padre Clemente, we sang excerpts from the song "Gloria" in Verdi's *Aida*. For the visit of the German ambassador and a Bavarian bishop whose congregations had donated money to build a new building for the Seminary, we sang the Trout of Schubert (*"En un claro arroyuelo, se precipita alegremente la trucha juguetona, que pasa como una flecha"*) and the German national Anthem (*"Deutschland, Deutschland über alles, Über alles in der Welt, Wenn es stets zu Schutz und Trutze, Brüderlich zusammenhält"*). For the Spanish missionaries who came for a month to spread the word of Christ in the Salvadorian countryside, we sang *Las Ranas* (*"cua, cua, cua, cua, canta la rana"*) and the Spanish National Anthem (*"Viva España, alzad los brazos hijos del pueblo español, que vuelve a resurgir. Gloria a la patria que supo seguir sobre el azul del mar el caminar del sol"*). For the Maryknoll Missionaries who came to build a church and an elementary school in the barrio Santa Barbara, we sang "Do-Re-Mi" from the *Sound of Music* (*"do, re mi, do mi, do mi, re, mi fa fa re mi fa…"*).

Finally, our most glorious performances took place during Holy Week at the cathedral of Santa Ana. On Holy Friday at 3:00 pm, the exact time that Christ died according to legend, Padre Chus chose the best voices to sing the Passion according to Saint John, the Gregorian version, as shown in the image here.

This was considered the most exceptional privilege, and the only seminarians eligible were the deacons from the Major Seminary, *San José de La Montaña*, in San Salvador, who came to Santa Ana for Holy Week. There were only four parts: one deacon sang as the narrator, another, as Jesus, and another as the other characters in the Gospel. We in the chorus sang the remarks of the people in the Synagogue: *"Quem quaeritis? Responderunt ei: Jesum Nazarenum. Dicit eis Jesus: Ego sum…Crucifige, crucifige eum"*. I loved this ritual with its Gregorian intonations and would become so full of emotion and uncontrollably would violate Padre Chus' order to keep my mouth shut during performance and would join the chorus with rapturous intonation: "*Crucifige, crucifige eum!*" Holy Week ended with us singing Handel's "Alleluia", in Latin of course, during Easter Sunday mass at the cathedral: "*Et Ressurexit, et Ressurexit!*"

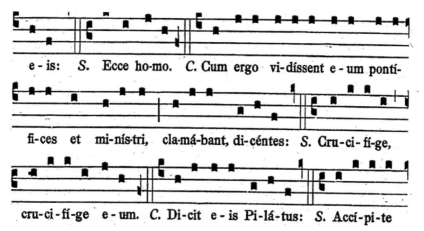

Passion according to Saint John, Gregorian Version

Other musical pieces that I remember fondly were: *La misa de M. Haller*, the Mozart Alphabet, *and "Es ust eub Ros' entsprungen"*. The latter piece is a traditional German Christmas choral, which, with intense astonishment, I heard again after 55 years one Christmas at Harvard University's Sanders Theater annual Christmas concert. My wife Carolina and Elena, my daughter, told me that they had never heard that Christmas carol before, which meant I was witnessing a very special moment.

Ernesto looked forward to my seminarian stories. As we would settle down for the night, like a little boy asking his mother for a bedtime story, Ernesto would ask me to continue: "*Sígueme contando tus mierdas, que me gusta oírte. Tu tendrías que haber sido un locutor de radio, cabrón*"

So, I continued with the story of the first day of my seminarian life.   On this day I was assigned an upperclassman, Ramiro Velasco, as my mentor and guide. Ramiro's job was to teach me the Latin associated with the mass ritual during recess using the *Liber Chori (1958)*, Latin language using the *Gramática Latina* by Ignacio Errandonea (1958), and Gregorian music using again the *Liber Chori*. After *el colegio* in the afternoons, different seminarians taught us *solfeo* with the Hilarión Slava method (1945) that is used throughout Europe and Latin America.

Hilarión Slava method (1945)

The ordinary mass ritual was my first encounter with Latin and my first lesson after school. The Bishop had a short temper towards the seminarians who stumbled in their Latin while officiating mass. He would stop the service and ask the seminarian at fault to repeat it again. The longest Latin responses were in the *Introito:*

- *"In nomine Patris, et Filii, et Spiritus Sancti."*
- *"Amen"*
- *"Introibo ad altare Dei."*
- *"Ad Deum, qui laetificat juventutem meam"*
- *"Dominus vobiscum."*
- *"Et cum spiritu tuo"*
- *"Confiteor Deo omnipoténti et vobis, fratres, quia peccávi nimis cogitatióne, verbo, ópere et omissióne: mea culpa, mea culpa, mea máxima culpa. Ideo precor beátam*

Maríam Vírginem, omnes, Angelos et Sanctos, et vos, fratres, oráre pro me ad Dóminum Deum nostrum."

I soon became aware that all types of learning needed to be absorbed through my eyes, not my ears. I couldn't sing, but I quickly learned how to read Gregorian and classical sheet music. While Gustavo practiced his melodic and angelic singing with his mentor, I was reading the notes aloud in the next room, keeping the beat using the right measures with the movement of my hand and arm, precisely the way an orchestra director would do. The music theory book, *Método Completo de Solfeo Sin Acompañamiento* by D. Hilarión Eslava, contained four parts. We studied only the first part of 58 lessons, which was plenty. Padre Chus became very impressed by my ability to quickly read any sheet of music that one day he decided to assign me as the chorus conductor for the Haller's mass, as ironic as this may sound given the fact that I could not sing, to be sung at El Colegio San José on Saturday, March 19, 1966, the feast of Saint Joseph.

Being assigned as the chorus conductor was the first indication that my superiors saw much more potential in me than I did. I had always regarded Gustavo as the one who had potential and was predestined to assume roles of leadership, not I.

Padre Chus also appointed me as the *Celador,* or Seminarian in charge of the student body, which is a sort of dean of discipline, a prefect, and team captain for the 1966 school year. This brought me in close contact with him daily as he imparted his directives to me for the day, which I then implemented with the seminarians. This was a prestigious position in the Seminary and implied I was not only a leader but also an example of the profound piousness and excellent comportment that needed to be emulated by the seminarian student body.

I assumed both roles with aplomb, dignity, oratory, and tireless determination. I felt chosen, important, accepted, loved, and proud. My posture became more erect, my steps firmer, and I held my head up higher. Disappointing el Padre Chus was considered tantamount to burning in hell, so I was determined to never let him down. The nature of the position as a leader and authority figure was not alien to me; I had plenty of practice with my three younger brothers Rafael, Teto, and Pirri whom I was responsible for when my parents weren't home. *"Chepito está encargado y ustedes le hacen caso a Chepito, ¿entendido?"* my parents would order before stepping out of the house.

For the Haller's mass, written for four voices, Padre Chus first ran through each voice part at the piano independently from the rest of the group and later joined everyone together for a rehearsal I conducted. I became very attentive to each voice intonation, diction, and dynamic wanted by Padre Chus. Using visible gestures with my hands, arms, head, and face, learned through the years by watching other directors in church, such as *el Chele* Walter, and Celada, I conducted the chorus.

The most challenging aspects were keeping the right tempo through the different movements of the score, as indicated by Haller, having the voice groups enter at the right measure, and maintaining the singers' concentration and complete attention on me, without forgetting to keep the chorus synchronized with Padre Chus at the piano. A chef insisting that his Edwardian 10-course meal be served at the precise moment for a large discriminating party would have sympathized with my predicament. I memorized the Latin libretto and the choral score with emphasis on the starts and endings of each voice part, including Gustavo's, the soloist, by studying them and practicing them in solitary. Above, I've included Gustavo's solo.

The conductor's sheet music was printed big on thick European size pages with wide spaces between the staves, which needed to be placed on a wide wooden music stand adjusted enough for me to read it at a distance. I learned that day that the best way for me to memorize anything is by standing up and moving my arms and hands as I visualize the content.

Missa Tertia

for two Equal, SAB or SATB Voices and Organ

M. Haller, Op. 7b

Gustavo's Solo

Choral music has often brought me to tears and made the hairs on my arms stand on end. This reaction was not conducive to conducting. My seminarian brothers, especially Gustavo, produced the most sublime of angelic voices that I, during rehearsal, in the center point of the quadraphonic sound, overcome with joy, came to the verge of fainting and had to repeatedly compose myself. *Qui tolis peccata mundi miserere nobis.*

The day of the Saint Joseph celebration, up at the back of the church in the close confines of the choral balcony, unseen by the congregation, my emotional syndrome reached pathological levels during the Gloria section of the mass. Haller's dynamics and tempo called for his music to be sung *allegro*, but I directed some sections with alternating *allegrettos* and *fortes* and *pianos*, always *accelerando*, especially on the line *"Laudamus te, Benedicimus te, Adoramus te, Glorificamus te,"* finishing with the loudest and fastest *"Glorificamus te."* Here, I let go entirely, moving my arms, hands and fingers, as my immediate emotions dictated, arriving at an orgasmic peak.

Leonard Bernstein would have been very proud of me. My demeanor was infectious. Padre Chus took his eyes away from his sheet music at the organ repeatedly, trying to understand my movements and not fall behind the chorus. The seminarians looked at me at first with the widest eyes, expecting me to drop into a trance or an epileptic fit, but gradually joined me, infected with my spiritual ecstasy until the entire chorus was transfixed, transcended to a never felt, almost magical, ineffable state.

After the mass, the church already emptied, we walked ceremonially out through the side door into the school's sunny courtyard. It took my eyes a long moment to adjust to the bright light of the patio after the dark confines of the upstairs choir balcony in the narthex, which was made darker by the fragrant clouds of Frankincense that accumulated about the church. The director at that time of *el Colegio San José*, Padre Catedral, officiated the *missa solemnis*, and several other Salesian clerics stopped to thank us for our outstanding performance, commenting on the exuberant Gloria. The feast of Saint Joseph had just been launched with a big bang. Padre Catedral, adjusting his heavy, black-rimmed eyeglasses, asked to meet the conductor. The entire chorus turned towards me, pointing, *"es Chico."*

Padre Catedral looked at me with incredulous astonishment, probably wondering how a hyperactive and
undisciplined kid, whose face he would hit with white
chalk for disrupting his class years before, could be the
chorus conductor. As he smiled at the irony, he asked the
chorus and the other priests to applaud me. "It has been
many years, maybe since my time in Rome, that I had not
had the pleasure of listening to such a sublime performance," he said.

I corresponded with a smile, thinking too of the irony
of being tone deaf on the one hand and on the other being
associated with a high-quality musical performance. I
knew the congregation had been deceived and ethically
should have corrected their admiration towards me. My
poor musical abilities could not have created such a production, but at that moment, far from being humble, I
wanted to make sure that Gustavo knew that I also could
be successful. For once, he was not getting all the attention.

I had just emotionally, with impetus, transmitted a
sublime vibe to the chorus, but I knew nothing about the
specifics and mechanics of conducting a musical performance. Padre Chus had done it all, but he was not
recognized and decided to let me have all the glory.

Towards the end of that year, Padre Chus assessed
that my piano practice had paid off and assigned me to be
the accompanist of the chorus instead, and he assumed
again its direction. Once, he decided to give Gustavo the
chorus *batuta,* restoring the social dynamics between
Gustavo and me.

"¡Ernesto! ¿Ya te dormiste cabrón? ¿todavía me estás
escuchando, puta?" I asked.

"Sigue hablando, no mames pinche pendejo que te es-
cucho," Ernesto said, his voice muffled by his pillow.

"Lo último que te quiero decir esta noche es que también
estudié griego," I said.

During the same year of propaedeutic courses, Padre Chus added Ancient Greek to our curriculum. We already had Latin, Philosophy, and World Literature. Padre Camilo Girón oversaw our World Literature course. He made us read Gogol, Fyodor Dostoyevsky, Dickens and Shakespeare. The only thing I still remember in Greek is Our Father. Πατερ ημον ο εν τοις ουρανοις, αγ ιασθητω το ονομα σου, ελθατω η βασιλεια σου (Páter hemón hoén toisuranóis, aguiaszéto tónomásu, elzáto hebasiléiasu).

On another night, I told Ernesto about my schooling in the art of orating. The final indication that my superiors were planning something larger for my future, something that my own assessment of my personal skills would never have envisioned, came after I won the Seminary oratory contest. Oratory, or as we seminarians called it Rhetoric, a polished, eloquent, high level of public speaking, was fostered and admired in the Seminary with the assumed purpose that one day, from the pulpit, the priest would be able to propagate the word of God and persuade his congregation to achieve higher levels of compliance with his commandments. The seminarian needed to learn the craft of public speaking well, knowing that being a motivational speaker would also pay off with higher donations from his parishioners. Padre Chus was a master in Rhetoric, becoming our model to emulate. We digested and analyzed his sermons and speeches. He knew we were always watching him, so was careful with his daily utterances and prepared his public speeches meticulously. He rarely disappointed us.

The works of Cicero, the Ancient Rome orator (his speeches against Catiline), and Demosthenes, the Greek orator (his speeches against Philip of Macedon) were scrutinized and their literary devices and strategies imitated, not unlike the emphasis placed on these classics in the curriculum of some prestigious U.S law schools where also The Federalist Papers and the speeches of Abraham Lincoln and M.L.K., Jr. have a prominence.

Our oratory skills were also honed during monthly "consiliums," community meetings with the Bishop. In these meetings we had to be ready to speak publicly, recite a poem, describe a piece of art, sing a song, or give a emotive sermon with plenty of biblical quotes, all in the spur of the moment, without warning, if we were called on by the Bishop. Some seminarians opted for an easy way out by reciting Cicero: "*Quo usque tandem abutere, Catilina, patientia nostra? Quam diu etiam furor iste tuus eludet? Quem ad finem sese effrenata iactabit audacia? ...O tempora, O mores!*" When they would say "*O tempora, O mores*" their voices would acquire a long vibrato and the vowels a crescendo and elongation. Manuelón, a much older, extremely bright, seminarian whom the Bishop had plucked from the Metapán country side without any schooling, often gave us an inspiring impromptu sermon quoting the bible extensively. I, on the other hand, turned to my favorite, simple poem titled "*Más Allá*", written, I believe, by Pedro Antonio de Alarcón (1833-1891).

¡Más Allá!

Por un áspero camino
un cansado peregrino
busca la felicidad;
y cuantos al paso halla,
todos le dicen que vaya
     ¡Más allá!
Y cruza por los estrados
de los palacios dorados
buscándola con afán;
y entre el rumor de la orgía
siempre una voz le decía:
     ¡Más allá!
A gentes de las montañas
pregunta si, en sus cabañas,
con ellos habita la paz;
y ellos bajan la cabeza
y le dicen con tristeza:
     ¡Más allá!

Further On!
Along a rough road
a weary pilgrim
looks for happiness;
the people he meets on the way
all say to him:
     Further on!
And he passes through the halls
of gilded palaces
in his eager pursuit;
and as he listens to the sound
of orgy
a relentless voice says to him:
     Further on!
To the people of the mountains
he puts the question
if in their cabins peace abides;

Penetra con desaliento
por los claustros de un con-
vento
y se postra ante un altar;
y entre el rumor de las pre-
ces
oye a veces, sólo a veces:
    ¡Más allá!
Al fin, en el camposanto,
con ojos llenos de llanto,
busca la felicidad;
y una figura huesosa
le dice abriendo una fosa:
    ¡Más allá!

but, lowering their heads,
to him they sadly say:
    Further on!
Discouraged
he enters a cloistered convent
and prostrates himself before
an altar;
and amidst the murmuring of
prayers
he hears at times, only at
times:
    Further on!
At last, in a churchyard,
his eyes flooding with tears,
he looks for happiness;
and there a bony figure,
digging a grave, says to him:
    Further on!

I lost the original copy of my winning discourse in the oratory contest. I remember that I quoted Saint Paul's letter about love to the Corinthians extensively. The point I tried to make in my speech, as I remember, was that the strict rules of the Seminary with a great emphasis on punishment and guilt did not push us to greater levels of compliance if love was not the motivator. *"Love is patient. Love is kind...Love never fails."* I knew nothing about love, only about sin, punishment, hell, and remorse. In my speech, I used several appropriate rhetorical devices Cicero and Demosthenes would have used. I entered into the contest seeing it as an intellectual exercise, although I knew that my voice, while reciting Saint Paul's words, had to show great emotion and passion to excite the student body and the judges, who among them was Padre Chus, Padre Camilo, and the Monsignor Barrera. I declaimed my phrases as I had done it with the psalms four years before. The seminarian audience loved a well-constructed, logical speech, but logic did not move their hearts. What moved them was the simple literary devices that played with language, such as anaphoras (repeating the word 'love' at the start of several sentences, like Saint Paul does), epithets, metonymies, and especially puns and synecdoches, such as "The more I sigh, the more I love you, and the more I love you the more I sigh."

The seminarians detested the *ad hominem* attacks. The speaker using it to win a logical or moral debate was booed because he had run out of logic and relevant content, and they were also suspicious of trying to win an argument by appealing to an authority. The one device the seminarians most loved was the apophasis, bringing up a subject by denying it: "I refuse today to talk about the guilt we seminarians feel after sinning, and even though confession may ameliorate it, we often succumb to the same sins soon after. No, today I want to talk about love." The entire Seminary, as I finished my speech, exploded into a vociferous *"Bravo, Bravo, Bravísimo"* song. Again and again, they sang it and sang it. Being acclaimed by my peers filled me with extreme pride.

Bravo, bravísimo

I had touched a sensitive chord in the social structure and climate of the Seminary. The song was repeated several times, resonating in the lunchroom, where the participants had to give their speeches during lunch hours, and spilled above the walls facing the street, reverberating within the walls of adjacent houses, waking up the dwellers from their after-lunch siestas. My prize was a new bible.

After winning the contest, Monsignor Barrera pulled me out of class very often to take me with him on his travels around the county. My job was to repeat the same speech in his meetings with catholic religious orders and organizations, *los cursillistas*, every time producing an emotional reaction. The 1966 high school graduation committee at the Colegio San José chose me to be the class valedictorian, in part due to my success with my speech that had by then reached the ears of both parents and students.

Those academic successes and awards did little to assuage my inner insecurities, thinking them to be granted upon me in great measure by chance. I found them inexplicably humorous. When I come to reflect about these things, I have concluded that I have often walked through life reacting to its vicissitudes with laughter, finding even amusing the innocuous which at times offended the more serious ones of my friends and family. I often became a teaser and a provocateur based on a desire to find logical explanations for human affairs, smiling through all the while.

Gustavo hated me for that as much as now my brother Teto, my wife Carolina, and my daughter Elena on whom often my inquisitive, benign smirk produces a visceral reaction. Their anger increases proportionally to my subsequent attempts to explain the situation by asking more questions, seen by my interlocutors as mockery, where the right thing to do in their opinion is just to shut up. The Rector Huesca at the Palafoxiano would often pull me aside from group discussions and activities just to admonish me for not being serious and somber as becoming of a priest, and Padre Chus at the Juan XXIII would often tell me to learn the calmness and seriousness that Gustavo portrayed.

On the other hand, those academic successes in the seminary created an expectancy that only great things could come in my life, haunted by an intense hope that its true secrets and hidden treasures, that I had already concluded would be nothing but marvelous, were just lying around the corner. Those treasures were there and I had done nothing to create them. I can only be accused of reacting with great expectations to what is often hidden in life.

That night, by this point of the trip through my past, Ernesto was dozing off, but still tried to pay deep attention to my long stories that I had felt compelled to recount to be transported to a moment of my life when I felt safe, happy and accomplished. I needed to infuse my being with positive intentions about my immediate future that at this precise moment had become very uncertain. I think I would have continued talking to the wall if needed, had Ernesto fallen asleep, which most likely he did every night. Our friendship grew stronger during those nights in the back porch of Alicita's house through sharing common, daily experiences we've had, our hopes, and our desires.

It soon became only natural that we would continue our search for a better life together as a team. I felt strong, safe, and unafraid in America with him at my side, and my desire for higher educational attainment was contagious and I saw it as having positive effects on his future. Ernesto soon started to talk about going to university, just like me. "Maybe we could apply to the same university and study together," he told me one day.

Later, during the first week in Boston in the month of July, Ernesto and I would into Boston State College, Northeastern University, and UMass Boston's admissions office thinking that the application process could be completed right then and there, to start our studies in September. We were shocked about the process. I didn't know enough English and Ernesto didn't know anything about the significant role of academic transcripts and records in applying to college. He just carried his GED diploma into the admission offices and pulled it out first to show the officer. Next, he would proudly show his graduation gold ring, maybe issued by El Monte Union High School. Somehow Mrs. Phillips at El Monte Adult Education Center had managed to order rings for her GED graduating class. That would have been sufficient evidence in Guadalajara, not in Boston. We didn't have any money. What were we thinking? We were extremely naïve. Ernesto was devastated and gave up on his educational dreams.

Back then, he couldn't have foreseen that I would be starting as a Freshman at Boston University with plenty of financial aid a year later, and that most likely he could have been my classmate. Neither could he have known that he would be engaged with his future wife Sandra. "I am accepting you, Francisco, because we are under pressure to increase our diversity," Dr. Fields, a black admissions officer told me in my interview, "but I am sure," he continued, " you will drop out around November because you are working nights full time washing dishes at Howard Johnson's and because you do not know enough English to understand academic material," he added with a smile as to lessen the impact of his words.

Poor Dr. Fields. He had no idea of the magnitude of his words. They instantly fueled my motivation to prove him wrong. The almost innate desire immigrants carry within themselves to succeed and their willingness to sacrifice it all to do so is alien to a native born, black or white. Dr. Fields had failed to focus on my seminarian background, and the ambition that propelled me as a recent immigrant. His mistake was to accept me based only on my ethnicity, as if that meant something academically.

Come September 1974, I worked from 4:00 pm to 12:00 am washing dishes at Howard Johnson's, got up early to be inside Morse Auditorium at 7:00 am, prepared with a portable reel-to-reel tape recorder that I had brought to Boston from LA, taken from my cousin Alicita's garage, and sat in the front row ready for Professor Henry Marcucella to impart his Psychology 101 lectures. I transcribed incomprehensible sections of his lectures at home in the afternoons.

After one of his lectures on the sense of vision, I distinctly remember pausing and repeating the tape countless times trying to understand the word "threshold", in this sentence: "...the term absolute *threshold* refers to the minimal detectable intensity of stimulation in any modality". With the help of Eric's mother, Claudia Aschaffenburg, friends, dictionaries, textbooks and workbooks, --Principles of General Psychology by Kimble, Garmezy, and Zigler, 1974 edition-- by the end of the first semester, I didn't need the tape recorder. It gave me great satisfaction to prove Dr. Fields wrong.

Chapter 30: ¡Adiós! Los Angeles.

In Temple City, we had access to Alicita's house during the day while she and Ana were at work. We continued working nights at the electric ornamental welding factory. By this time, we had already let go of the idea of one day returning to our countries of origin. We sensed that our life adventure was at its beginnings, and there was no reason to look back.

What happened next was inevitable. A week later, Laurie phoned me and spoke to Alicita while I was at my night shift at the factory. *¡Chepito! Una de tus novias americanas habló por teléfono. Dejó este número para que le hablaras. Hace un poco de frío en las noches. Aquí les traigo una colcha y una almohada,* Alicita said lovingly, as she entered the back porch early Saturday morning.

As it so happened, Laurie lived in Temple City, Lower Azusa Rd, blocks away from mine. She soon made it a habit to come see me around 1:00 am almost every night to spend a couple of hours with me. This was further indication that the police were not at all concerned about protecting her or finding us. Otherwise, if they had believed a crime had been committed, they would have easily found out where we lived by following Laurie. I don't remember ever being afraid. I saw her visits as perfectly normal. Another possibility was that the gringas' parents, realizing their mistake and knowing the culpability of their daughters, pressured the police not to follow up with charges against us.

During Laurie's visits, Ernesto pretended to be sleeping. Laurie told us that Debbie was sent to Wisconsin to live with her grandparents and that she still professed her immense love for Ernesto in the letters she had written to Laurie asking Ernesto to write her back. Ernesto never did. We had already moved on and considered the adventure over.

Throughout the time we stayed at my cousin's house, my English continued to improve. I could now understand around 50% of speech, utter some phrases, and ask some short questions. Laurie enjoyed having a mostly silent audience anyway. I attentively loved watching her mouth as the English words spewed out of it. I seldom dared to interrupt her. I would look and examine the movement of her lips, her tongue, and the flickering of her eyes. She found my intense gaze very loving and sexy. I took her visits as my after-midnight English lessons and she took them as a series of reassuring and solidifying love encounters. Ms. Phillips at the El Monte Adult Education was impressed by my sudden improvement in my English-speaking ability, even though I struggled to stay awake in class.

"Your family does not see when you leave?" I asked Laurie one night.

"No. My room is on the first floor and it has a wide window that I keep open at night. My parents go to sleep early and are heavy sleepers. I just jump out of the window to get here. I walk one block on Lower Azusa Rd, turn left on Temple City Blvd, continue for seven blocks, turn left on Broadway, walk one block, turn right on Cloverly Ave, walk a short block, and then I am here on your street, Wedgwood Street. I walk eight blocks in total. Nobody walks around here, day or night. Chances are that I will never run into a person. Police cars, at night, gather around the bad areas of the city, not around where I live. I love you and want to be with you."

Laurie spoke fast and clearly, hugging me and kissing me profusely. I understood her desire, but my heart had been closed, inert, cold, since my break up with Norma. Her professions of love did not find any resonance in me.

One of those Saturday mornings, on June, 1973, Ernesto and I went to Arcadia for lunch with one of our classmates. Along the way, we talked about our future. Right there and then, inside the green Plymouth, we decided it was better to get away from Los Angeles to find a new fortune somewhere else. The professor could have been right. Although everything seemed calm now, we still had persistent doubts as to whether the police had closed the case against us. Although that would have been true, our conclusion was that if the police stopped us for any other reason, say in a driving violation, and, even if the officers were probably overwhelmed with other more serious cases, they would act cruelly if they somehow made a distant connection with the two *gringas*.

In that case, although very remote, the police would pre-judge us as two dirty, undocumented immigrants, and they unscrupulously would imprison us because, as such, they would consider us guilty before having the opportunity to prove we were innocent. Our mental concern was based, then, where to escape, find peace, permanent shelter, work, and education. I was also frustrated by my slow process of learning English and wanted to go as far as possible from California, as far as possible from Spanish.

"¿Tú sabes que hay gente en Los Ángeles que han vivido aquí más de cinco años y no saben inglés, puedes creer eso?" Ernesto told me that morning.

"Eso es imposible. ¿Entonces para qué diablos venir a este país si uno no aprende a hablar inglés?" I said.

I considered not learning English while living in the US a sad waste of potential that reduced the opportunities fellow immigrants could have in their search for a brighter future to the maximum. In that case, better to go back to your country of origin.

We rode on East Colorado Blvd crossing Pasadena. On the right-hand side, we suddenly noticed an American Airline travel agency at the American Express office. *"Bajémonos y veamos para cuales ciudades viaja esa aerolínea. Esto parece ser una señal de nuestro destino,"* I said, certain that my luck with divine intervention would pay off again.

Posters of faraway lands colored the walls, enticing us to travel. We soon gravitated towards a carrousel display in the middle of the room. On it, there were small pamphlets inserted in its grooves, their front and back covers picturing multiple cities' landmarks. We turned it several times. We focused on the pamphlet in front of us. Each pamphlet described a popular destination of the United States: Chicago, New York, San Francisco, Dallas, Miami, Boston, etc.... We looked at the pictures and tried to understand the small text below them. I remember, unlike those you would see today, the pamphlets were mostly text, with one picture on the front and three pictures on the back cover.

"¡Ernesto! ¡Púchica! No sé nada de ninguna ciudad de estas. Solamente me acuerdo de que Boston es una ciudad muy histórica llena de cultura y de educación. Y yo me quiero ir a donde no haya ninguna gente que hable español y quiero vivir con gente educada. Estoy seguro de que en Boston no hay ningún Latinoamericano. Sólo gringos viven en Boston. Ahí voy a aprender inglés perfectamente. ¿Imagínate un lugar donde solamente oigamos inglés? Y no te olvides que tenemos que ir a la universidad. En Boston hay muchas universidades. Yo me acuerdo de que leí eso en el Seminario."

Ernesto agreed with me on the spot. We bought one-way overnight tickets to Boston leaving the next Sunday, July 8, 1973, that cost $154.00 each. This gave us one week to say goodbye to our friends and embark on our newly formulated narrative for our future lives. We were reinventing ourselves. I felt special and high above the rest, a mentality I have always used as a motivational device. Some felt resentful and tried to bring me down to reality. I ignored them. We were leaving Los Angeles to go to college in Boston. We were leaving everybody else behind. LA treated us like dirty Mexicans. LA was not good enough for us. The Seminary had made me feel special, unique, and born to achieve great things in life, as the rectors often reminded us, *"Ad Maiora Natus."* This also created in me a sense of superiority, a snobbish attitude that often made me act professorial in my dealings with people. Later, this ingrained outlook would help me excel academically at Boston University and later at Harvard.

In LA, however, most of my Mexican acquaintances couldn't relate to me, treating me as a weird guy who was always in the clouds and good for nothing. I didn't matter to them. I did not fit their existing laborer categories. Some Immigrant girls, however, saw potential in me, generated by how I stood out from the crowd. I became the one who was an immigrant like anybody else of their group, but unique in the sense that I was not Mexican, a guy deeply different from them, and a foreigner amongst his Latin people.

Our friends in Arcadia were extremely impressed by our plans. We never shared the incident we had with the girls and the possible involvement of the police, which was another determining factor pushing us away from LA.

When we got back to Temple City, I told Alicita that we would be moving out of the back porch within a week. She made a face that people who don't understand what it is being said to them make. She and Ana, living in their hectic, detached world, and with different work schedules than ours, had long forgotten about us. I knew we wouldn't be missed. *"Buena suerte,"* she finally said, as a stranger would to another just before boarding a plane at the airport. Her fear of losing Ana's protection and the possibility that I could make another compromising mistake that could attract immigration's attention, forced Alicita to be cold. Had she known about the girls, she would have become aware of a real danger and would have never permitted my return to her house in the first place.

We quit our jobs at the factory, cashed our last check, and sold the green Plymouth for $100 to one of Ernesto's friends to be delivered the day of our flight, with the added benefit of a ride to the airport. That last week in LA, we bounced all over to say goodbye to our ESL classmates and platonic girlfriends, most of them from the El Monte Adult Ed. Ernesto took me to the professor to say goodbye. He was impressed to hear we were going to Boston to study and told us that Boston, with the historic Harvard, was still the best educational center of the United States. However, he added, the place was overrated, and it was already on a decline, judging by the fact that some great professors, friends of his, were leaving the Boston area to come to California's universities. His remarks were most probably the product of his jealousy. He saw us as two brave and enterprising young immigrants who were on the verge of a promising and unexpected educational adventure that he regretted not having had after high school, due to his contentment with the life he was leading, and fear of leaving his reassuring family ties behind.

Laurie came over the night before our departure and cried upon hearing our decision. She read aloud the airplane ticket. "Boston?! Tomorrow?! Please, please, take me with you! I am miserable at home. Nobody pays attention to me. I won't be a burden. I will help you get ahead. We could start a new life together!" I just fixed my eyes on her in silence. She understood. "Will you at least write to me?" she said, trying to clear the growing lump in her throat. "I'll write," I said. I never did. Many times, in my life, when a clear purpose and goal was set in my mind, I felt compelled to ignore all sentimental contexts, all human processes, activated during or just before taking action. I have generally opted for quick action, above all else, when my purpose has been crystal clear. My task orientation could have been cruel, but I have felt that had I stopped to think about how other people felt, I could have been unduly delayed or completely derailed from my plans in life. Some people probably felt walked over, which was never my intention, and interpreted my actions as an indication of an overpowering personality, and at times chauvinistic, someone who loved to just have his way. The truth is in those moments, I just wanted to keep moving, advancing, to feel accomplished, and I was in a hurry. Come to think of I, I am eternally in a hurry.

That short moment in front of the carrousel display at the American Airlines travel agency, on East Colorado Blvd. in Pasadena, defined the rest of my life. I could have ended up in any other city in the United States, but we chose Boston. It's overwhelming sometimes to dwell on what could have happened and where else life could have taken me had I not gravitated towards the city I now call my home. But be reassured in the fact that my life has been just a series of impromptu decisions, accidents, improvisations, and chance. I am so grateful for where my path has led me, potholes, twisting turns, dead-ends and all because I knew each day promised me a treasure.

Epilogue

At present, I work full time as a substitute at Boston Latin School, waiting for my wife Carolina to retire. I have been covering different subject matters, but when I am assigned to a Latin class, my entire being is transported anew to the Seminary and become fully involved. I often surprise the students with my ability to still remember my declamations, "*O tempora, O mores. Quo usque tandem abutere, Catilina, patientia nostra?*" I also can recite declensions of nouns, pronouns, and verbs, which I do so aloud in their entirety to the rhythm of a walking beat, "*amaba, amabas, amabat, amabamus, amabatis, amabant.*" I don't have to be concerned about where to stress the short and long vowels, as most of them do, because it matches perfectly to the ones in Spanish.

I see the bright faces of the Class VI students studying the relative pronouns and quizzing each other, and I tell them to put music into it with pleasure, to practice with a rhythm. It is easier to remember that way: "*qui, quae, quod; ...quem, quam, quod...*" For sure I graduated from BLS, or so they believe.

I also volunteer on Saturdays, teaching Citizenship classes to Latinos who are preparing to take the exam and be interviewed by U.S. immigration officer. These classes offer me the time to rethink what this great country of America has created as a democracy and it brings me back almost in a complete circle, to those days as a laborer in California when I had to struggle to get food on my table by working nights welding ornamental gates, and when I had to wash dishes overnight in two restaurants in Boston while attending school during the day. My Citizenship students work up to 70 hours per week, sometimes without the benefits of overtime pay because their employers often cheat them out of their earnings. These brave, hardworking, and determined people inspire me to solidify my belief that America is built on and made by immigrants, and it depends on them to maintain its values as a democracy. As Bret Stephens, New York Times writer wrote: "People who have known tyranny tend to make the most of liberty. People who have experienced desperation usually make the most of opportunity. It's mainly those born to freedom who have the knack for squandering it."

I am also teaching Spanish to adults at the highest level at the Brookline Adult Education Program. This also has awakened in me a renewed interest in the Spanish masterpieces from *Don Quijote* to *Cien Años de Soledad*. I have reread more carefully the poems of Espronceda, the plays of Garcia Lorca, the short stories of Borges and those of Unamuno, prompting long literature discussions with Gustavo over the phone and every time I visit him in Puebla. I am also in the process of reading Tomas de Aquino's Summa Theologica, something that I never did in the Seminary, and other classics that I never fully understood the first time around. These include the latest translations of *the Iliad*, *the Aeneid*, and *La Divina Comedia*, as well as other works Padre Camilo made us read, but I barely understood at that time, such as *Taras Bulba* by Gogol and *Crime and Punishment* and *Insulted and Injured* by Dostoevsky.

It is as if I want to relive my life, to recapture it in the confines of my study, but this time I would do it well, with understanding. In reading classic literature, I aim to recapture those moments, those memories, to feel a sense of eternity, or maybe to be forgiven for not having paid attention, as if I were seeking redemption, divine absolution, for perhaps having taken life too lightly. I don't buy books anymore, and my local public library has become the go-to place for all the books I feel inspired to read or reread. The other supply of books, the lighter reading, comes from Teto. He gives me paperbacks of espionage books by David Silva, and crime books by David Baldacci, Lee Child, and Michael Connelly. I have become addicted to the Jack Reacher novels, but only skim the L.A. crime scene books

Teto loves. Reading books he has just read adds another layer to our connection as brothers, and even if I never fully read them, it makes me happy to know he enjoys sharing his interests with me.

Finally, in my pursuit of mastering tasks that I before executed poorly, I started re-learning French at the start of my retirement and have continued with it since then. Every Tuesday morning one can find me at a French literature class offered by Brookline Adult Education reading Proust with a group of fellow French enthusiast. Presently, we are reading *Le Côté de Guermantes*, the third volume of seven, of Proust's *La recherche du Temps Perdue*, with the aim of reading them all. I understand everything I read and listen to, but my oral language is yet to become as fluent as a native speaker. My desire is to one day live in France or Belgium for 6 months, one of my bucket-list items, but I doubt I will ever get the chance. Still, one can dream!

The rest of my time I use to learn new pieces on the piano and to play the music I learned in the Seminary. Needless to say, my life in retirement has developed into a structured adventure, as I promised it to be, but I still do not know or understand everything about myself or the life I have led so far and doubt I ever will.

I have tried to live by principles, and have learned that they are often broken, but never lost, and that when I do stray away from them, they are always there as a point of reference, as an anchor. Your principles can nourish you when you get lost, like crutches or foot holds, but there are times in life when one needs to take extreme actions at the expense of those principles. In my life, during the periods when certain life situations put me in a position of fighting for survival, I had no choice but to compromise my principles in that moment. I have committed numerous necessary sins. Maybe there was another way out that would have provided me with a chance to preserve my integrity, but in those moments, I felt like I had no time to weigh the odds. I do not see those moments as a personal failure, but only temporary suspensions of my values. In the business of life, especially when faced with adversity, nothing is absolute. One must be ready to quickly adapt to new circumstances and demands.

In those periods of my life, principles become situational, relative, and temporarily expendable, especially if I was trying to survive. In a way, this attitude negates the absolutism taught in the Seminary where dogmas were *impermutable*. There is a Latin phrase attributed in the Seminary to Thomas Aquinas that states "*In extrema necessitate omnia sunt communia,*" meaning "In extreme needs all things are held in common", a mindset sometimes implemented by the Roman Empire during times of poverty. In cases of desperation in life, one at times has to act out of the confines of the law, a distinction I had to make several times throughout my journey to where I am today.

The Catholic Church accepts killing in a war, if the war is just, if it is in self-defense. During my first year in this country, I felt as if I were attacked by the elements of the American culture, and I needed to go to war, so to speak, so I could survive, conquer, and succeed. At times, the strategy had to be total submission to those forces. In addition, my thinking and moral attitude changed gradually from the absolutism and dogmatic position of the Catholic scholastic philosophy, to the phenomenology of Teilhard de Chardin, consisting of the trade-offs of cost-benefit analysis, to end up adopting probabilistic assessments before making life choices. In other words, I went from believing in absolute truths to coming to terms with relative positions and understanding that often a person's actions are not a reflection of her as a person, but a consequence of the current situation she may be in.

I have also learned that people at times disappoint you because you held unrealistic expectations about them; expectations that spoke more about you than about their needs. It is never wise to lose hope or faith in them. Friends, your family, and especially your children will frequently surprise you with their personal transformations and accomplishments.

My time in the Seminary taught me that a modicum of competition propels you to do better. My perception that my dear friend Gustavo was my competitor helped me achieve higher levels of self-development than if I had let myself be dragged down by my insecurities born from growing up in a dysfunctional nucleus family. Competition helped me develop a persistent work ethic that most certainly made me a better person. There were times when I was really competing with myself, not with Gustavo, seeing as my paranoiac nature led me to assume that all our interactions were tinted with an air of personal competition when often they were not. I attribute this impulse to my desire to escape what my father was, to be better than what I perceived he turned out to be, an unfair image distorted by a permanent veil of alcoholic stupor. I did not see it at that time, but now I think my relationship with Gustavo provoked in me envy and jealousy. Envy for his exceptional natural intellect and jealousy for what *muchachas poblanas,* perceived to be striking good looks. Nietzsche preached that in the labyrinth of our inner souls, were we to seriously look, rest the instincts and passions that make our understanding of this world, and states, "envy and jealousy are the private parts of the human soul." This secret admiration mixed with envy I felt towards Gustavo, in a paradoxical sense, fueled my desire to try harder in my youth.

I have also learned that one must take risks in life. It is impossible to understand beforehand the magnitude of their consequences, positive and negative. If nothing is risked, nothing is gained. In my life, the risks I have taken, luckily, have led to mostly positive consequences. I seized whatever I deemed to be a worthy opportunity when I was presented with one. I became obsessed with not making my life a series of missed opportunities and growing into an old man full of regret. I wouldn't agree with what Romain Gary wrote in his book *La promesse de l'aube*. He states that "*La vie est pavée d'occasions perdues.*" (Life is paved with los opportunities). I believed in the contrary, "*La vie est pavée d'occasions saisies.*" (Life is paved with seized opportunities). I am aware that the conclusion of many of my risky actions could have ended badly, particularly when I acted impulsively to move things along, to make sure they were completed. Yes, my life could have been a total disaster based on my actions during my first year in this country, but up to now it hasn't been, and for that I am grateful.

My over optimism when approaching life has let me discover the extremes of what I can do. I believed that saying yes when asked if I could do a job would prove to be the right approach, even if I knew nothing. I had never been concerned about making a fool of myself. The unattainable has always attracted me. One can always learn on the job with the help of others who often quickly notice that one is defenseless and feel the human need to help or find themselves for the first time in the position of showing off publicly their abilities, which they may seldom get the chance to do. I've taken so far what life has given me as a full glass of milk, even though many times the glass was empty. With persistence and help from others, however, I often filled that glass up, concretizing perfectly an otherwise uncertain self-fulfilling prophecy. Often, I jumped easily over the gaps of the suspension bridge, purposely ignoring them, landing happily on the planks that led me to the other side of the river.

One reason for this is that the continued series of successes in the Seminary permanently ingrained in me the personal outlook that success was the likely outcome whenever I tried something new, regardless of the nature of the endeavor. Not knowing anything about a topic did not deter my engagement with it, but rather increased my desire to explore it and to master it, without holding back. Breaking the codes of the unknowns, which life presented me, developed frequently into an obsession. This led me often to achieve the gratifying feeling of mastering something at its highest quality possible, unless constricted by my genetic endowment. Being tone and rhythmically inept did not prevent me from practicing the piano every day, and although I am by no means a master, through repetitive practice, I have achieved an intermediate level that allows me to enjoy Chopin's nocturnes, ballades and sonatas, Mozart's and Schumann's sonatas, and Schubert's impromptus.

I am writing this memoir out of a great desire to complete it, but I never excelled at writing. Undoubtedly, I failed many times miserably. My perceived failures only made me change course, adapt, like the time, after being accepted at B.U. as a Pre-Dental student, an aspirational goal at that time, I soon realized that my goal of becoming a Dentist was a gross overreach of my capabilities, seeing as the Seminary had not provided me with any Bio or Chem Lab courses, essential requirements for pursuing medicine, and decided quickly to change majors.

Sometimes one is not in control of one's life. Other people control it. Even though it may seem that the world is about to end, and submission is thought as betrayal to oneself, one has to let it happen. In those precise moments one may not have any other choice.

Now, years later, the events I have recounted in this book during the first year in this country, feel like they happened to a completely different person who lived a completely different life. When I was younger, I never quite understood what it meant when older adults would sigh and lament how time goes by too quickly, but now I am very much aware. Elena is about to start her third year at Union College, Alejandro recently got engaged and is getting married next Spring, and Eric and his wife welcomed their eighth baby to the family in accordance with the traditions of Orthodox Judaism.

As this book ends, I should clarify that this is merely the first volume of my life that recounts the time leading up to and during my first year in the US. If my energy is sustained and I have the continued support of my family, I am determined to start and complete a second volume. This volume will begin with when I met my first wife, Eric's mother, married my second wife, Carolina, and continue with detailed accounts from my years working in the Boston Public Schools. Such a book will give me the chance to reflect on and share the ups and downs of my life after arriving in Boston in much more detail, including my experiences raising three children (all of whom will probably be happy to finally be mentioned in more than two sentences each).

If I had a second chance at life, I would repeat my long years in the Seminary and the first year in the US to the fullest. I have been an ordinary man who has not done anything extraordinary, but foolishly has thought of himself as extraordinary, fully embracing the Seminary's motto, *"Ad majora natus,"* ingrained in my brain since I was 13. I came to America on an 11-day tourist visa, changed it to 110, stayed for a lifetime.

Made in United States
North Haven, CT
27 November 2021

11615295R00209